The Promise of Anglicanism

The Promise of Anglicanism

William L. Sachs

and

Robert S. Heaney

scm press

© William L. Sachs and Robert S. Heaney 2019

Published in 2019 by SCM Press
Editorial office
3rd Floor, Invicta House
108–114 Golden Lane
London EC1Y 0TG, UK
www.scmpress.co.uk

SCM Press is an imprint of Hymns Ancient & Modern Ltd
(a registered charity)

Hymns Ancient & Modern® is a registered trademark of
Hymns Ancient & Modern Ltd
13A Hellesdon Park Road, Norwich,
Norfolk NR6 5DR, UK

All rights reserved. No part of this publication may be reproduced,
stored in a retrieval system, or transmitted,
in any form or by any means, electronic, mechanical,
photocopying or otherwise, without the prior permission of
the publisher, SCM Press.

The Author have asserted their right under the Copyright, Designs
and Patents Act 1988 to be identified as the Author of this Work

978-0-334-05844-1

Scripture quotations are from the New Revised Standard Version of
the Bible, Anglicized Edition, copyright © 1989, 1995 by the Division
of Christian Education of the National Council of the Churches of
Christ in the USA. Used by permission. All rights reserved.

British Library Cataloguing in Publication data

A catalogue record for this book is available
from the British Library

Typset by Manila Typesetting Company

In honour of
James Theodore Holly (1829–1911)
Constance Padwick (1886–1968)
Florence Li Tim-Oi (1907–92)
John S. Mbiti (1931–2019)

Contents

Acknowledgements		ix
Introduction: Anglicanism's Dilemma		xi
1	The Meaning of Promise	1
2	A Contested Genesis	26
3	Catholicity and Contextualization	57
4	Catholicity and Communion	84
5	Testing Anglican Coherence	117
6	Renewing Communion in Mission	150
7	Distinctive and Faithful Practice	182
Conclusion		220
Index		234

Acknowledgements

The idea of being in communion, which is central to this book, was realized among those who contributed to its creation. Disparate persons encouraged the authors' progress, sharpening both our ideas and their expression. A range of staff and scholars at the Virginia Theological Seminary provided support and insight for this work. They included Mitzi Budde and her team at the Bishop Paine Library, Hartley Wensing, and Molly O'Brien at the seminary's Center for Anglican Communion Studies, a number of student assistants at the Center, and inquisitive and able 'GCM' students.

Church leaders in a variety of fora throughout the Communion engaged with developing ideas that contributed to this work. Special thanks are due to SPG and the Council of Anglican Provinces in Africa at the Senior Leaders Roundtable meeting in Nairobi in November 2017; John Kafwanka and the participants at the Global Episcopal Mission Network conference in April 2018; audiences in the Diocese of Liberia and at Cuttington University in December 2018; the Consultation of Anglican Bishops in Dialogue meeting at Liverpool Cathedral in June 2019; and the 'Building Dialogue' conference at St George's College, Jerusalem, in June 2019. Robert Heaney is a member of the Lambeth Conference 2020 Design Group, and gives thanks for their generous collegiality and commitment to the promise of Anglicanism. Robert Allen, Bob Bottoms, David Cox and Ann Hallisey read portions of the manuscript and offered valuable suggestions. The creation of this book proved to be a lively conversation.

We are especially grateful to our editor at SCM and his cohorts. David Shervington embraced the idea of this book and encouraged its realization. Beyond words appearing in print, David has envisioned a range of occasions for discussion of the idea of Anglican promise. We are grateful for his tireless efforts.

In the midst of a number of commitments and challenges, God's gift of loving families remains a source of inspiration, grace and peace. We especially recognize and honour the place that our spouses occupy at the centre of our lives and our hearts. Thank you, Austin and Sharon.

Pointedly the late Lamin Sanneh asked: 'Whose religion is Christianity?' We have cited his work to enliven not only the book's argument but the passion that prompts it. God's people are wondrous and variegated. Anglicanism as faith in God revealed in Christ cannot be confined if it is to embrace the range of human experience. In this spirit we write and we hope.

Introduction:

Anglicanism's Dilemma

The Limits of Anglican Assurance

Until recent years, references to 'Anglicanism' could be made with the assurance that they would be readily understood. Descriptions of Anglicanism as a faith tradition typically trace it to the first century and a half of its English development. The basis of Anglican identity has seemed obvious since those early years. Anglicanism has been embodied in the Book of Common Prayer and the threefold ministry of bishops, priests and deacons. Anglicans have prized both the Bible and a historic, sacramental worship. From these sources a rich legacy of spiritual and theological writings and hymnody has flowed. The idea of the *via media* became prominent, elevating emphasis on balance and breadth in church life. Anglicanism's sources are unmistakably English, stamped by the place and manner of their emergence.

English experience can be cited to argue for the distinctiveness of Anglican identity. Even though Roman Catholic, the medieval English Church retained evidence of earlier influences and carried a distinctive imprint, for example in the Sarum Rite of the medieval Mass. The Synod of Whitby did not merge English church life into a seamless Roman garment.[1] Late medieval reform proved influential, for example in the movement of John Wyclif and his spiritual heirs.[2] One need not romanticize late ancient and medieval English religious experience, or political life for that matter, to make the case for a distinctively English form of development. Before there was a Church of England, there was a distinctively English church.

THE PROMISE OF ANGLICANISM

To speak of the promise of Anglicanism, it has proven tempting to limit discussion to the rise of the Church of England. Various authors follow this tack. It is commonplace to speak of Anglicanism's identity, integrity and even its future with little reference beyond England. In part, confusion over Anglican identity has arisen not only from a variety of religious experiences and priorities labelled 'Anglican', but simply from imprecise usage of the term. It refers to the Church of England but encompasses far more than English experience alone. 'Anglicanism' must not be equated simply with English life.[3]

Anglicanism has not remained coterminous with the Church of England, though its origins lie there. The early stages of Anglicanism's development arose as extensions of English church life throughout the British Isles and to colonial settings. The Church grew to North America, then the South Pacific, then Asia, Africa and elsewhere. Growth continued beyond English colonial domains and even into former colonial areas of other European nations. From the mid nineteenth century on, Anglicans saw themselves as global and prized the idea of being a communion of regionalized churches, or provinces. The conviction of a lasting English stamp never wavered but did not prove final.

Nevertheless, given its English origins and lines of development from England outward, its continuation of ancient Christian forms and its blend of synodical and episcopal authority, Anglican identity has appeared self-evident. Descriptions of Anglican life have manifested predictable casts. The authors of works assessing Anglicanism typically presume that this faith tradition's significance and the hallmarks of its identity require little explanation. Of course, many published works have elucidated particular aspects of Anglicanism's origins or interpreted features of its development. But the basic subject, 'Anglicanism', has needed no justification. It has virtually explained itself.

The concept of promise, in both its religious and its secular meanings, includes specific and broad meanings. On the one hand, a promise is a commitment to fulfil a specific task. On the other hand, a promise is an open-ended vision of an intended way of life awaiting fulfilment. For Christians, the task of being God's people has specific as well as broad aspects. By being faithful, Christians such as Anglicans seek to guide people in faith, building the Church as an expression of God's promise to redeem life, personally and socially. Given the seeming clarity of Anglican identity, this Church's nature and intention should be assured. But the promise of Anglicanism does not rest on easy assurance about its identity.

Even though Anglicanism's basis has been presumed, its nature has been questioned and its intention has been unrealized. There have been ragged edges to Anglican identity and seeming paradoxes about Anglican experience that have defied convenient resolution. Thus, the co-editors of an extensive collection of Anglican spiritual writings have noted that different groups among Anglicans, representing different readings of Christian tradition and church expression, like to claim that they are the real heirs of the classical tradition established in the earliest years of Anglican life. Agreement on Anglicanism's nature has never been complete.[4]

Part of the confusion over Anglicanism's identity has resulted from the complexity and incompleteness of the historical process that created the Church of England. For example, the term 'comprehension' represents an intention of the English Church that could not be achieved in formal, establishmentarian terms. Yet 'comprehension', often debated and at times challenged, remains a foremost Anglican ideal, derivative of the Church of England but used broadly across Anglican life. It could not be achieved formally, in its place of origin, but has been pursued diversely and in de facto ways among Anglicans, as we shall explain.

The legacy of parties represents both Anglicanism's expanse and its incompleteness. For several centuries, the outlooks of High versus Low Church parties in the Church of England created rivalries that fostered different understandings of Christian sources and church life. A later, Broad Church cluster has been identified with theological liberalism. The labels retain current expression. Thus, the editors of one collection of Anglican historical documents invoked the term 'catholicity' early in the introduction to their volume.[5] Similarly, authors sympathetic to Low Church ideals have made the Bible and mission central to their explanations of the Church. Various authors have also fostered the conviction that to be Anglican is to be both catholic and evangelical in some measure. The ideal of melding diverse streams has offered some Anglicans the sense that their Church could be Christianity's meeting place. Yet it is difficult to equate Anglican promise with church unity. Anglicanism itself has proven to be splintered.

As we shall explore further, the priorities of theology, religious practice and church life embodied in these parties have infused Anglican life beyond England. Anglican mission gained impetus from High and Low Church influences, seen in the Society for the Propagation of the Gospel (SPG) and the Church Missionary Society (CMS and later known as the Church Mission Society). Anglican mission has carried such influences far from English shores, into settings where they would be adapted to contextual influences. We will depict mission as a key to the nature of Anglicanism's promise, though not simply as celebration of Anglican expanse.

Because there are limits to the assurance we can have about Anglican identity, it appears problematic to speak of Anglican promise. The fact that there has been variety in church life has fuelled debates about the Church's nature. Often such debates have centred on which form of liturgical expression and which theological interpretation should be dominant. Anglicans have also debated the proper relation of the Church to the state, the locus of church authority and the role of episcopacy. These debates have recurred, the lines of difference seemingly sharpening more than being overcome. Lately, Anglican debate has elevated ideals such as justice and orthodoxy. The prominence of such debates is our touchstone. We shall address the role of debate over faith and the Church in Anglican life, speaking of 'contestation' to emphasize both its extent and our analytical view. We view contestation as a principal clue to the promise of Anglican life. The incompleteness of Anglican identity, and repeated debate over it, suggest the nature of Anglicanism's promise.

ANGLICANISM'S DILEMMA

The term 'contestation' could appear troubling and paradoxical. It seems to grant more truth to instances of intra-Anglican conflict than to this faith tradition's biblical foundations and apostolic worship and ministry. The promise of Anglicanism surely must be depicted in terms of adherence to revealed truth and faithful expressions of it. Consensus about the faith appears to be the appropriate basis of promise, not divergences among those who claim its mantle.

The reality of contestation throughout the history of Anglicanism is not remarkable, in one sense. All faith traditions reveal instances of internal tension that can produce dispute and even division. The most apparent and recurring cause of contestation in religious life concerns differences over proper forms of practice, that is, faithful expressions of religious ideals and beliefs. Differing interpretations of theological doctrines have erupted into controversy and disaffection as their implications for living faithfully have diverged. Thus, the history of early Christian doctrinal differences inevitably became social as well as intellectual. Similarly, efforts to stem difference theologically often had social and even political repercussions. Formulation of the Nicene Creed, a benchmark in the history of doctrine, did not end disputes over belief and biblical interpretation, nor limit such differences to clusters of theologians and church leaders.

Our point is that contestation has been a recurring fact of human history and religious life in particular. It is especially apparent amid cultural differences and disputes over the translation of religious ideals into social realities. As we shall see in the case of Anglican life, the same religious ideals, largely affirmed by all who claim Anglican identity, have been applied in various ways in different situations, often fuelling conflict. Yet in such contestation we will locate Anglican promise.[6]

Even as contestation has arisen over the nature of the Church and the proper course of its development, those who have written about Anglicanism felt able to presume that their subject and their own intentions were readily understood. There may have been competing versions of the Anglican narrative, representing divergent points of Christian emphasis, but the playing field on which they met was clearly demarcated. It was trans-Atlantic life, framed by the assumed priority of English history and culture. But the limitations of this playing field have become apparent. Far more people and their experiences were excluded than included. The players proved unrepresentative of the breadth of Anglican demographics. Debates between Low and High Church figures would prove quaint as the field on which they competed, and the very game that was being played, changed. By the middle of the twentieth century, the familiar presumptions that framed earlier debates about Anglicanism could no longer be sustained.

Anglicanism has become defined as much by its extensions and varieties as by its points of origin. English forms have been retained, but their meaning and expression have varied from one Anglican setting to another. As Anglicanism has become variegated, it has become hotly contested. Anglicanism's majority now resides in the Global South, and voices from across that region frame Anglican belief and life alternatively, reflecting different personal and cultural narratives. Anglicanism's widening swathe of adherents illustrates that the religious ideals which arose in England have proven adaptable to a multitude of contexts. Faith has arisen, and church life has developed in new ways, encouraging novel forms of leadership and religious expression. For example, grassroots movements of spiritual renewal have arisen on various continents. Further, the alignment of Anglicans and grassroots movements for social justice, such as in South Africa, gave the Church a different cast. The forms of worship and ministry resemble their English origins. But the tenor of Anglican identity has proven different elsewhere.

How then is Anglicanism to be understood? In what sense is it possible to speak of its promise? This faith tradition appears to be a confusion of ideals and realities posed from diverse and sometimes conflicting points of view. From English origins, it acquired both grounding in local contexts and affirmation of a larger religious identity. There are historical and theological givens that frame its life, namely forms of worship and ministry. But the effort to secure a faithful and coherent identity that could unify has been a challenge that has intensified as Anglicanism has become variegated. It would be challenge enough if Anglicanism were simply diverse. But Anglican experience reveals forms of conflict over proper interpretations and expressions of Christian tenets and Anglican ideals, and over appropriate relations of Anglicans to one another amid their differences. Such conflict has fuelled alternative forms of church life, each claiming to be legitimately Anglican. The very meaning of being Anglican, as well as of being Christian, is in dispute. Church life is fragmented, making its promise elusive.

Contestation seemingly has dominated Anglican life in recent memory. Since the middle of the twentieth century, various movements among Anglicans have influenced the shape of church life and sparked profound debate. Three movements in particular, reflective of life at the Church's grassroots, have absorbed the agendas of church leadership circles. These three movements have been as celebrated in some Anglican locales as they have been decried in others. Indeed, these movements have proven divisive within some Anglican provinces, making the reality of conflicts among Anglicans unmistakable. With conflict has come a lessening of the Anglican ability to presume the nature of their identity.

We cannot assess any of these movements in the detail each deserves. However, we must cite them to establish the serious, some would say dire, situation the Anglican world now faces. The first such movement that changed the Anglican profile was the liturgical revision movement, which gained momentum after World War Two. The appeal of an enhanced, more Catholic ceremonial widened as former British colonies gained political independence, and as some church leaders in the Global North sought to distance church life from its host cultures. The rise of autonomous church life included the task of creating or revising the Book of Common Prayer for new and older provinces of the Anglican world. The necessity of adaptation was apparent to some church leaders and the intention spread. Revision of worship became a widespread Anglican project.

A more Catholic, sacramental emphasis arose in much of Anglican life. In some places this trend was protested vigorously, for example, in the United States. There, efforts to preserve the

Episcopal Church's Book of Common Prayer in its 1928 version came to naught in 1979 when a new version was authorized. There was irony in that a proposed revision of the Book of Common Prayer of the Church of England failed to gain parliamentary approval in 1928. In the one instance, the 1928 Prayer Book was defended as the true embodiment of the Church's tradition. In the other instance, it was defeated as an assault on tradition. The times and circumstances differed, of course. But the irony must be noted. Anglican life proves contextual.

The second movement which broadened the Anglican playing field was the admission of women to ordination as priests and then as bishops. Unlike the methodical steps and formal approval that marked each stage of Prayer Book revision, and the creation of new versions in former colonies, the steps towards the ordination of women happened inadvertently, irregularly. It was not planned or widely noted at the time, but early in 1943, Bishop Ronald Hall of Hong Kong ordained Florence Li-Tim Oi to the priesthood. Such a step was deemed necessary under the circumstances of war in East Asia; as such, it appeared singular. But the argument that the Church faced a variety of novel circumstances, and must expand its ministries, would take hold.

By the early twenty-first century, the presence of women in the Church's priesthood and episcopate was prominent in some parts of the Anglican world and unrealized elsewhere. In some places the admission of women to holy orders triggered protests and even defections from church ranks. The number of defectors was not large, but the noise of their defection reverberated within and beyond the Church. Advocates of the ordination of women insisted that such an opening of church leadership was a natural fulfilling of the gospel's intention. In modern circumstances, the restrictions formerly placed on women's roles were deemed an anomaly needing correction. Ancient and medieval cultures had precluded what the gospel intended.

Opponents of the ordination of women perceived such a step as a repudiation of Christian tradition, especially of its Catholic inheritance. By this logic, the Church must reflect the ideal of Vincent of Lérins, namely, that it embodies the faith which was once delivered to the saints.[7] That is, the Church must express immutable, timeless truth, which has been fully revealed. Amid the whirlpools of modern culture, the Church must maintain its historic deposit, in belief and in practice. We shall consider the role of practice in Anglican life and will depict it as the fulcrum of some of the Church's most acrid disputes as well as the basis of its promise.

Advocates of the ordination of women have viewed Christian tradition not as complete or as revealed once for all time, but as awaiting further revelation pointing towards an eventual completion. The ordination of women became more than a question of the shape of Anglican ministry. It acquired symbolic importance as an expression of the nature of Christian tradition and the Church's transformative intention for culture. Even as various Anglican provinces reached a live and let live stalemate over the ordination of women, the fault lines that this issue represented would deepen.[8]

In the early twenty-first century, the tensions that liturgical revision and the ordination of women had stoked ignited into conflict of an unprecedented extent among Anglicans. Issues of human sexuality, especially steps towards the acceptance of homosexual persons in all aspects of church life, created an apparently irreparable fracture. The issue symbolized two distinct views of the Christian faith and Anglican tradition competing for primacy. Was the Church's truth indeed complete and inviolate? Or was it in the process of being fulfilled? Passions ran so high, and the divergence proved so distinct, that any effort at a mediating position seemed futile. Division over sexuality hijacked Anglican life, creating division that was difficult to transcend.[9]

The issue of sexuality subsumed aspects of colonial and post-colonial experience in parts of Africa and Asia. Especially in East and West Africa, Anglicanism had grown dramatically and assumed a biblically literalistic cast in the process. Such an inclination gained strength from the conviction that the faith had been delivered complete in the earliest Christian years. It was also fuelled by a widespread search for indigenous voices of African and Asian experience, though this search was not confined to those who rejected homosexuality as antithetical to Christian intention. Anglicans of the Global South emphasized the faithfulness of their values and their commitment to charting a pattern of church life that reflected the purity of their faith. We trace the sources of this way of being Anglican to contextual influences that foster particular ways of reading the Bible and Christian tradition. We shall attend to this reality throughout this narrative.

The result of widespread changes in church life has been a multiplication of the stresses affecting Anglicanism. The meaning of the term 'Anglican' as a historic Christian tradition has been challenged from without and within. The Church's challenges from without, including wars and political upheaval, economic disparities and rivalries with other faiths, receive attention in these pages. Recent Anglican experience has focused both on finding internal consensus and on securing constructive roles in new social circumstances. The Church's relation to culture became a point of division by the early twenty-first century. The charge that one or another expression of church life and leadership represents a surrender of the faith to culture is cited by ecclesiastical factions. This accusation signals the hardening of divergent theological positions and strategies for church life. Anglican factionalism represents fear that one's opponents are placing the Church in irretrievable jeopardy. The extent of division among Anglicans has clouded the Anglican prospect. How is it possible to speak of Anglican promise?

We are not dismayed by Anglican conflict, historically or in the present moment. As we shall describe, the Church has always been contested. We take this reality as a basic mark of its history, indicating the nature and dynamism of Anglican development. Contestation reveals a faith tradition that is unfolding, that is reshaping itself through lived experience in multiple contexts, facing social challenges amid societies in political and economic disarray. Amid such challenges, Anglicans have proclaimed Christian faith and built transformative ministries in their settings. Yet they may frame the faith that inspires their life differently. It should not be surprising that there is difference, nor that no particular formulation of Anglican identity encompasses the breadth of contextual life. The depth of allegiance to the Christian faith in its Anglican guises is as striking as the extent to which Anglicans can differ over its expression.

To speak of 'Anglican promise', then, is to speak of more than a fixed identity. It is to speak of a process of development that has shifted repeatedly as the Church's situation has changed. We will speak of forms of discontinuity, primarily the efforts of Anglicans to shape their Church and live faithfully in their contexts. We will look beneath the surface of Anglican life, citing persons and situations that illustrate the Church's dynamism, its affirmations and its perceptions of its possibilities. In considering how Anglicans have lived their lives and shaped their Church, we will uncover broad patterns of promise. Even as we speak of 'contestation', we are struck by what has become possible for Anglicans. As we unfold the story of Anglicanism in a revised way, we will not gloss over the reality of contestation. Instead we see in contestation a habitual Anglican search for a way, for common prayer and even for unity. The promise of Anglicanism proves paradoxical, arising out of contestation, of difference stridently proposed. Anglicanism proves unfinished; it is ever in the process of becoming. More than its English origins, this is its truth.

Contextualization and Promise

We argue that even as it has grown, Anglicanism has proven disparate and incomplete. Its fecund experience only partially reflects its English sources. As the English Church gave rise to mission branches, church life became both broader and more contested. Anglicanism's promise seemed matched by Anglican divergence. As we have suggested, a case can be made that the promise of Anglicanism appears diffuse, found in different ways across different settings of church life. Anglicanism has become a patchwork quilt of cultures and expressions. Its variety has fuelled contestation, while at the same time there are instances of Anglican life that defy the narrative of division. The promise of Anglicanism must be seen in terms of how instances of faithfulness arise, how they relate to difference and how contestation itself occurs. We find there is more to the reality of Anglican life than the finality of divergence.

We will show that what we mean by Anglicanism's promise surfaces in the midst of contestation. Anglicans differ, and dispute key matters of belief and practice. But the finality of division does not necessarily result. The reality of contestation, and its various portents, reflects the reality that Anglican life occurs primarily at local levels, where the faith is lived by most of its followers. The unfolding of Anglican life beyond England became a grassroots phenomenon, the Church arising in one context after another. This contextual character of church growth was sharpened because, in the settings of mission, Anglicans were compelled to respond to local circumstances, to cultivate local ties and to create local forms of governance. Anglicanism has arisen as much from intercultural exchange as from contestation over the shape of church life.

Mission has always entailed the translation of the Bible and the essential aspects of church life into vernacular expressions. But contextualization as a function of mission has meant more than translation. Contextualization has meant absorption of forms of local culture, or at least critical response to them. Between the polarities of syncretism on the one hand and rejection of culture on the other, mission requires ongoing assessment of the culture in which the Church is set. Christians must ask, as Anglicans have repeatedly, how to speak in compelling ways that both distinguish the Church and engage it in a context in redemptive ways.[10]

Not surprisingly, Anglicans have disagreed over the nature of contextualization as a function of the Church's mission. Conservatives, who may speak of themselves as orthodox, often fear that faith and tradition may be compromised, resisting what they see as accommodation to culture. Progressives, as liberals now are termed, see particular adaptations to contextual life as essential to mission. However, Anglicans of all theological sorts have been compelled to adapt to novel cultural circumstances. Adaptation must not lapse into cultural absorption and must retain a capacity to critique as well as to affirm the life of a given place. Contextualization signals a dynamic, unfolding life of faith in community. For Anglicans, forms of contextualization have led to the differences that surface in contestation. But there is more to mission and to Anglican intention than difference. Contestation reflects forms of contextualization that feature promise.

Given Anglicanism's confusions and conflicts, that argument seems untenable. However, we will show that Anglicanism, historically and at present, has been engaged in ongoing, religious formation, the promise of which entails proclaiming the gospel, defining the Christian life and building the Church in ways that prove faithful while featuring contextual focus. Both Anglicanism's distinctiveness and its challenge arise from its intention to engage the life of a context faithfully. Across Anglican history, the Church has never proven complete, but has been built continuously. Such a process entails contestation, that is, debate about the proper forms of church life in one or another context. Building the Church requires remaining in conversation even amid divergences. The promise of Anglicanism resides in historic forms of tension that have proven as generative as they have divisive.

Our argument for the promise of Anglicanism, explaining this theme's broadly religious dimensions and particularly Anglican aspects, begins in Chapter 1, 'The Meaning of Promise', as we consider the reshaping of Anglicanism's story around the theme of promise. We then consider biblical and early Christian sources of the meaning of promise before summarizing how promise infused reform movements during the Middle Ages. In Chapter 2, 'A Contested Genesis', we analyse the rise of the Church of England in terms of the theme of promise. We will present the emergence of the Church of England as contested and unfinished, drawing insights from these realities for the theme of promise. Chapter 2 also considers the rise of mission from the Church of England, which we locate with the work of Thomas Bray, in the late seventeenth and early eighteenth centuries. Bray served in Maryland as commissary, or agent for church affairs, then became the catalyst for the creation of the SPG. This marked the beginning of the

Church's turn to international mission and not simply overseas chaplaincy. Bray and his colleagues, and later the founders of the CMS, perceived a biblically mandated sense of promise and a means to catholicity for the Church of England.[11]

The Church of England's mission was bound to English identity and British political and cultural influence. Such influence has never ended, and we will assess its legacy. But as the Church's mission unfolded, the idea of an Anglicanism that should transcend English experience became increasingly compelling. Beginning in Chapter 3, 'Catholicity and Contextualization', we argue that in mission Anglicans developed an ideal of catholicity. This emerging tradition encompassed widely dispersed peoples and cultures yet retained faithful and coherent patterns of church life. This emerging Anglican catholicity forms a key part of our analysis. The Church could not presume catholicity. Rather, in the challenge of contextualization that arose in its mission, the Church found the basis for a universal identity. Catholicity, the genesis of Anglican identity as intercultural and international and, hence, Anglican promise, early on became associated with the task of contextualization. That is, mission entailed evangelism and ministry intended to build the Church in a variety of cultural contexts while retaining consistent features. Until the second half of the nineteenth century, the organization of Anglican mission focused on adaptive strategies that promised to ground church life by assuring its continuity with Christian tradition and English precedent. Early on, the Church's relation to culture became a pivotal issue.

From the late nineteenth to the late twentieth centuries, the catholicity of Anglicanism also relied upon the emerging ideal of communion. In Chapter 4, 'Catholicity and Communion', we find that the appearance of diverse branches of the Church of England, many moving towards indigenous ministries and synodical self-governance, compelled attention to Anglican unity. As we shall explain, the unity that was once lauded because of the centrality of the Church of England was increasingly questioned. The sheer expanse of Anglican life prompted missiological, theological and ecclesiological tension and promise. But the ideal of catholicity, and hence the prospect of unity among

ANGLICANISM'S DILEMMA

Anglicans, was posed on an increasingly problematic basis. The notion of an Anglican Communion was of intercultural inception and Western control. The Bishop of London, the Archbishop of Canterbury, Lambeth Conferences, Primates' Meetings and Anglican Consultative Councils have played leading roles in practices of communion according to particular Western conventions. Communion remains a vital ideal and a crucial arena of Anglican consultation. Although the apparent fragmentation of communion may be taken as evidence of Anglican decline, we argue that Anglicanism has been a locus of ongoing contestation, from which promise has emerged and can emerge again.

Yet, as we describe in Chapter 5, 'Testing Anglican Coherence', the contested state of Anglican mission and life beyond the British Isles and North America has only been considered through particular lenses. The creation of church structures, such as synodical governance, and international webs of consultation that characterize the Communion have been central to discussions of the state of Anglicanism. However, consideration of church structures, which historically have been deferential to the Global North, does not exhaust analysis of Anglicanism. The past and present of Anglican promise reflect the ability of this religious tradition to find contextual footing with commitment to catholicity of belief and practice. The promise of Anglicanism surfaces through analysis of this balance, focusing on life at contextual levels.

Our argument centres not simply on Anglicanism's abstract catholicity, but on the role played by the ideal of catholicity in the dynamics of mission. Anglicanism has never presumed to be complete but has been understood developmentally in contested ways. Anglicans have repeatedly debated the shape of mission and the boundaries and porosities of their cultural adaptations. A danger, which some perceive amid current divisions, is that of allowing church life to be defined more by cultural influences than by theological ones. The other danger, also widely perceived, is that of asserting forms of religious or cultural authority from beyond, which would subdue indigenous cultural authenticity. We will argue that there has been a characteristic Anglican pattern of seeking contextualization, which has afforded the Church both local footing and catholicity of ministry and worship. Contestation has been both fruitful and divisive because of the Church's focus on contextual mission. This dynamic is a core aspect of Anglican life now.

We understand Anglicanism to be an international fellowship that has arisen on the basis of a contextually centred faith tradition. Accordingly, we will consider what 'context' and 'contextualization' have meant, and explain why we hold that contextual life, seemingly the periphery of Anglican experience, proves central to its identity. It could be argued that disparate forms of contextual life inflame division rather than point beyond it. But we will show that Anglican contextual life centres on practice, and that the contested state of Anglican life reflects ongoing searches for effective and faithful forms of mission and ministry in the Church's varied contexts. We will not approach contextual realities uncritically, nor glorify division in church life at any of its levels. We will argue that conflict often reflects a commitment to contextual expression of Christian promise with broad impact. Disparities between contextual life and the dynamics of church leadership circles will be an important theme in our narrative.

As colonial-era initiatives, styles and dependencies diminished, a reality that could be seen as decline, mission initiatives arising contextually increased. As Chapter 6, 'Renewing Communion Through Mission' describes, a kind of Anglican decentralization is unfolding. There has been no let-up in mission, especially in areas of the world where political unrest and social instability are pronounced. Chronic economic and health issues demand services few but the Church can provide, and education at all levels relies upon what the Church organizes. In these arenas, Anglicans prove adept at garnering resources and acting without urging from the Global North. Anglicans act on the basis of contextually initiated efforts, often assisted by wider consultations and partnerships. Anglican life continues to be a vibrant catholicity from below.

As we assess the ways in which Anglican life, through cross-cultural mission, has been and continues to be renewed, we will consider the extent to which these transitions at contextual levels prove both coherent and faithful. Chapter 7, 'Distinctive and Faithful Practice', focuses on the meaning and distinctiveness of Anglican religious life contextually. Using illustrative situations and individuals, we will identify patterns of mission and ministry that characterize the Church's relation to its cultural settings. We will find that Anglicans believe the Church requires further development, framed by its English origins and its catholic aspirations, guided by biblical parameters of faith and practice. The translation of ideals into particular expressions and church priorities varies from locale to locale and is often the stuff of Anglican contestation. But there are faithful patterns of seeking to discern God's mission through the Church that prove distinctive. Anglicanism's promise lies in its contextual approach to mission.

In conclusion, we will consider continuities and changes in the Anglican notion of promise. While focusing upon the practices of church life at contextual levels, we must address the limits of consensus and coherence. It will be important to ask if Anglican life was as clearly defined in prior eras as it can be tempting to assume. Was the Church of England, or its Irish, Scottish and Welsh counterparts, ever complete? For that matter, was the Anglican ideal of communion ever finished or universally honoured? We do not believe that Anglican promise has ever relied upon achieving like-minded confessionalism. Rather, while assuming the Church must identify key forms and practices, Anglicans have debated their nature and meaning.

A variety of Anglican transitions occurred during the twentieth century.[12] Prominent among them has been the growth of Anglicanism in the Global South, to the point that the majority of Anglicans are now found outside Great Britain and North America. There was also widespread adaptation of Anglican liturgy, in the Global North as well as the South. Anglicans shifted significantly towards a eucharistic emphasis and created Books of Common Prayer that reflected the Church's growth in new nations. In altering their worship, Anglicans took paths that arose contextually, reflected wider consultations and acted in parallel fashion to create similar forms of Prayer Book worship. We will use this example to argue that patterns of continuity and change are inherent in Anglican life, marked by contextual differences but enacted in comparable fashion and resulting in comparable outcomes. In that sense, contestation can inspire promise.

Notes

1 Barbara Yorke, *The Conversion of Britain*, London and New York: Routledge, 2006. Richard Fletcher, *The Barbarian Conversion*, New York: Henry Holt, 1997.

2 Anthony Kenny, ed., *Wyclif in His Time*, Oxford: Oxford University Press, 1986. Anne Hudson, *Lollards and their Books*, London: Bloomsbury, 2003.

3 Cf. Rowan Williams, *Anglican Identities*, Lanham, MD and London: Rowman and Littlefield, 2004. Martyn Percy, *The Future Shape of Anglicanism*, London and New York: Routledge, 2017. Paul Avis, *The Identity of Anglicanism: Essentials of Anglican Ecclesiology*, London: Bloomsbury T&T Clark, 2008.

4 Geoffrey Rowell, Kenneth Stevenson and Rowan Williams, *Love's Redeeming Work: The Anglican Quest for Holiness*, Oxford: Oxford University Press, 2001.

5 G. R. Evans and J. Robert Wright, eds, *The Anglican Tradition*, London and Minneapolis: SPCK/Fortress, 1991.

6 Antje Wiener, *A Theory of Contestation*, Heidelberg and New York: Springer, 2014. Marc Howard Ross, ed., *Culture and Belonging in Divided Societies*, Philadelphia: University of Pennsylvania Press, 2009.

7 For example, Marc Stewart, 'Everywhere, Always, and By All', in *The Living Church*, online, 23 February 2017, www.livingchurch.org.

8 Cf. David Hein and Gardiner H. Shattuck, Jr, *The Episcopalians*, Westport, CT and London: Praeger, 2004. Frank G. Kirklpatrick, *The Episcopal Church in Crisis*, Westport, CT and London: Praeger, 2008.

9 Cf. William L. Sachs, *Homosexuality and the Crisis of Anglicanism*, Cambridge: Cambridge University Press, 2009.

10 The works of Lamin Sanneh are especially helpful on the issue of contextualization. See his *Translating the Message*, Maryknoll, NY: Orbis, 1989, and *Whose Religion is Christianity?* fourth edition, Grand Rapids, MI: Eerdmans, 2003.

11 Daniel O'Connor et al., *Three Centuries of Mission*, New York: Continuum, 2000. Kevin Ward and Brian Stanley, eds, *The Church Mission Society and World Christianity, 1799–1999*, Grand Rapids, MI: Eerdmans, 1999.

12 William L. Sachs, 'Introduction: A Century of Anglican Transition', in William L. Sachs, ed., *Global Anglicanism c. 1910–2000, Volume 5 of the Oxford History of Anglicanism*, Oxford: Oxford University Press, 2018.

I

The Meaning of Promise

Reframing the Anglican Story

What has been the promise of Anglican life? That is, what have Anglicans intended and on what basis? There is no lack of vivid suggestions, but there is a frustrating lack of consensus. The obvious marks of Anglican identity find expression in various ways in English religious life. Even the Church of England's role as religious establishment has not resolved the matter. Within the Church of England, the idea and function of the religious establishment have been questioned repeatedly. Within strictly English bounds, 'Anglicanism' is a term that defies coherence. But its seeming uniformity masks theological and liturgical factions. The Church is a mix of varied expressions. No one formulation of its identity conveys the whole.

Of course, the greater problem concerns the Church's expansion beyond England. The success of its mission can be attested by the variety and durability of churches that arose and now claim Anglican identity. But the extent of Anglican expansion deepens the sense that Anglican life is incoherent. We use the term 'expansion' descriptively, without particular valuation. Anglicanism became larger in its numbers of adherents, especially during the twentieth century. It has also become more dispersed across continents and cultures globally. The result has been that, across its variations, Anglicanism is defined disparately. Variation, which we see as the fruit of contextualization, set the stage for contestation. The extent of contestation now and the issues being contested belie easy assurances about Anglican identity. Promise seems forestalled, even though all sides in the recent Anglican dispute over sexuality invoke this ideal. The conflict over sexuality echoes the prior tensions over liturgy and the ordination of women, exacerbating differences of biblical interpretation and the nature of church tradition in particular. Yet it has proven more divisive than prior disputes. Differing positions on sexuality, especially homosexuality, have subsumed various other tensions and cast such differences more widely across Anglican life. This conflict alone seemingly forestalls the ideal of Anglican promise. But even amid such division, we find portents of promise.

To explain how this is possible, we take a broad perspective on the nature of religious tradition and on the meaning of conflict in religious life. Our goal is to reframe the Anglican story. That is, we intend to tell the Anglican story from a different perspective and, in so doing, to highlight both the dynamism of Anglican tradition and the possibility that contestation has been the pathway to promise for Anglicans. It should be apparent that we discount claims for the finality of Anglican identity in strictly English terms. It should also be clear that we view religious faith and tradition dynamically. We affirm the truth of Christian revelation and we honour the historic framework of Anglican life in worship and ministry. However, efforts to form the Church and to live faithfully in the midst of diffuse cultural patterns lead to variations of Anglican expression. The Church is never complete, but is ever in search of ways to incarnate more fully the faith it has inherited. It is a human fellowship journeying in the midst of realities that challenge its intention. Alert to the frictions that have arisen, how Anglicans have moved from ideals to expressions is our focus.

The development of religious life in all instances requires the creation of normative patterns of belief and practice. Religions do so through identifying core aspects of human experience of the divine. Often expressive of human origins and of the beginnings of the particular religion, these accounts, and the customs that embody them, are passed on from one generation to another. Religious life links the past to the present. For Christians, this means close attention to Jesus, to his earliest followers and to the Scriptures as witness to their words and actions. By virtue of being handed down, generation to generation, such accounts form a religious tradition. Yet religious traditions must be lived, not simply passed on. As such, a tradition readily becomes contested. What we term 'contestation' is, paradoxically, emblematic of the Anglican approach to a Christian tradition that ever unfolds.[1]

All religious traditions utilize interpretations of the past, especially with reference to founding figures and a period of origins. Interpretations of the past propose actions that enhance the possibility of realizing an envisioned future. Teleology is implicit in tradition; that is, tradition intends to do more than to hallow the past or to frame life in the present, as pivotal as those emphases must be. Religious traditions seek to attain certain ends; they are inherently purposeful; they are laden with forms of promise unrealized and glimpsed partially. The theme of promise is integral to all religious traditions. In Judaism, for example, promise is embodied in the covenant between God and the Hebrew people. Promise centres on the destiny of this people and the land promised to them. In Christianity, as we shall see, the scope of promise broadens beyond one people and one land. All people can become heirs of the promised redemption and receive the gift of unity in God's eternal kingdom. Christians are called to a treasure in earthen vessels, that is, the Church, which intends to foreshadow the eternal realm. As an expression of Christian faith, Anglicanism shares the ideal of this promise. But given Anglicanism's confusions and conflicts, it seems improbable to speak of promise among Anglicans now.

As our Introduction outlined, conflict among Anglicans is historic, and the extent of conflict and resulting division has seemingly intensified. Yet conflict, we suggested, has been a facet of building the Church, a by-product of a faith tradition that is growing and diversifying. Contestation, we will reiterate, inevitably arises, challenging Anglicans to clarify what they intend and by what means. Contestation brings needed debate that serves church growth when it is accompanied by a sense of mutuality, which lately has frayed. Paradoxically, contestation on major questions of Christian faith and life can illuminate Christian promise more vividly. The challenge is to shift the focus of contestation from what various factions in a dispute fear and oppose to what they envision and aspire to become. To be a Christian, and to be the Church, is to engage in a process of becoming, whose telos requires clarity and faithful grounding.

There is no denying the depth of recent contestation among Anglicans, nor that it concerns basic aspects of faith. The conflict that has fractured Anglicanism has an intense religious and moral focus. Division over sexuality surfaces in profoundly different approaches to human identity, moral priority and proper practice in Anglican life. This conflict reflects divergent interpretations of Christian sources and their application. Anglicans are not engaged in such conflict alone. It must be understood as part of larger tensions that afflict all world religions now. As we indicated, and as Sachs has assessed in print, this conflict pits people and factions of conservative, or 'orthodox', conviction against those who uphold liberal, or 'progressive', views. For each side, issues of religious and moral purity are at stake. As the reality of alternative Anglican factions dramatizes, people of one theological and moral ilk may refuse fellowship with those who take the opposing view. The resulting division seems insurmountable.

Yet several factors mitigate this situation. The first, as we shall describe further, is that this is hardly the first time Anglicans have faced intractable difference. We do not diminish the fact of division, but neither do we make it definitive of Anglicanism's nature, historically or in the present. We see meaning and direction in Anglican disputes. Second, many Anglicans in the Church's multiple contexts do not define their faith or their lives by disputes that may occur at some remove from them. We do not discount the reality of local issues arising in parishes and dioceses across the Anglican world. But issues such as sexuality that seemingly divide the Church as an institution hardly touch most people in their local domains.

The contextual focus of Anglican life proves central to understanding the meaning of promise.

Lastly, division over sensitive theological and moral issues must be considered closely. What seem to be stark differences reveal common concerns and affirmations, but also different forms of emphasis and expression. In his broad assessment of divergences between religious liberals and conservatives, this is the conclusion of Jonathan Haidt. He is able to frame moral life in an all-encompassing way, citing six patterns of moral dichotomy that people generally use to frame their convictions. Thus, Haidt contrasts care versus harm, fairness versus cheating, loyalty versus betrayal, authority versus subversion, sanctity versus degradation and liberty versus oppression. His categories, reflective of research on several continents with special attention to religious groups and faithful people, prove suggestive for our argument. The very framework conveys the seriousness of moral concern for most people most of the time. Most people, Haidt concludes, tend to hold common foundations, in the sense that they reason morally in similar ways. Also, most people in their situations face personal and group challenges, testing their convictions and compelling adaptive stances in light of new circumstances. Morality does not begin in reason, he also finds. Reasoning is secondary, the product of conviction proposed by intuition, by sensitivities and perceptions, and by group affinity. Religious faith is grounded in such perceptions first, then explained in rational terms.[2]

What distinguishes people and their groups, and can ultimately divide them, is that different moral questions arise that reflect different kinds of contextual issues. Context here can mean just the neighbourhood or local area in which one lives, but in which vexing moral questions can surface. The issues that arise, how they are framed and what are deemed proper responses can vary across diverse contexts that reflect cultures and simple local values and priorities. Haidt also finds that people can be bound in moral conviction in ways that transcend context. He traces divergent moral priorities, and even a readiness to contest different moral conclusions, to differences of temperament. Some people emphasize care, while others focus on authority. Some lift up fairness, while others value sanctity. His six dichotomies reflect how moral conviction arises for most people. But moral conviction finds divergent emphasis and expression.

Even with apparent depth of conviction, moral absolutes are difficult to sustain. Adaptive challenges arise as life changes, circumstances in one's locale shift, new realities and insights become unavoidable. One's moral inclination may not alter greatly, and one's basis of moral conviction may not change. But the necessity of ongoing moral assessment means that Haidt describes a dynamic and unfinished process. It is not unlike the dynamism of Anglican life, with its contextual focus, its search for ever more faithful expression amid change. In addition, Haidt's framing of moral conviction in a way that transcends ideology shapes our consideration of promise. In the ways that Anglicans have framed their life, and even in the ways they have disputed with one another, we see a similar dynamic. Anglicans have sought the same ends using the same theological and historical resources, albeit valuing them differently. The hope of realizing faith's promise animates Anglican pursuits.

As we have approached the promise Anglicans have envisioned, two points of emphasis have already surfaced. The first is that Anglicans have sought to realize the Christian intention primarily in their localities, through a biblical, sacramental and pastoral tradition applied contextually. To a notable degree, Anglican theology is local theology; Anglican life is local life. At the same time, Anglicans have envisioned a larger unity that is both faithful to Christian sources and expressed compellingly in a myriad of contexts. Anglicanism is neither strictly magisterial nor entirely confessional. It claims the grounding of apostolicity understood as the continuation of gospel witness across time and cultures. Thus Anglicanism emerges in mission. Its challenges have become global on the one hand and contextual on the other. It can be vexed both by large-scale moral differences and by particular demands of resources and leadership. Anglican life occurs at various levels, and so its promise must be viewed. We now consider what the promise of Christianity has meant biblically and how it animated early Christian life, before we turn to the unfolding of Anglicanism's journey towards promise.

Promise as a Biblical and Early Christian Theme

In the New Revised Standard Version of the Bible (NRSV) the word 'promise' occurs 72 times. Nearly half, or 34 occurrences, are in the Christian Bible, or New Testament. In Luke 1.55 the word is found once in a Gospel text. This is Mary's song of praise, where she declares: 'He has helped his servant Israel, in remembrance of his mercy, according to the promise he made to our ancestors, to Abraham and to his descendants forever.' Mary speaks of promise as fulfilled, with events unfolding that confirm it, a prominent theme in Luke and Acts. Jesus speaks of himself in this way in Luke 20.17, a reference to Psalm 118, where he uses the imagery of the stone that, once rejected, has become the chief cornerstone. Acts 4.11 echoes this reference. In part, then, the New Testament gives a message of completion: that which had been promised, from the time of Abraham, has been fulfilled in the person of Jesus.

But fulfilment of historic promise in the person of Jesus does not mean that the task of building faith has been completed. Though Jesus advises his followers to stay in Jerusalem for the time being (Luke 24.49), the implication is that further events will unfold. Indeed, the message of Luke, and of the other Gospels, is that a new promise is unfolding as the old one is fulfilled. Taking Luke as illustrative, the Gospel depicts a new way of life, only beginning to unfold, to which followers of God in Christ must respond. Such a transition from old to new promise is apparent when various individuals ask Jesus what they must do to inherit eternal life, and he confounds references to keeping the law (Mark 10.17; Luke 10.25; 18.18). Indeed, the word 'inherit' is found 16 times in the New Testament. Matthew 25.34 makes reference to inheriting God's kingdom, a clear sign that new promise awaits fulfilment. Similarly,

Luke 17.20–37 describes the coming of the kingdom of God, with the message that while this new entity is imminent, it is as yet unrealized.

In the Gospels, the nature of this kingdom centres on a new way of life, personally and collectively. Thus Matthew 5–7, the Sermon on the Mount, gives the most elaborate and distinctive description of what it means to be part of what God in Christ is doing. The 'great commandment', found in Matthew 22.35–40 and Mark 12.28–34, offers a refinement on Jewish law that offers God's kingdom to all, Jew or Gentile. Similarly, the Lord's Prayer, in Luke 11.1–4, explains what it means to be in daily relation to God and to others. The parable of the Good Samaritan, in Luke 10.25–37, gives a practical, ethical illustration of this relation, contrasting the new reality of God's kingdom breaking into history with its predecessor, the law and those who would guard it, which has proven incomplete. Promise unfolds in the life and teaching of Jesus but awaits fulfilment in the life of the Church.

Other New Testament references to the theme of 'promise' occur in Acts and the Pauline epistles, where the message is amplified. Galatians 3.29 makes it plain: 'And if you belong to Christ, then you are Abraham's offspring, heirs according to the promise.' One who follows Jesus Christ is an inheritor of the promise God made to Abraham. Hebrews 9.15 depicts Jesus as the 'mediator of a new covenant, so that those who are called may receive the promised eternal inheritance'. Romans 4.13 insists that 'the promise that he would inherit the world did not come to Abraham or to his descendants through the law but through the righteousness of faith.' The implication is that faith in God, revealed in Jesus Christ, has been reframed. As Paul describes in 1 Corinthians 15.45–49 and Romans 5.12–21, Christ is the second Adam. The human race has begun anew, moving from death to life, to use resurrection imagery.[3]

Thus not only the ancient covenant with the Hebrew people, but the creation of humanity as a whole, has been re-enacted in Jesus. His followers inherit a new promise. The Jewish people are not displaced, though their role in salvation history at times would be debated vigorously and persecution of Jews over centuries would declare that some followers of Jesus would reject them, even brutally. More appropriately, the gift given to Jews has been fulfilled in Christ. References to 'inherit' in the Gospels suggest the means by which one becomes worthy. Moral criteria and self-sacrifice reflecting trust in Jesus loom as the way to the kingdom of God. Yet the biblical message does not assume that God's promise has been fulfilled. It is the promise of final redemption and realization of the kingdom of God, which is to be anticipated and sought in earthly life, but not necessarily realized, though this point also would be debated. How to understand, embrace and remain in God's promise has been the substance of Christian debate for two thousand years. Christians have consistently agreed more on the basic categories of their faith than on their proper expression. While the promise awaits fulfilment, what believers must be and do to merit it has resisted consensus. The proper shape of the Church as the company of believers and the repository of faith's promise has evoked repeated debate.

The apostle Paul (c.5–c.67) never knew Jesus during his lifetime, but Paul's experience of the resurrected Jesus inspired conviction that has stamped Christianity indelibly. For Paul, the promise of Christian faith resided in the Church. But given Christianity's infancy then, the Church could not be presumed, it had to be formed. The process of its formation, often contested, centred on both its ideals and its realities. On the one hand, the Church had to be enacted in distinctive ways, befitting its faith. On the other hand, the Church could only be construed in ways that were understandable, utilizing social models from the Roman world that were readily recognized. In a word, Pauline Christianity sought to be socially transformative of its world, taking extant forms of social relations and remaking them along the lines of faith. It is the transformative impulse in church life that historically has accounted for much of the sense of promise in Christian life, while contextual realities fuelled efforts at transformation.

For Paul, the Church begins as the company of people who respond to his preaching, or who in some way have begun to appropriate faith in Jesus Christ (1 Thess. 1.6; 2.13). They have begun to acquire a corporate identity as followers, as believers. The gospel is the foundation of the Church (1 Cor. 2.2; 3.6, 10; 4.15). The existence of growing groups of believers is evidence of the power of God. It is evident in the presence of the Spirit, and in lives changed as a result (1 Thess. 1.6–10). Central to the change is their sense of community, of acquiring a mutual possibility, of shared promise we might say. Although they waited for Jesus' return, as the end of Luke's Gospel counselled, they were a people of destiny, who were called to live as holy people even as they waited for history's culmination (1 Thess. 1.9–10; 4.13–18). Thus they created community, a sense of fellowship, evidence of being one body, united in faith (1 Cor. 1.9, 12). Spiritual formation as believers also served as corporate formation, that is, their emergence as a body, a fellowship, akin to a family.[4]

To describe who and what they were becoming, the earliest Christians had recourse only to models from the ancient world. Of course, they used the family as something of a metaphor. They also adopted the term *ecclesia*, originally a Greek term for an assembly of the city's citizens. In Christian hands, ecclesia acquired images of a distinctive fellowship, those joined by a unique bond, living a new and redemptive way of life, and not simply an assembly as their ancient predecessors understood it. At the heart of their fellowship was a common meal, modelled on the Last Supper of Jesus and his disciples (Luke 22.7–23). In their common meal, early Christians felt the presence of their Lord and saw themselves not only as replicating the past but creating the power and clarity of the original meal in their own midst. That such a common meal became central early in Christian experience is attested by the Didache, a first-century teaching document, which gives instructions as to the meaning and performance of the meal, as well as to baptism and other early practices and teachings of the early Church.

But within a few decades of the birth of Christianity, the common meal became one of the most contested aspects of Christian life and even a source of division. Paul's first letter to the Church at Corinth suggests the nature of this dispute. In chapters 8 and 10 he speaks of not eating food offered to idols, of developing proper knowledge, and of avoiding arrogance and puffery. The reference to idols may be as much metaphorical as it is literal. Food, and meals, and one's place at the table, could reflect idolatry, especially the idolatry of self-importance, as readily as they could express genuine faith. But there was a still larger issue, namely that of table fellowship, a carryover from the Jewish origins of Christianity. Galatians 2.11–14 records Paul's realization that the early Church's common meal was divided along Jewish and Gentile lines. The issue would become acute at Antioch, with old divisions intruding upon the intended fellowship. Habitual issues of appropriate foods, and who was suitable to eat with whom, threatened the Church's life. Values of purity in religious identity and practice were the source of the dispute. These values have challenged Christian unity ever since and have surfaced repeatedly in Anglican disputes.

The reality of differences among Christians, some of them severe, has been apparent since the earliest Christian times. Late in the second century, the philosopher Celsus (n.d.) belittled Christian truth claims by noting that the followers of Jesus were divided into competing sects with divergent views. Some 70 years later, the Christian theologian Origen (185–254) responded to Celsus' charge, as historian Robert Louis Wilken explains. 'Differences, [Origen] pointed out, not just on "small and trivial things" but about "the most important matters" were, as any philosopher would recognize, a mark of intellectual seriousness.'[5] Debate over the person of Christ, and the meaning of the incarnation, occupied a series of early Christian councils, starting with Nicaea in 325, and extending to Ephesus (431), Chalcedon (451) and later gatherings at Constantinople (553, 680). By 787, another council at Nicaea engaged the issue of veneration of icons, which would further challenge Christian unity. The reality of difference has been a historic reality facing Christian life, even as key aspects of church life seemed clarified.

We do not have the opportunity here to give an extensive review of these or other early Christian disputes. But the direction of our argument should be clear. The theme of promise was prominent in early Christian life. To realize the promise of faith in the risen Lord, the first Christians had to be clear about what they believed, and about how they organized and practised their faith. Yet even as they agreed readily on the lineaments of church life, such as the common meal, and even as the Church grew and became elaborated, the meanings of core practices and beliefs of the Christian faith were contested. As Christian history characteristically is written, it is apparent that there were disputes with groups who were deemed heretical, and who posed alternative forms of organization to the Church, such as Gnostics and Donatists. But even among those who would become the mainstream of Christian development, there were fault lines over practice, often concerning questions of purity of belief, worship and ministry. The promise of the Church was not easily realized, nor clearly articulated. The Church's development was never complete, and those who now are seen as major contributors to it often lent colorations and distinctions that embodied different points of emphasis and expression in its life. It is important to acknowledge that there were differences in church life and to identify what prompted them.

For example, the second- and third-century Christian author, Tertullian (160–220) advanced an exclusionist, perfectionist view of the Church, a stance befitting his Montanist views. While speaking of the divine Spirit's presence in the Church, he also depicted proper church life in terms of discipline. In practical terms, this meant that Tertullian challenged the readmission of adulterers to the Church even if they were penitent. Preoccupied with the Church's necessary unity, he spoke of it in terms of holiness and of unity in belief and practice. For him, the Church's deposit was clear. Yet, the Church was unfinished: it bore a sense of promise not in what it was, but in what it must become. Having received its form, the Church must realize its calling. Comparing the Church to a ship at sea, and also to a military camp, Tertullian blended dynamism with strictness in his sense of promise.[6]

At points, a somewhat later early church leader would agree. Fourth-century bishop and theologian Basil of Caesarea

(330–79), one of the so-called Cappadocian Fathers of Asia Minor, echoed earlier images of the Church's distinctiveness and mission. But if perfectionism was the mark of Tertullian's view, agreement and unity shaped Basil's sense of the Church's intention. In homilies and other writings, Basil depicted a Church that intended to create a social whole, of clergy and laity bound together in common loyalty and endeavour, with particular emphasis on charity and good works. Basil intended for the Church to be engaged constructively in the life of the city, to instil a new sense of social whole, of the polis as a family. Unlike the emphasis of Tertullian, Basil held that one should not press too hard on those in theological error if they showed signs of repentance. The Church's task was to search for harmony, for an order that would redeem all human relations. In that sense it was catholic.

There was a certain rigour in Basil's faith and its application. He was an ascetic, one who viewed the world sceptically, with wariness of uncritical acceptance of social patterns. But Basil viewed the world as real and necessary, that is, as the setting in which the Christian faith must be lived, in which Christian intention must be realized. Thus he worked to better the world while advancing the identity and role of the believing community. Motivated by awareness of an invisible, spiritual world, Basil worked to secure the life of faith in the visible world. He uplifted the Church's pastoral role, invoking images of individual and communal life as a journey. In doing so, he readily adopted resources from the secular world. Even as the late Roman world showed signs of fragmentation, Basil, like his Cappadocian colleagues, adapted its categories and modes of expression to advance the Church's life.[7]

The decline of the Roman world, which became irreversible by the late fourth century, had a formative influence upon the rise of Christianity. On the one hand, the Church benefitted from Roman example in building its organization as well as its theological convictions. Though his actions later could seem more intrusive than beneficial, the Emperor Constantine intervened in church life in 325 at the Council of Nicaea. There he shaped the historic creed that resulted, but his action was not surprising. In 313 Constantine ended Roman persecution of Christianity, which had flared periodically since the time of Jesus. Indeed, Constantine became a catechumen himself. In a sense, the promise of Christianity seemed fulfilled. During the fourth century, the numbers of Christians across the Roman world grew by tens of millions. Late in the century, the emperor Theodosius made Christianity the Roman world's favoured religion, even enacting legal disabilities against other faiths. Christianity's triumph seemed complete. But as the basic outline of the Church and the faith seemed clear, profound differences remained among Christians. By the time of the fifth century, it was possible to speak of 'catholic' Christianity. That is, to a considerable extent, Christianity had acquired consistent, or 'universal', characteristics. These included the threefold ministry of bishops, priests and deacons, the central role of worship, and the priority of baptism and the Eucharist among the Christian sacraments. Nicene Christianity had been articulated and was advancing, even as the Church faced social and theological rival groups, especially Arians and Donatists. The office of bishop had come to embody the Church's belief and teaching, though there were rival Arian and Donatist bishops. As we shall see, the office of bishop also would represent the Church's mission and thus dramatize its promise.[8]

As Bishop of Hippo Regius on the coast of North Africa, in modern Algeria, Augustine (354–430) embodied the Christian Church's challenges and promise. His remarkable corpus spanned a variety of theological and pastoral occasions and topics. In part, his writing was tendentious, reflecting controversies with Pelagians and Donatists; in part, he wrote as a philosopher and rhetorician, befitting his classical education; in some measure, he wrote works of mystical reflection, such as his treatment of the Trinity. In large measure, he wrote as a bishop of the Church, setting out the life of faith in community. In doing so, he gave lasting definition to the meaning of the Church being catholic. In Augustine's hands, the Church avoided the excess porousness of Pelagianism and the excess exclusivity and purity of Donatism. Thus, he left a definitive imprint on catholic penitential thinking and practice. His focus was the ongoing process of salvation in the entire community, on relations among Christians and with the Church. He took care to delineate a variety of sins, with increasingly stiff degrees of penance required. But his emphasis was on preserving church unity. Bishops would play a role in forgiveness, but in most instances the burden of overcoming sin and its attendant divisions lay with the local faith community. In one sense, the Church's promise for Augustine lay in securing reconciliation.[9]

The Church's worship proved to be central. The sacraments and preaching complemented one another to join diverse people into one community, faithful to its Lord, joined spiritually to prophets and patriarchs. Liturgy imparted a sense of wholeness and purpose, grounding the Church internally and motivating it externally. As Wilken shows, for Augustine the Church was 'an ordered, purposeful gathering of human beings with a distinctive way of life, institutions, laws, beliefs, memory, and form of worship'.[10] The Church must be clear and consistent about what it intends and what manner of life it imparts. Augustine's goal was to interpret, to explain and to invite. As a result, the Church must be open to a diversity of customs and traditions in its local settings, while adhering to its basic affirmations and practices. Yet such adherence is never complete, always something of an aspiration. The Church's promise lies in unity amid diversity.

The importance of such promise was heightened by the Church's circumstances in Augustine's day. It was an age of decline in civic life, in historic institutions and even in Rome itself. Augustine lived to see the city of Rome sacked, though even this tumultuous event did not signal the empire's collapse. However, the sack of Rome did become the occasion for him to write his lengthiest and most noted work, *The City of God*. There he distinguished the Church from earthly institutions, however glorious and historic. Like earlier Christian writers, especially those motivated by ascetic disciplines, Augustine sought to distinguish the Church from civic and political life, while maintaining that Christians could not disengage from them. Prior to his life as a Christian, he had been a member of the Manichees, a world-rejecting sect, which drew a stark contrast between body and spirit, the world and faith. But as a Christian, even as the world that had formed him disintegrated, Augustine extolled the visible Church, its worship, belief and offices, including that of bishop. It was impossible, he held, to speak of the city of God in its eternal sense without invoking the Church, where the eternal is represented on earth.[11] Promise for Augustine lay in the life, ministry and mission of the Church. Social disarray should strengthen its purpose and enliven its mission. Thus, as Rome declined, the Church grew.

Mission, Promise and Divergence

The origin of Anglicanism has habitually been traced to 597, when Augustine, a missionary sent by Pope Gregory, arrived at Canterbury in Kent. The intention was not simply to convert Aethelbert, king of the Anglo-Saxons, and his domain to Christianity. In addition to evangelism, the intention was to draw all of Britain and Ireland into the orb of the Roman Catholic Church which was emerging across Western Europe. Christianity already existed in portions of the British Isles. Patrick had already conducted his mission to Ireland. St Columba, who in the sixth century had set up religious foundations in Derry, Durrow and Kells, also founded what would become a centre for 'Celtic' Christianity with Iona, in some sense, as its locus. Though Iona and its 'Celtic' character have been romanticized as a spiritual Camelot, there was ample fact to fuel modern imagination.

The signal aspect of Augustine's mission was to convert and to incorporate the populations of the British Isles to Catholic Christianity. His focus on converting a ruler began the process of aligning Church and state across Britain, which would become an intricate and not always desirable relation for the Church. At the time, the conversion of Aethelbert was a pragmatic step that would facilitate papal influence among the Anglo-Saxons. Indeed, Augustine's ministrations would produce large-scale baptisms, as the Anglo-Saxon population became Christian. Not all aspects of the mission proceeded smoothly. Existing Christianity among the British population, notably several bishops, initially resisted Augustine's efforts to draw them into Roman allegiance. Augustine himself became a bishop, and also founded sees at Rochester and London. There is tangible evidence to support the idea of his success.

He also founded a monastery and a school at Canterbury, lending further shape to how mission would be conducted and what conversion intended. To embrace the Christian faith would be to start down a pathway of personal development in the context of sacred community in one's locale on the one hand and to launch the Church's role as a catalyst for social development on the other. In the Middle Ages across Europe, monasteries became principal sources of local education and pastoral care. They were contextual embodiments of an extended ecclesiastical network. They illustrated the promise of the Church's catholicity.[12]

Deep divides remained between Christians with allegiance to Rome and those who claimed an earlier form of Christian confession. These differences were apparent in divergence over the style of monastic tonsure, the dating of Easter and how the Church was organized, more locally, or with greater sway from beyond.[13] For the time being, the mission of Augustine and the pre-existing Church of the Britons coexisted. But Rome's influence could not be deterred. In 664, the Synod of Whitby confirmed that Roman patterns of tonsure and the dating of Easter would prevail across the British Isles. Unity was proclaimed, though it was never complete. Across Western Europe, a particular order of church life, centred on Rome's authority, arose.

Extensive forms of mission defined the early Middle Ages, consistently focused on evangelism and faith community formation in local settings. The work of holy people can be cited in various places and eras, including Martin and later Gregory of Tours, Boniface, and Cyril and Methodius, all on the European Continent. Across Britain as well, Augustine's example was extended by the likes of Columbanus then Aidan, as the medieval Church consolidated. Various historians have described how the Church became rooted in local life while developing sacred centres such as monasteries and even islands where pilgrimage and spiritual enhancement were possible. The Church became grounded in one context after another by comparable means.

The Christian Church's life was rich in various respects. It became the support not merely of the rich and powerful, but of ordinary people in the midst of life's passages. The Church adapted to local customs and vernaculars, infusing them with meaning and purpose, explanation and consolation, wonder and promise, all grounded in the gospel and the sacramental life. Parish churches and monasteries created sacred canopies uniting local life into a coherent whole. That is, the Church became the framework of local life, its ministries providing social coherence and religious grounding in an unpredictable world. The Church's pattern of regular, sacramental worship and pastoral care, enlivened by annual observances such as Christmas and Easter, and by regular festivals, often focused on saints and holy remembrances, gave life indelible direction and unity. Thus the British Isles, like the rest of Western Europe, was drawn into Roman Catholic Christianity.

A similar pattern repeated itself from locale to locale. In the process, the various localities were knit together in stated allegiance to Rome. The obvious representatives of unity to Rome were the Church's archbishops and bishops. Mission seemingly fused a myriad of contextual faith expressions into a unified, Catholic Church. Over the course of the Middle Ages, Catholic practice and belief would be elaborated and Rome's dominion enhanced. In that sense, the promise of Christianity of biblical origins, echoed by patristic direction and hope, seemed fulfilled across Europe. Yet the Roman Catholic achievement was never complete; it could not erase differences of belief and practice that reflected more contextual patterns of regional and local church life. The seeming uniformity of medieval Catholicism subsumed tensions and differences that would later evoke calls for reform and movements to secure it.

Nevertheless, the achievement of medieval Catholicism was impressive. How such elaboration of church life occurred is a fascinating story, which we can only summarize briefly.

The rise of the penitential office, encouraged in late ancient times by Augustine, is an important example. What began as an idea, of forgiveness and of the Church's possibility in offering it on God's behalf, extended over the Middle Ages into the idea of purgatory, and fuelled the Church's prerogative to interpret and apply it.[14] Of course, the administration of penance occurred contextually, in the work of local priests, monastics and bishops. But local practice was accountable to Roman authority, should religious or political circumstances warrant. Part of the growth of the medieval Roman Church can be seen in the increasing flow of religious business towards Rome, that is, of decisions on various ecclesiastical matters that could only be determined at Rome as its hierarchical system took effect.

Thus, in the early medieval centuries, mission began as conversion and as contextual development of the faith in monastic and parochial life. But as Rome became Christianity's functional centre and, arguably, the arbiter of much of European life, mission entailed not just incorporation into the faith but fealty to Rome's authority. Such loyalty became the formal test of catholicity. In this sense, catholicity meant unity that had acquired a legal character, enforced as much by the Church's own institutional capacities as by its alignment with kings and princes. The medieval Church's capacity to inspire hearts and minds, to order belief and morality, and eventually even to rally Crusades and Inquisitions bespoke its claim to being Christianity's centre, the guarantor of its truth and efficacy. It could be argued, and has been repeatedly, that the promise of the Christian faith requires such unity around a sacred centre, namely Rome.

The Roman Church's claim to be the centre Christianity required would gain tangible credence with the reign of Charlemagne. He envisioned the rebuilding of the structure of the Roman Empire, of its administrative network as a unifier of Europe. His emphasis upon a learned civil service enhanced the Church's sense of its own network and thus framed the growth of its own administrative and connectional ideals. Ancient Rome's empire itself had been an extended network of culture, loyalty and administration. As the empire waned,

Christianity inhabited its outline and captured its intention, creating a new, religious *lingua franca*, but otherwise adopting ancient civic forms. One cannot say, with Gibbon, that the Church hastened the end of the Roman Empire. In various respects, Christians and the Church faced severe challenges because of Rome's decline. More importantly, early medieval Christianity across Europe reanimated ancient Rome's form and its pursuit of social unity.[15]

Christianity's unity, despite the centralizing influence of the Roman Church, was neither assured nor complete. The life of an extended institution requires a designated centre to give it purpose and form. That is, all institutions required focused purpose and the authority designed to achieve their ends. However, the life of no institution, even the Church, can be summarized solely by the activities of its designated centre. Whatever matters are addressed, and apparently resolved, by centralized authority and its governance take on different meanings and expressions at the institution's peripheries. Of course, the extent of Roman Catholic dominance was not complete: the emergence of Orthodox Christianity became elaborate by the eleventh century, and Coptic and non-Chalcedonian expressions of the faith forged their own life. It could be argued that they were beyond the periphery of Roman influence; but they dramatized the disparate forms of Christian expression.[16]

But as medieval life, and the Church as well, consolidated, the periphery of Roman Catholicism also elaborated. In a sense, the unity of Christianity across Western Europe was always incomplete. Timing, conviction and circumstance introduced distinctions from one context to another. We have noted that there were distinctions among Christians of the British Isles and Ireland. Even more, distinctions can be made between the Christianity of various early medieval tribal groups. The Franks are a notable instance to whom much scholarly attention has been given. When comparisons are drawn between Germany and Scandinavia and Spain, further differences can be seen. Unity of offices, beliefs and ideals in broad compass did not ensure unity of application and practice across Europe.

THE MEANING OF PROMISE

The English Sarum Rite, a form of the medieval Mass, is an example of the phenomenon we wish to underscore. The rite was the particular creation of Osmund, Bishop of Salisbury, in the eleventh century. Incorporating enhanced ceremonial, apparently of French influence, the Sarum Rite is thought to be formative of distinctively English worship. It was a contextualized form of a more general liturgical form, the Mass. Thus, the creation of Catholic Christianity represented the achievement of a religious culture defined in terms of an institution centred at Rome and joined administratively to it. But within the bounds of Catholic offices, practices and beliefs, there were variations from one context to another. The Church's periphery was a mottled assortment. While certain groups could be defined as heretical, notably the Waldenses and Cathars, over the course of the Middle Ages novel movements arose across Catholic Europe, not all of which could be deemed out of bounds. They arose on the periphery of the institutional Church, where they evolved different visions of Christian community, often reflecting local social experience. Intense interpersonal and group experience bespoke a more authentic Christian life than the formalized Catholic Church and its authorities embodied. The groups that diverged from Roman Catholic life claimed they could revive the essence of Christian faith and point the Church towards realization of its promise.[17]

By the eleventh century in Western Europe, the theme of reform had begun to arise across the Catholic Church. It began in the monasteries as an impulse to cleanse the Christian world of perceived impurities. In his history of the great monastery that began at Cluny in France a century earlier, Raoul Glaber wrote in 1050 that the reforms at Cluny embodied the biblical vision of a new heaven and new earth. He meant that Cluny gained unusual influence, becoming a centre of social and political as well as religious reform. It sought to be distinct from civil power yet hold dominion over it. This variation of the Augustinian ideal led Cluny to help inspire the Crusades, given the careers of bishops, archbishops and popes that it shaped.

At the heart of Cluny's approach to reform lay an emphasis upon order and identity. In a fragile, disordered world, the Church took the initiative to define the boundaries of acceptable belief and practice within the Church and in society. Not surprisingly, some rulers, such as Henry I of England (c.1100), aligned with Cluny and endorsed its approach to reform. Although Cluny and the reform initiative to which it gave impetus partly served to secure the Church's uniqueness, it also served to enhance earthly power. Friction between Church and state would be prominent throughout the late Middle Ages and into the centuries of Renaissance and Reformation. England would offer its own examples of such tension. But a shared interest in preserving social and ecclesiastical order would repeatedly link religious and secular rulers. Thus, the first wave of reform in the Middle Ages came from the top down. We could say that reform of Church and society began at the centre, from the designated sources of religious and social authority.[18]

But from the twelfth century onward, reform of the Church also began on the periphery, that is, in contextual settings apart from the locus of formal authority. The distinction between centre and periphery has been developed by social theorists to explain spatial, power and resource differentials within organizations and societies, as well as among them. In modern studies, the emphasis often falls on economic development, and on relations between the so-called industrialized world and the so-called developing world. The distinction can also be used to highlight grassroots movements that arise more or less spontaneously beyond the sanction of formal authority and present cultural challenges to them. The reform movements of the twelfth century had this character; one in particular set the stage for the far-reaching initiatives that created the Church of England and other branches of the Protestant Reformation.

On 16 April 1210, almost a year after they first met, Pope Innocent III approved the new religious community that had gathered around a native of Assisi, Italy named Giovanni di Bernardone. Already he was known as Francis of Assisi, to mark his commitment to a devout life. The mendicant life, as it would be known, occurred in community marked by piety, poverty and service, following Jesus' example. Unlike the precedent set by Cluny and other monasteries derived from Benedictine example, Francis and his followers did not settle in one locale. Nor did they inspire a new network of monasteries, linking one locale to another. Franciscans focused upon their religious vocation of prayer and service. They lived mobile lives, seeking fresh opportunities for witness to the example of Jesus. The peripatetic Francis had a notable encounter with an Egyptian, Muslim sultan, a visit which deepened his devotion to prayer.[19]

Franciscan piety and communal life spilled beyond the bounds of order as the Church's hierarchy intended. The example of Francis and his followers conveyed a sense of religious promise to other groups across Western Europe who were not interested in submitting to formal authority. Familiar distinctions between clergy and laity, and between men and women, faded. The Poor Clares, for example, became a notable women's movement following the Franciscan example. A variety of groups, loosely known as spiritual Franciscans, gave further testimony to the grassroots appeal of the religious ideal. By the late Middle Ages, various groups, in one locale after another, strove to embody the idea Francis helped to popularize: lives of piety, poverty and service, collectively known as the *vita apostolica*, or the apostolic life. It was an intense and spontaneous movement, at the Church's periphery, especially among lay persons seeking to find authentic faith and community beyond what the Church's centre recognized.[20]

Reform, on the eve of the Protestant Reformation, had a variety of sources. Some arose intellectually, such as the humanist theme of the Renaissance. Some arose among elites, as the impetus of Henry VIII would illustrate in England. In the end, contextual, popular movements, often seeking to embody the apostolic life, proved determinative. So we shall also discover as we consider the rise of Anglicanism. Its promise has repeatedly emerged at the periphery of church life, more than at its centre.

Notes

1 Jaroslav Pelikan, *Tradition*, New Haven, CT: Yale University Press, 1986. Edward Shils, *Tradition*, Chicago: University of Chicago Press, 2006.

2 Jonathan Haidt, *The Righteous Mind*, New York: Vintage, 2013.

3 Cf. William Kurz, 'Promise and Fulfillment in Hellenistic Jewish Narratives and in Luke-Acts', in David Moessner, ed., *Jesus and the Heritage of Israel*, Harrisburg, PA: Trinity Press International, 1999, pp. 147–70. Also Darrell L. Bock, *A Theology of Luke and Acts*, Grand Rapids, MI: Zondervan, 2012.

4 N. T. Wright, *Paul: In Fresh Perspective*, Minneapolis, MN: Fortress Press, 2009. James W. Thompson, *The Church According to Paul*, Ada, MI: Baker, 2014.

5 Robert Louis Wilken, *The Spirit of Early Christian Thought*, New Haven, CT: Yale University Press, 2005, pp. 111f.

6 David Rankin, *Tertullian and the Church*, Cambridge: Cambridge University Press, 1995. Montanism was an early Christian movement encouraging the idea of further prophecies driven by the Holy Spirit in the Church. Modelled after its founder, Montanus, the movement also emphasized a strict personal ethic and sought to distinguish the Church from the world. Cf. Christine Trevett, *Montanism*, Cambridge: Cambridge University Press, 1996. Also, Peter Thonemann, ed., *Roman Phrygia*, Cambridge: Cambridge University Press, 2013.

7 Philip Rousseau, *Basil of Caesarea*, Berkeley, CA: University of California Press, 1998.

8 Peter Brown, *The World of Late Antiquity*, New York: W. W. Norton, 1989 and *The Rise of Western Christendom*, Oxford: Wiley-Blackwell, 2013. Brown's work, in these and other books, links bishops to the promise of late ancient Christianity in that the office of bishop acquired ideals of holiness translated from early monastic communities. Early Christian leadership was thus presumed to unite Christlike attributes with oversight of church affairs. One way in which these impulses blended was in the importance attached to practical forms of compassion such as care for poor and infirm persons.

9 Mark Ellingsen, *The Richness of Augustine*, Louisville, KY: Westminster John Knox Press, 2005. Wilken, *The Spirit of Early Christian Thought*, pp. 188f.

10 Wilken, *The Spirit of Early Christian Thought*, p. 191.

11 Wilken, *The Spirit of Early Christian Thought*, p. 191.

12 Yorke, *The Conversion of Britain*. Fletcher, *The Barbarian Conversion*.

13 Cf. W. J. Sheils and Diana Wood, eds, *The Churches, Ireland, and the Irish*, Oxford: Ecclesiastical History Society, 1997.

14 Jacques LeGoff, *The Birth of Purgatory*, Chicago: University of Chicago Press, 1981.

15 Chris Wickham, *The Inheritance of Rome*, New York: Penguin Books, 2010.

16 Cf. Diarmaid MacCulloch, *Christianity: The First Three Thousand Years*, New York: Penguin Books, 2009.

17 Frederick Thomas Bergh, 'Sarum Rite', in *Catholic Encyclopedia*, New York: Robert Appleton Company, available online at www.newadvent.org/cathen/13479a.htm [accessed 22 May 2019].

18 Edwin Mullins, *Cluny: In Search of God's Lost Empire*, New York: Blue Bridge, 2006. See Edward Shils, *Center and Periphery*, Chicago: University of Chicago Press, 1975.

19 Dominic Monti, *Francis & His Brothers*, Cincinnati, OH: St. Anthony Messenger Press, 2009.

20 Katherine Ludwig Jansen, *The Making of the Magdalen*, Princeton: Princeton University Press, 2000.

2

A Contested Genesis

An Unfulfilled Settlement

The ideal of the *vita apostolica* offered a basis for discontent with certain practices of the medieval Roman Catholic Church. Images of apostolic Christianity also furthered the intention of securing the essence of faith and practice. Early Christianity became idealized in a broad way that informed the growth of humanism, reform-minded religious orders and groups on the Church's margins, such as the Lollards in England. Thus, while late medieval Catholicism provided a sacred canopy for life in Western Europe, the Church's capacity to realize essential aspects of the Christian faith became contested in various places. When a German monk named Martin Luther proposed his Ninety-five Theses to further reform of the Church in 1517, the Protestant Reformation began. Luther proved to be the tipping point of an array of religious as well as political and social reform movements.

Luther's central themes were readily understood and widely emulated. First, he affirmed the idea of *sola scriptura*, or the central religious authority of the Bible. Indeed, he devoted himself to a translation of Scripture into German, a tangible expression of his emphasis on making the Bible accessible to all believers. Second, he grounded the Christian life less in the Church's historic authority than in an emphasis on salvation by faith rather than works. His criticism of Catholic devotional practice awakened the idea that all believers can find God directly, though faith is most readily sustained through the Church. Luther levelled particular criticism at the practice of selling indulgences, or seemingly buying God's forgiveness while expanding the Church's coffers. Luther's anger at the Church's excesses would be clearly and repeatedly stated, and widely absorbed. Yet more than anger and protest were entailed. Luther launched a widespread reframing of Christian life, the relation of the Church to the world and the workings of the Church itself. His initiatives were the initial focus of Protestantism.[1]

Thus, the Reformation was both protest against Roman Catholic abuses and reanimation of basic Christian principles. As Luther's ideals echoed across Europe, the ranks of Reformers grew. They differed in how they understood the proper expression of Christianity's biblical and apostolic ideals. For example, John Calvin applied the principles Luther advanced in different and distinctive ways. With the collaboration of civil authority in Geneva, Calvin remade worship, reframing the sacramental dimension and heightening the dimensions of teaching and preaching. He also applied strict doctrinal standards, emphasizing the sovereignty of God and God's guiding hand in human affairs. To integrate faith and life, Calvin devised an elaborate system of pastoral care across Geneva. Thus, as Luther's model grew in some portions of Europe, Calvin's model grew in others, notably Scotland, as well as Switzerland.[2]

More than Luther or Calvin, the ideals of Reformation evoked other energetic and even radical initiatives. A sectarian impulse arose, intent on applying literal, apostolic and biblical ideals to the Church's life. In the Netherlands, for instance, a quietly charismatic leader named Menno Simons cast a vision of peaceful Christian community on society's margins that would exemplify charity and pacifism. The Reformation's ideals knew no boundaries and could not be confined to one or another channel of influence. Nor could the Reformation be guided by existing religious and political elites alone. Eventually a kind of stasis emerged, after years of contestation and even civil conflict. Certain European provinces and cities bore one or another Reformed imprint, while others remained predominantly Roman Catholic.

THE PROMISE OF ANGLICANISM

It is important to note the scope and manner of the Reformation across Europe. It arose as a form of discourse at the levels of church leadership. Martin Luther's protest against what he deemed to be abuses of Christian intention in the Catholic Church were presented as theses, then debated, published and debated further. But the ideas he floated quickly gained social as well as religious currency, and the nature of discourse broadened, to encompass patterns of religious life as well as social and political relations. Discourse, it became apparent, occurs in informal and widespread ways, as well as formal occasions within higher institutional echelons. We note the work of Michel Foucault on the theme of discourse, for he has described discourse as a means of constituting knowledge, together with social practices and use of power in the relations that result. We also note Foucault's emphasis on discourse as a habitual means of contesting inherited ideas and transforming the social relations that ideas would frame.[3] In speaking of Anglicanism's promise, we shall make repeated use of the theme of discourse as the basis of contestation, that is, of presenting challenges to inherited assumptions about the Church's nature and truth. Such an impetus came from the Reformation and led to widespread variations in church and social life, even among Protestants.

It is also important to observe that in retelling the familiar story of the Reformation, and then of the rise of the Church of England as one branch of it, we are reframing the nature of the story. Histories of the Reformation, as well as of the Church of England, make note of the broad impact of religious reform and of the variety of reform impulses. However, most assessments of the rise of Protestantism emphasize the rise of tradition and focus on its coherence and later forms of continuity. Various treatments of the rise of Calvinism from Geneva embody this approach.[4] We take a different tack in our consideration of Anglicanism. We acknowledge the rise of a distinct tradition, framed by various forms of discourse, we might say. We also note the multitude of efforts to articulate, in the past and the present, the nature of Anglicanism as a coherent and faithful tradition. Yet we will also emphasize

A CONTESTED GENESIS

the incompleteness of Anglicanism, its disputed aspects and the series of conflicts that have marked its history. In such forms of contestation, we will locate essential aspects of Anglicanism's promise, as a form of church life and Christian tradition that has ever been emerging, in the process of being realized. In this sense, not only in its forms of consensus, Anglicanism has reflected its Reformation heritage.

At one time or another, from 1534 to 1660, Christianity in England bore many of the marks of Reformation on the Continent. A variety of religious impulses, bearing the imprint of Roman Catholicism and various Protestant strands competed for hegemony. As historians have traced, the English Reformation absorbed much of the Protestant impulse from the Continent, notably the Calvinist one. But while not entirely unique in religious terms, the dynamics of reform in England were framed by the vicissitudes of the monarchy, arguably more so than on the Continent. In search of a new religious equilibrium, English life swung from disavowal of the papacy to embrace of reform, to rejection of reform, to embrace of a moderate reform, then, later, towards radical Protestantism and finally to Restoration. In short, the predominant form of religious life swung from the predilections of one ruler to the next, back and forth.

Throughout these political and religious swings, one or another sort of reform trajectory appeared, or even, under Queen Mary, rejection of Protestantism and return to Roman Catholicism as the state religion. The search for a national religious solution would never be complete, even as a new framework for religious establishment was created after 1660. Throughout the swings of political and religious life there were two defining themes: first, that England was in search of a unifying religious framework; second, that reform was incomplete. English life was caught between pursuit of a reformed Church and state, and encounters with realities, especially religious variations, that complicated their realization.

The English Reformation is said to have begun with passage of the Act of Supremacy in 1534. Already, in 1533, the Act of Restraint of Appeal had signalled that King Henry VIII was intent on eliminating papal influence from England. Henry's use of a passage from the book of Leviticus to justify his intention to divorce Catherine of Aragon signalled that he held a modicum of faith and biblical knowledge. But he sought divorce in order to marry a wife who would give him a son and sought religious justification for his intention. By the Act of Royal Supremacy in 1534, Henry excluded papal authority from England. Otherwise, Henry resisted the impetus for reform that was appearing on the Continent. Indeed, he persecuted early English Protestants such as Robert Barnes. Movements towards actual reform awaited Henry's death and the accession to the throne of nine-year-old Edward VI. The council that ruled in his stead embraced reform and Reformers, and Continental influence became noticeable. Reformers, especially those drawn towards Calvin, found a haven in England. The reign of Edward also permitted Thomas Cranmer to advance versions of the Book of Common Prayer in 1549 and 1552 that reflected Protestant influence. The Church of England was emerging as a definitively Protestant body.[5]

Cranmer envisioned a Church of England that was ever more Protestant in belief while holding to forms of ministry and sacramental life that were historic. In effect, Cranmer was the first to envision a reformed Church whose breadth could unify the nation. But realization of this vision eluded him. The reform permitted by Edward's reign proved brief. For five tumultuous years after Edward's death in 1553, Mary held the throne and moved England back towards Rome. In the process more than 300 accused Protestants, including Cranmer, were executed. As Eamon Duffy has argued, clearly there were localities as well as religious and political leaders who welcomed the return of Roman Catholicism. But few welcomed the mass executions that became Mary's legacy. By the time of her death and Elizabeth's accession in 1558, England on the whole seemed ready to reject Rome and embrace Protestantism. But the manner of that embrace would immediately be contested.[6]

Elizabeth's long reign, from 1558 to 1603, seemingly created conditions for the religious 'settlement' for which historians have credited her. With Cranmer's work as the prelude, the Elizabethan years allowed for the coalescence of what is now known as the Church of England, and the foundation of Anglicanism. For instance, John Jewel and Richard Hooker produced statements of the Church's belief and practice that have become basic reference points. The outline of ideals ascribed to the Church, and its Anglican descendants, gained clarity. The Church of England became traditional in its worship and ministry. Valuing apostolic precedent, it absorbed Protestant influences, especially an emphasis on biblical authority. It aspired to be a via media, offering clear but broad order, a moderate tone capable of embracing diverse views of worship and doctrine, and faithful teaching and pastoral care. The pastoral dimension of church life, and the extent of local, parish autonomy, became lasting points of Anglican emphasis. An Anglican spirituality rooted in Scripture, prayer and sacramental life began to emerge.

John Jewel (1522–71) is a notable source of the Church of England that emerged during the Elizabethan reign. For much of Mary's reign, Jewel was on the Continent in the company of Protestant Reformers. When he returned, his opinions took a moderate course, emphasizing the Elizabethan intention of uniting the nation. Bishop of Salisbury for the last 12 years of his short life, Jewel wrote an *Apology of the Church of England*. This work embodied a new effort to move from protest to concrete proposal. In effect, Jewel focused more on the shape of the Church than on its doctrine. He envisioned catholicity but not Catholicism. The Church should retain its historic worship and ministry while giving centrality to the Bible's authority. In effect, the Church must return to the sources from which it has sprung. Importantly, the Church must also be grounded in the nation. The promise of Anglicanism was rooted in its capacity to unite national life, as Jewel proposed. That ideal has not diminished even as it has gained nuance.[7]

Even as an encompassing, national religious framework took shape, it remained incomplete. Resolute pockets of recusants remained, continuing Roman Catholic allegiance underground. Also, a growing, grassroots Protestantism sought more thorough measures of reform than the Elizabethan state

Church allowed. This movement, eventually producing its own spectrum of belief and practice, was known as Puritanism. As it evolved, Puritanism accrued religious, political and even military power. This development should not be surprising. Puritanism became politicized in the House of Commons and mobilized militarily in response to the social and religious ostracism it faced at the hands of royal and religious authority. At the higher levels of English life, the reality of power dynamics was apparent, evoking the Puritan response and likely contributing to the growth of Puritanism as a protest movement.

As a result, under Elizabeth and her successors, James I (ruled 1603–25) and Charles I (ruled 1625–49), the ideals that animated both Catholics and Puritans impinged upon the Church of England's development. Though the core ideals of later Anglicanism were becoming plain, their meaning was not uniformly resolved and their application was often contested. The Church of England had begun to emerge, but its nature and expression were contested. It could not claim, in a practical sense, to unify England.

For a century, from 1558 to 1660, the tension that defined English religious life centred on which sort of religious imprint could advance sufficiently to unite the nation. The coalescence of ideals later instinctively ascribed to the Church, and to its Anglican heirs, arose more in the process of contestation than from abstract reflection. Thus, Richard Hooker (1554–1600), one of the architects of the Church and its tradition, advanced his ideals in the process of challenging Puritan convictions. Acclaimed for the idea of the *via media*, a religious embrace of moderation between extremes, Hooker combined an idiosyncratic sacramental theology with a strong sense of the union of Church and state. His approach has informed later High Church Anglicans on the one hand, and defenders of religious establishment on the other. Hints of Calvinism as well as rationalism in his thought intensified his broad, lasting appeal. But that appeal has changed since his lifetime. The contestation that framed Hooker's work has faded from view, while the ideals he advanced have endured beyond the circumstances of their formulation. Diarmaid MacCulloch depicts Richard Hooker

A CONTESTED GENESIS

as one who proposed that the Church should be a meeting point, a synthesis. 'A Synthesis was essential because of the paradoxical nature of the Elizabethan Church Settlement, with its peculiar arrested development in Protestant terms, and the ghost which it harboured of an older world of catholic authority and devotional practice.'[8] A synthetic approach reflected the needs of Hooker's time, addressing divided loyalties and pointing towards national religious unity.[9] Yet contestation intensified, and unity proved elusive.

The sort of contestation that characterized the English Church, and would frame Hooker's efforts at a synthesis, are illustrated by a recurring controversy over the wearing of vestments in worship. Already, during the reign of Edward VI, one prominent cleric, John Hooper, had refused to wear the surplice, a billowy white robe. Hooper had spent time with Continental Reformers, especially Ulrich Zwingli in Zurich. Returning to England in 1548, he refused to wear vestments in worship, but was mollified by the assurance that vestments were things indifferent rather than either banned or prescribed as items of faith. The distinction between indifference and matters required by faith loomed large in sixteenth-century English discussions and has surfaced repeatedly in later Anglican debates. Often such a distinction has either promoted division or promised reconciling discussion. It has been something of a frame in subsequent Anglican contestation. Such a distinction has not been unique to Anglicans. But, arguably, it has been given more weight as Anglicans have sought a meeting point between their Catholic legacies and Protestant affirmations, in England and beyond.

Offered the office of Bishop of Gloucester, Hooper initially hesitated. Bishops typically were vested in rochet and chimere, the latter a more ornate form of surplice. Hooper also paused over the required oath of allegiance to the sovereign. Eventually, encouraged by various Reformers and persuaded by Cranmer's quiet pragmatism, Hooper agreed and assumed episcopal office in March 1551. His tenure, and this phase of the controversy over vestments, proved brief. Two years later Mary's reign began, and Hooper's fate was execution.[10]

With the accession of Elizabeth, however, the issue of wearing vestments reignited, flaring especially from 1565 to 1567. By then the range of opinion had become nuanced, encompassing more than sheer opposition or mere endorsement. Some urged that wearing vestments could wean people from error. Others insisted that garments such as surplices were dangerous distractions that could hardly be considered edifying, a quality dear to Reformers. It was unclear whether vestments could be seen as things indifferent and thus more readily negotiated.

At the centre of the storm was Thomas Cartwright, a Cambridge don and emerging Protestant reformer, who challenged the idea that the Church of England in its Elizabethan form faithfully represented apostolic Christianity. Vestments, and bishops who enforced their usage, he held, were not embodiments of the earliest Church, whose true expression motivated Protestant initiative. In 1566, Matthew Parker, Archbishop of Canterbury, had not only sought to enforce conformity in clerical dress, he had considered refusal to conform as an attack on the Church's authority and, by extension, that of the queen. Yet some refused, and more than three dozen clergy were removed from their positions. Cartwright persisted in his protest, even concluding the Church could not be reformed properly while bishops held authority. Deprived of his office in 1570, Cartwright did not lose his influence. He spent some years among Reformers on the Continent, and with influential English benefactors supporting him became a leading voice of the emerging Puritan movement until his death in 1603.

If Puritans deepened in their convictions, Elizabeth and her bishops hardened in their emphasis on uniformity. The question of vestments was more symbolic than literal; the surplice embodied a struggle for the shape of the Church and its grounding in national life. The Elizabethan Settlement, as such, was enforced even as its limits were apparent. Thus, the Act of Uniformity of 1558 prescribed use of the Book of Common Prayer and assessed fines for failure to attend church weekly. Though this advanced the idea of a meeting point, a synthesis, the political approach envisioned religious uniformity as the pathway to national unity. But in actual terms unity could not be compelled. A notable recognition of the reality of Puritan dissent occurred with the Hampton Court Conference of 1604.[11] The new monarch, James I, convened religious leaders in response to a Puritan petition for further religious reform. An easing of some Catholic practices resulted. More significantly, a new translation of the Bible, now known as the King James Version, was commissioned. However, these steps were not enough to stem Puritan fears of further proscription of their convictions. Such fears were justified with the accession of Charles I in 1625. In his hands, the Church became a principal means for encouraging political loyalty. Worse, in Puritan eyes, religious measures imposed by Archbishop William Laud challenged Calvinist theology and moved church life in a more Catholic direction. Laud elevated the sacraments as necessary channels of divine grace, a step that suggested a return to the pre-Reformation Church. Efforts to squelch dissent alarmed Puritans and elicited sympathy for their cause. Their ranks grew, with Parliament as their forum, and then their vehicle for revolution.

The executions of Laud in 1645 and Charles I in 1649, along with the military triumph of Cromwell's regime, meant that the Church of England was dismantled as the state Church. Religious loyalists were forced to an underground status of sorts. Bishops ceased to function, at least publicly. A majority of the clergy renounced bishops and the Prayer Book for the new Puritan religious confession. Something of the private, localized nature that had characterized Elizabethan Puritanism was forced upon the once dominant Church. During the Interregnum, deprived of political advantage, it struggled to survive. Its lands were confiscated; its bishops were prohibited from functioning; and two-thirds of its clergy swore allegiance to the Puritan religious and political order. A loyalist Church of England remnant was forced to exist as isolated pockets of distinct practice. The future of the Church of England was uncertain; survival entailed adaptation to unprecedented circumstances. But it was amid this situation of diminished prospects that the promise of Anglicanism emerged.

When its survival could not depend on legal status, the Church's identity began to coalesce as a spiritual tradition grounded in Scripture, liturgy and pastoral practice. Later generations have cited Jeremy Taylor (1613–67), for instance, for whom the time in religious exile had a formative influence. Less known but just as influential, Gilbert Sheldon (1598–1677) lent a pastoral emphasis that included attention to faith formation in families and local communities. The contextual emphasis in later Anglicanism drew from this example; parish life would become central in a way that had not been the case previously. Sheldon's influence was secured when, early in the Restoration era, he became Archbishop of Canterbury. Indeed, he exercised influence that helped to secure the status of the Church of England once the restored monarchy was in place. Henry Hammond (1605–60), a cohort of Sheldon's during the Puritan rule, sustained an emphasis on the Church's liturgy, an apparent carryover from the Laudian era. Just as important, Hammond and Sheldon quietly established links between pockets of religious loyalists during the time of proscription. Their intention was partly political: they created a network of opposition that awaited the possibility of a revived monarchy and an established Church. The intention also was religious, but in novel circumstances. They were compelled to advance what it meant to be the Church apart from the public advantages it had presumed. That intention became embedded in Anglican self-understanding as the Church became more than English. A search for the Church's essential nature in theory, and its realization in fact, deepened and has never concluded.[12]

The result was fresh attention to securing the Church's distinctive features. What had been inherited from Cranmer, Jewel, Hooker and even Laud began to be reframed in a new way entirely. Now the Church of England was not a defined tradition to be preserved as much as a nascent tradition yet to be realized. The Interregnum, lasting little more than a decade, from 1649 to 1660, cast the Church's nature in a different light. To be sure, some familiar sources of identity remained. Even in diminished circumstances, there were still a few bishops who attempted to function out of sight of Puritan authorities. Sheldon, Hammond and their colleagues created a new basis for the Church's pivotal office, for they emphasized the episcopate's pastoral and teaching roles. They also wondered what they would do if compelled to select a new generation of bishops. Fortunately for them that challenge never arose; it awaited future generations and the challenge of mission in different social contexts.

Though John Dryden would use the phrase later in the decade in a different circumstance, *annus mirabilis* suitably describes 1660. With stunning swiftness, Puritan rule collapsed. The movement had never been as unified or complete as it is now tempting to believe. It had been a spectrum of Protestant groups united in opposition to Charles I's use of power and to William Laud's impositions upon their religious sensibilities. When Oliver Cromwell died, however, Puritanism lost its unifying figure and collapsed. When Charles II returned from exile to assume the throne, opposition to monarchy dissolved. Just as startling, Charles struck a moderate tone that promised political amnesty and religious toleration. It was not immediately clear whether moderate Puritans such as Presbyterians would be incorporated into a new national Church or would be proscribed. Nor was it clear that the Church of England would be reinstituted with anything like its prior public form and role. Any religious sense of promise seemed focused on a national Church that would unite as many of England's Protestants as possible. The ideal that was posed for the revived Church was 'comprehension', that is, a broad religious establishment reflecting the diversity of national life as well as the fact of monarchy restored. The circumstances seemed propitious for realization of some plan of comprehension, somehow encompassing Church of England loyalists with at least moderate Puritans such as Presbyterians and perhaps even Congregationalists.

When Charles II issued the Declaration of Breda in April 1660, he advocated religious toleration as well as pardon for crimes that reflected the Interregnum. A leading Presbyterian divine, Richard Baxter, represented a segment of former Puritans who were receptive to the idea of a broad established Church. But, within five years, such hope was dashed by a Parliament that was intent on a reversion to prior Stuart, and even Laudian, ways of Church life. The efforts of Gilbert Sheldon and Edward Hyde, Earl of Clarendon, in particular made comprehension an elusive goal. Thus, the Act of Uniformity of 1662 prescribed the form of public prayer, the sacraments and other rites of the Church of England according to the Book of Common Prayer. The reissued Prayer Book of 1662 made plain that the Church was being revived in its familiar sense. For example, episcopal ordination was required for all clergy. As a result, over 2,000 clergy refused to subscribe and were expelled from their livings and from the Church of England, in what became known as the Great Ejection. Moderation of any sort, even that of Richard Baxter, was overwhelmed by a rush to revive the established Church. By 1665 the legislation had been achieved, a body of enactments known as the Clarendon Code after Edward Hyde. The Corporation Act of 1661 required all municipal officials to take communion in the established Church. The Conventicle Act of 1664 forbade unauthorized gatherings for worship. The Five-Mile Act of 1665 prevented nonconformist clergy from coming within five miles of incorporated towns or the place of a former pastoral charge.[13]

If Anglican promise is seen to reside in the advantages conferred by establishment when uniformity is not possible, the political achievement of the Clarendon Code would represent a high point, even a singular moment in the Church's history. To this day, the Prayer Book of 1662 remains the Church of England's recognized standard, and the fact of religious establishment is intact. But greater realities loomed as the established Church faced an ever-expansive religious pluralism in England. More, the Church's internal life bore critical differences of outlook and practice that would harden into lasting church parties. The result has been that religious uniformity, though sanctioned legally, could not be achieved practically. The presence of religious dissent, within and without the Church, was reality, and differences multiplied further before the end of the seventeenth century. The hope of comprehension gradually became the granting of toleration by an established Church that was compelled to acknowledge difference and sanctioned disadvantage. The nation could only be called united by the intermingling of a religious system and a political framework that achieved a momentary stasis.

Charles II's instinct towards recognition of religious minorities bespoke his Catholic sympathies. Even more, his successor, James II, seemed intent on actual Catholic allegiance until he was forced from the throne. Yet the 'Glorious Revolution' of 1688 complicated rather than clarified the Church of England's prospects.[14] While the Church's leadership was united in opposition to James's religious drift, not all welcomed his removal from the throne. Worse, some did not believe his successors, William and Mary, could be recognized as king and queen. Nine bishops, including William Sancroft, Archbishop of Canterbury, refused to swear allegiance to the new sovereigns. Joined by over 400 clergy, these bishops formed the Non-Juror movement. They were deprived of their posts but created a network that persisted for a century. In turn, the ideals of the Non-Jurors cast a wide net. Their emphasis on the divine right of kings, and on the rights of the Church, informed the rise of the Tory, High Church party. Ironically, given its theological priorities, the High Church party would spend the 'long eighteenth century' from 1688 to 1832 in opposition to the prevailing political and religious winds. The Church aligned with the Whig political hegemony, an alliance that, in High Church eyes, submerged the Church's religious distinctiveness. To Whigs, on the other hand, the alliance of Church and state as they had forged it, secured not only political stability but religious establishment.[15]

The Whig achievement secured a pastoral and spiritual identity that left a lasting imprint on the Church, and Anglicanism generally. The Church intersected the dominant culture in ways that ministered to it without necessarily endorsing it. Though clergy, even bishops, lived in ways that bespoke the mores of the age, they generally exercised religious office and asserted moral norms based on convictions of faith more than social habit. The pervasive latitudinarian theology may have reflected English philosophical rationalism, but it arose from substantive engagement with theological and social questions. The breadth of outlook fostered the advance of religious toleration at home and encouraged the first stirrings of ecumenical discussion abroad. The Church of England's leadership began to see itself as part of the fabric of a wider Christendom. Secure in their identity as established, church leaders could begin to express more respectful views of the varieties of Christian experience. Eventually the range of respect would also encompass non-Christian religions, especially as England's diversity grew. Hints of later Anglican promise were latent in these early inclinations.

Such consideration reflected the moderate and inquisitive temper of church leadership at its best. But closer to the Church's grassroots there were initiatives resulting from quite different perceptions. A broad sense spread that the Church's ministrations and their grounding in vital faith were inadequate. Such holy discontent has been a prominent strand of Anglican life and a source of its sense of promise. It became apparent as the Church of England awakened to opportunities for mission at home and abroad.

The First Stirrings of Anglican Mission

Since the middle of the twentieth century, theologians and historians of Christian mission have spoken of the *missio Dei*, the mission of God. By this term, they mean that mission is not the Church's institutional initiative. Christian mission represents divine initiative to which the Church responds. Mission must focus the Church's life as its organizing principle. But the Church cannot equate its actions with God's intentions. Nor can the Church assume that God's mission has ever been fulfilled. Rather, the Church embodies the dichotomy between what is intended by God and its fulfilment in human terms. Ideals of faith must be realized amid social and political realities, involving the Church in matters of cultural style and the use of power. The gospel embodies unchanging truth, which people of faith are challenged to realize in their personal lives and their faith communities.

As a result, mission compels the Church to face questions about its identity in practice. The emphasis on mission as the Church's priority must be more than confessional: this emphasis must translate into effective action. The essence of the gospel message need not change. But the manner of its expression must vary with shifts in contexts and circumstances. The Church must always assess its relation to the world because it must be grounded in this relation. When it is, there will be occasions when the forms of church life are adapted or even reconfigured by the situational demands of mission.[16] We shall return to the theme of practice, seeing patterns of life in Christian community as a basis of discourse among Christians and sources of contestation about the proper way of expressing the gospel in particular circumstances. Discourse, we emphasize, is not merely what is spoken, but what is expressed in actions as well as words. The practices of the Church loom large in our approach, for its faith appears in both stated and unstated ways. Similarly, as we develop the history of Anglican mission, we shall cite the centrality of context, for the life of the Church resides not in the abstract, but in specific settings.

Such dynamics in church life have reflected the challenge of mission in varied contexts for Anglicans. Much of the promise we find in Anglicanism is associated with a capacity for mission. In turn, the capacity for mission has arisen largely informally and unexpectedly, at the Church's grassroots, often remote from titular church authority, often outside the bounds of church precedent, in circumstances both foreseen and unforeseen. The capacity for mission has reflected a complex, contextual instinct among Anglicans. We trace this capacity to a pastoral emphasis rooted in an incarnational theology which prizes local life and faith community amid it. We shall attend to this theology throughout this narrative. Now it suffices to note the local nature of Anglican attention to mission. The ministries of the Church of England from the Glorious Revolution onward reflected this local emphasis. A leading bishop early in this era, Gilbert Burnet, wrote a manual on pastoral care that became a classic. Other notable figures, including William Wake and William Warburton, advanced ideals of church life that had lasting import. It is ironic that the eighteenth century would later be identified with sleeping congregations, inept clergy and moral laxity. By its own standards, the Church functioned well.

But for some the Church's ministries lacked adequate confessional and practical vitality. The rise of evangelicalism in the Church of England cast a different religious vision. The key figure of the early eighteenth century, of course, was John Wesley, abetted by various figures, notably George Whitefield, from the late 1730s. Mission for evangelicals meant proclaiming a redeeming faith to unreached persons. Whitefield and Wesley took their preaching outdoors, and Wesley built a network and system of organization of prayer and ministry that would point beyond the established Church but leave a powerful imprint on it. For scores of Anglicans, promise has centred on a dynamic awakening of personal faith and the focus on mission it encourages. Mission, in this case, focuses upon evangelism, that is proclaiming the gospel to those who have not heard it, with the intention of conversion, then building the Church.[17]

Within the Church of England, evangelicals were not alone in emphasizing mission, nor evangelism. Before evangelicalism arose, a priest of the church, Josiah Woodward, alarmed at the apparent decay of public morals, organized small groups of young adults to promote a 'reformation of manners'. A series of publications, including books and pamphlets, helped to popularize the effort. Group members made religious witness in distressed areas among wayward people. Their example was absorbed by evangelicals who linked an awakened faith to moral improvement. Implicit in this programme was the assumption that the Church's ordinary ministries fell short. There were unredeemed circumstances and unreached people for whom local, unofficial and untraditional measures were required. The promise of Anglicanism acquired a strong emphasis on such perceptions and the mission initiatives that resulted.

If England had unreached populations, the growing North American colonies offered entirely uncultivated soil. To be sure, something of the English establishment was translated across the Atlantic. Replications of the established Church were possible in some colonies, the most complete likeness being in Virginia.[18] But even there, innovative measures were needed to allow for the uniquely colonial circumstances. Innovations were required to extend the Church's ministries and to provide adequate church governance. No bishop ever crossed the Atlantic or was consecrated for service there prior to the American Revolution. In such absence, church leadership in colonies where establishment was possible fell to a commissary, or administrator, appointed by the Bishop of London. The commissary performed no sacramental functions but administered church affairs within the domain of religious establishment.

The combination of distance from London and authority to act allowed commissaries freedom for initiative. One in particular took creative advantage. Although only briefly the commissary in Maryland, from 1699 to 1700, Thomas Bray acted to advance the Church's mission there. He divided the Church of England there into parishes that replicated the English format. At the same time, he established more than a dozen libraries and encouraged learning as part of faith formation. He also placed particular emphasis on instruction prior to baptism for entire families and worked to raise baptismal emphasis in the Church. Bray saw need of religious instruction for African slaves and Native Americans in Maryland and encouraged this work. But his brief stay there produced little tangible result. The libraries which marked his Maryland work also identify Bray as founder of the Society for Promoting Christian Knowledge (SPCK). He was an early influence in linking mission, faith formation, education and better training for clergy. The emphasis on mission grew when, soon after returning to England, Bray launched the Society for the Propagation of the Gospel in Foreign Parts (SPG, now the USPG), which has become the Church of England's oldest mission agency. The logic behind these efforts and the vision of reaching native populations were early signs of the promise later generations would find in Anglicanism. Thinking only of the Church of England at this time, Bray glimpsed the need for reaching more people with a vital faith. He identified actual needs and possibilities for extending the Church's reach. He perceived that it was called to be lively in its faith and effective as the religious establishment. These ideals were seen as interdependent.

From the time of its founding to the eve of the American Revolution, the SPG sent 600 'agents', clergy and lay workers and teachers, to North America. A considerable number went to New England, including two of the first, Patrick Gordon and George Keith, who arrived in 1702. Although SPG literature reveals an early and continuing concern for mission among the slave and Native American populations, only small efforts resulted. Few SPG recruits, especially the clergy, wanted to be assigned to mission with non-English populations. Instead, like Gordon and Keith, they intended to minister among the English-speaking people.[19] The reasons were apparent. Not only was life more comfortable, SPG workers assumed that any cultural differences between English life and English populations could be readily overcome. Initially, they were less sanguine about the prospects of mission to Native American and slave populations.

Of course, as in England, signs of irreligion and compromised morality were apparent in colonial society. Inspired by the example of the societies for the reformation of manners, the SPG intended to elevate the standard of social morality in the colonies. In this sense, they worked unabashedly as agents of colonial authority. For the established Church, the maintenance of social order has been a consistent emphasis and a profoundly felt responsibility. Colonial circumstances did alter this emphasis in notable ways. In colonial New England especially, the Church of England arrived not as the religious establishment but as the rival of Puritan prerogative. In other words, the fact of Puritan establishment cast the Church of England in a position of religious rivalry, not unlike dissenting groups at home. As the Church of England and Anglicans at large would soon discover, they could not presume the advantages of establishment in England, even if they enjoyed such status nominally in a colony. This reality became apparent in New England.

The results were impressive. By the American Revolution, one-third of all Church of England clergy in what would become the United States had SPG affiliation. Of these 77, 40 would leave as part of the Tory exodus to Canada and the West Indies. The growth of the Church in Massachusetts and Connecticut in particular reveals the imprint of SPG missions. This work centred on presenting the Church of England as a reasonable and pastoral faith. George Keith in particular helped to establish reading rooms and forms of religious instruction that embodied this moderate, rational faith, reflective of English latitudinarianism. The approach drew converts, including three senior faculty of Yale College in 1722. The Church gained social influence that marked it as a de facto establishment. Such social standing would also follow the Church's growth after American independence.

Consistently a few church leaders, especially in England, called on the North American Church to extend its sense of mission to the Native American and slave populations. Thomas Secker, who would serve for ten years as Archbishop of Canterbury until his death in 1768, made an especially strong appeal. But even Secker had difficulty translating the English sense of residence in a parish with the peripatetic and challenging circumstances of the very mission he hoped to encourage. Secker hoped to build a depth of faith in these populations such that they would both participate liturgically and deepen in their Christian conviction as a result.[20] But little came of Secker's urging. The ideal of a Church truly adapted to new contexts, with indigenous leadership, lay in the future. That aspect of the Anglican promise awaited further developments.

Yet the emphasis on mission to English-speaking populations could take dramatic turns as evangelicalism grew. In 1740, Alexander Garden, church commissary in Charleston, South Carolina, forbade George Whitefield from preaching in a parish. A verbal and print contest began, Whitefield charging that the Church lacked spiritual vitality. Garden posed the

Church as the guarantor of order and the true representative of Protestant theology. As the debate proceeded, Whitefield preached in public, as he would do generally. He became a celebrity throughout the North American colonies, even praised by the normally sceptical Benjamin Franklin. Despite his challenge to the Church of England, Whitefield followed the logic of mission awakening within it. He sought to enliven religiously torpid populations and a spiritually inadequate Church as he saw it. Like Wesley, he provided a dynamic message that some church leaders resisted, and yet which extended the Church of England's witness to its faith. Unlike Wesley, he never launched an alternative church order and never fully left the Church of England. He was an independent evangelist who castigated the Church yet extended its benefits.

Not all evangelicals were as confrontational as Whitefield nor as divergent as Wesley's legacy proved to be. Beginning in the late eighteenth century, a group of lay persons with social and political influence as well as evangelical convictions coalesced in the Church of England. They became known as the Clapham Sect because several of them purchased homes near one another in a London suburb. Individually they had awakened to an energetic, insistent Christian faith. Together they pursued projects of mission and political reform that expressed a shared, faith commitment. Their awakenings, and their initiatives, arose outside the stated channels of church leadership. Yet they left a profound imprint on the meaning of Anglican promise. The best-known Clapham figure was William Wilberforce who has been cited for his avowed opposition to first the slave trade then to slavery itself. The centrality of mission to this effort becomes clear when the range of his coterie's interests is considered. The Church Mission Society (CMS) was founded at Clapham. The creation of a bishop for church life in India was a result of Clapham efforts. In addition, the first bishop in India, Thomas Middleton, began to undertake mission there, emphasizing education and evangelism. The Church of England was beginning to see itself as the steward of a faith that could not be confined to English people.[21]

Yet the framework of mission remained colonial and in retrospect its premises and activities can be debated. First, the colonial Church put a priority on securing order. Even innovations such as the office of commissary and mission itself were defended on the basis of securing English notions of order. The case for evangelizing colonialized peoples, and thus challenging their own cultural assumptions, could be made as an aspect of securing English-imposed order. Even efforts at education and moral reform acted to reinforce English social patterns and thus substituting one form of rule for another. The alignment of Anglicanism and colonialism has been and must continue to be considered in its full scope. The sense of promise we identify with Anglicanism has looked well beyond colonialism, even though the Church spread on the shoulders of colonial rule in many cases, and Global North influence elsewhere.

A partial response to the relation of Anglicanism and colonialism must begin by noting that, from the beginning of the eighteenth century and gaining momentum thereafter, a variety of persons and groups linked to the Church of England unofficially for the most part, reached two general conclusions: first, that the ministries of the established Church needed to be enhanced and not simply administered more efficiently. The needs of the Church centred on mission of greater scope and deeper religious and moral vigour. Second, there was a recognition in some circles that the Church of England must be more than a chaplaincy to English people in colonial settings. Instead, the pursuit of mission dictated that the Church, as an expression of the gospel, must declare that all peoples share a common humanity, endowed equally by the creator. In the fire of personal faith awakening, many evangelicals grasped this point. Such recognition dawned powerfully among evangelical opponents of slavery, as the Clapham Sect exemplified. The evangelical emphasis on the salvation of the individual and a life lived within clear moral bounds meant all people, regardless of culture or religion, shared a common need. Sin and salvation were clear categories which encouraged the conviction that all people must find saving grace.

At the end of the eighteenth century, doors were opening to a wider sense of the Church, albeit in ways that now seem controversial and perhaps compromised. The emerging sense of promise centred on the recognition that the Church of England was encompassing a widening set of viewpoints and initiatives even as it sought to coexist with religious and social difference. It aspired to be the Church of the nation even as it gained formal privilege to bolster its claim. The alignment of intention and reality became a daunting task that was encouraging mission initiatives, which would be absorbed into church life. Over time, this dynamic would become a pattern in the Church, especially as it spread beyond England and was compelled to seek indigenous forms. As this process unfolded, in one social and cultural context after another, the Church's inherent relation to the nation, and to national purpose, would be evident. But through mission it would become more than the Church of England: it would become truly Anglican.

The Dynamism of Anglican Promise

What can we conclude from this survey of the Church of England's emergence? First, from the Church's beginnings, its identity has been debated repeatedly and inconclusively in terms of finding uniform expression. Though a framework for the Church's life was secured, that framework did not unite the nation conclusively, nor did it eliminate varieties of party identity and differences of theology and practice among the Church's adherents. Second, in the wake of the Restoration, and likely informed by the experience of the Interregnum period, some church leaders began to develop forms of mission to extend its faith and life within England and beyond. Third, the rise of the Church of England, the sources of its variations and the eventual turn to mission reflected forms of discourse about the nature of the Christian faith and the proper shape of church life. As we have indicated, the discourse that can be cited occurred both formally and informally, both in the

Church's leadership circles and on its peripheries. It could be argued that the most influential forms of mission and reform that would appear in the Church of England, and would embody the emergence of Anglicanism, have occurred on its peripheries, that is, in various contexts removed from ostensible leadership circles.

Fourth, we have also begun to emphasize that the Church of England, and Anglicanism as a fruit of it, have possessed forms of religious and social dynamism. This point in itself reflects our intention to reframe the nature of Anglicanism away from static notions of identity and fixed institutional forms. We resist the temptation to ground Anglican identity at early moments of the Church of England's life when points of consensus can be cited and presumed to have lasting authority, notably the fact of religious establishment. While Cranmer's work could never be considered complete, he has been marked as a founder of the Anglican tradition. Similarly, the works of John Jewel and Richard Hooker have provided historical and theological benchmarks that have framed the Church's emergence. As we have suggested, their positions grasped key aspects of what was coalescing, though the contexts in which they worked mitigated their immediate impact. The Church of England was ever in the midst of complex, contested, unfinished patterns of definition, crisscrossed by religious, political and social dynamics that were unpredictable and unmanageable. The Church gained authority, lost it and gained it anew, though never as many of its proponents hoped. Yet the Church of England emerged to become the religious establishment.

It is impossible to diminish this aspect of the Church of England's development. The writings of the Church of England's founding figures have left crucial reference points which gain clarity as we consider the circumstances of their formulation. The controversies that beset the Church's early years, such as that over vestments, remind us that the Church has always been contested. There have been alternative viewpoints which have been presented in assertive ways, even seeking forms of compulsory allegiance. It is necessary to say that Anglican history, from England outward, reveals a series of debates often threatening division and alienation among protagonists. By such contestation, the Church has gained fresh energies and found fresh purpose, as we shall uncover repeatedly. Faithful intention and practical outcome in dialogical relation frame much of the history of the Church and its development into new patterns of life, all the while seeking faithful adaptation of the ideals from its formative centuries.

Perhaps the most obvious feature of the Church's deposit has the imprint of being the religious establishment upon its life in England and beyond. Anglican life has been framed by the legacy of religious establishment. The result has been as much a sense of pastoral charge as it has of institutional power and privilege. The first three centuries of the Church's life reveal various processes of proposing, clarifying, securing and exploring ways to advance the Church's intention in terms primarily of its faith, not its national presence. Yet the path of the development entailed aligning the Church with England's national life, though what this meant and how it was formed was contested repeatedly, within and without the Church. Indeed, it could be tempting to assume that Church and nation were indistinguishable. The separation of Church and state, an undisputed fact of American life, could not have been imagined in England during the Church's early years. The merit of religious establishment has been debated among Anglicans, and especially in England. But the Church has proven to be far more than the religious establishment. The Church has unfolded of its own accord, generating its own debates, seeking its own integrity in terms of its faith and practice, not simply its presumed national role.

The development of the Church of England resonated with a religious sensibility that was integral to the forging of the nation, as Linda Colley depicts it. She aptly notes that one must speak of Britain as a nation in qualified ways. Though created by the Act of Union in 1707, Great Britain was far from united. It was 'a patchwork in which uncertain areas of Welshness, Scottishness, and Englishness were cut across by strong regional attachments, and scored over again by loyalties to village, town, family, and landscape'. Great Britain 'was infinitely diverse in terms of the customs and cultures of its inhabitants'.[22]

In part, Colley continues, the British national identity arose on the basis of what was opposed, principally Roman Catholicism, especially that of the French sort. The fact of geography, namely being an island, clearly set Britain apart, giving ready justification for union. As the British national identity solidified, to the extent that it would, and as 'it was increasingly concerned to carve out a massive empire in foreign lands that were not even Christian', a further factor stood out. As Colley terms it, 'Protestantism was able to become a unifying and distinguishing bond as never before'.[23] Shared religious affirmation enabled national identity to arise, alongside without subsuming, regional, political and specifically confessional identities. Notably, Scotland would carry forward its own 'national Church', for example. Protestantism, as Colley describes, shaped patterns of loyalty, material life, politics, public expression and, we add, morals and mores. British Protestantism was irreversibly pluralist by the time of the Act of Union. A prominent national role was accorded to the Church of England.

More than fear of France and dread of Catholicism was involved. A popular, nationalist spirituality arose, mingling a British sense of promise with that of England's Church. Britons widely felt themselves to be divinely appointed, a modern chosen people, primed to 'build Jerusalem in England's green and pleasant land', as William Blake phrased it. Britain became the modern embodiment of ancient Israel. Britons have been blessed by God's providence, their prosperity and their intellectual and military prowess giving abundant proof.

But as leaders of the Church of England affirmed, especially those intent on advancing Christian mission, the nation and its established Church bore divinely decreed responsibilities. They could not presume the superiority of their ways nor that God's favour was assured. Failure to uphold their moral and religious roles at home and abroad would result in divine punishment, eroding the good life Britons enjoyed. Thus Protestantism 'gave the majority of men and women a sense of their place in history and a sense of worth'.[24] At the same time, the rise of national identity, though never seamless, afforded the Church of England social roots that fostered its religious motivation, particularly as mission became a priority for church life. The spread of Britain outward, creating international trade and colonial life, prompted the spread of the Church of England, with distinct advantages over its British Protestant counterparts. Through such spread, the conditions for the birth of Anglicanism emerged.

Colley's work proves instructive in several respects beyond her depictions of the Protestant dimension of emerging national identity. She emphasizes that national allegiance never replaced more particular forms of identity: geographic, political, social and religious contexts proved secure and even became variegated over time. We will extend this emphasis as we explore the significance of context for Anglican experience. Similarly, we will argue that some of the Church's notable initiatives have arisen more particularly than generally. Mission initiatives to extend the Church's ministries have often carried the imprint of one or another theological party within the Church, e.g. evangelicalism and Anglo-Catholicism. Arising from the Church's peripheries, reflecting the dynamics of particular religious and geographic contexts, novel forms of Christian life and ministry have been tested, seeking sufficient public response to justify recognition across the Church's life generally.

We have noted that the work of Thomas Bray in Maryland and in England proved instrumental in launching the SPG. Then the SPG secured sufficient legitimacy to become the principal source of eighteenth-century mission discussion and initiative. Similarly, the rise of evangelicalism on the Church and society's periphery encompassed Wesley's ministrations to working-class England until Methodism became a distinct religious body. Whitefield's peripatetic, trans-Atlantic ministries affronted church authorities but galvanized an energetic religious public. More conversant with Church and political authority figures, the Clapham Sect evangelicals nevertheless functioned at the margins of institutions while working to redeem, as they viewed it, both those institutions and the life of the nation as a whole.

Reference to the dynamism of the Church's life, especially on its peripheries, will be a recurring aspect of our description of the unfolding of Anglicanism's promise. There are various theories of the relationships between designated social and institutional centres and their presumed peripheries. With careful application, consideration of the relation between centre and periphery can illuminate Anglicanism's development within and beyond the Church of England. The centre typically is understood as the source of political dominance with power to define patterns of social relations that come under its purview. Domains that fall under this power, and may prove restive under it, are the peripheries. Often peripheral areas develop their own elites and amass local forms of power, while remaining subservient to the centre. It is apparent why this framework has influenced studies of colonial and post-colonial relations. But more than patterns of resistance loom, as the work of Pierre Bourdieu has explained.[25] We note Bourdieu's interest in forms of social capital linked to centre–periphery relations. That is, the worth of social and religious institutions reflects their ability to generate forms of meaning, including shared purpose, trust and common values. The cultural dimension that Bourdieu highlights can inform our consideration of Anglicanism's emergence in and beyond Britain's colonial realms as well as dynamics within the Church of England. Bourdieu reminds us that the practices which shape larger traditions often arise in local contexts then gain wider appeal.

We are all the more interested in theories of centre–periphery relations because they readily focus on patterns of discourse. We understand discourse to be the organization and expression of knowledge, especially its role in shaping social relations along lines deemed to be normative. When we speak of Anglicanism as contested, we are speaking of forms of discourse, invoking ideals of Christian faith and church life reflective of the Church's English origins. We also are speaking of an unfinished, emerging sense of faith community drawing not simply on the English past but on aspects of contextual life and culture that are given authority to inform, or even to define, the Church's priorities. As we shall explain, the Anglican sense of promise has been asserted and tested and reasserted in such circumstances, often contesting relations between the centres and peripheries of church life. In the process, such theological concerns as authority and incarnation have been reference points. The shape of contemporary church life, especially in one or another context, has been assessed against historical precedent deemed to confirm or to challenge it. The meaning of Christian tradition, in Anglican guise, has been contested.

By invoking 'contested' and 'contestation', we signal that the Church of England and Anglicanism have embarked on a continuous project of building faith community. In the process, points of theological emphasis and patterns of practice from the Church's origins and early development became reference points invoked by later generations. Such invocations have produced as much debate as they have unified affirmation. The drive to realize in fact what Anglicans have envisioned in principle has fuelled difference, some expressions of which have become lasting reference points themselves. We pay particular attention to what Anglicans have said, in what contexts and to what ends. The eighteenth-century SPG sermons advancing mission are an example, emanating as they did from a particular segment of church life in search of ways to realize its intention. Mission would take diverse forms, often prompted as much by divergence as by consensus. Thus, we speak of 'contestation' as the sign of an emerging Church.

We are uncovering the dynamism of Anglicanism's promise and the shapes such promise has been compelled to assume by circumstances the Church encountered as well as by the hopes it perceived. We are stressing that the Church, from its English origins onward, was compelled to revise its life continually and often divergently. But intermingled with challenge were increasing signs of opportunity for new forms of mission and ministry. We will discover further that there have been a number of instances where church figures, at the centre of religious life and on its peripheries, have taken steps they believed would close the gap between Anglican intention and reality. The Church has never been finished, but that does not mean it has been incomplete. It has been contested in a multitude of ways, but that does not mean it need be rent apart. The development of mission has been a vital reference point and organizing principle.

Notes

1 Diarmaid MacCulloch, *The Reformation: A History*, London: Penguin, 2005.
2 F. Bruce Gordon, *Calvin*, New Haven, CT and London: Yale University Press, 2011.
3 Michel Foucault, *The Archaeology of Knowledge*, New York: Vintage, 1982.
4 D. G. Hart, *Calvinism*, New Haven, CT and London: Yale University Press, 2013. See Carlos M. N. Eire, *Reformations*, New Haven, CT and London: Yale University Press, 2016.
5 Anthony Milton, ed., *Reformation and Identity, c. 1520–1662, The Oxford History of Anglicanism, Volume I*, Oxford: Oxford University Press, 2017. Peter Marshall, *Heretics and Believers: A History of the English Reformation*, New Haven, CT and London: Yale University Press, 2018.
6 Diarmaid MacCulloch, *Thomas Cranmer: A Life*, New Haven, CT and London: Yale University Press, 2017. Eamon Duffy, *The Stripping of the Altars: Traditional Religion in England, 1400–1580*, New Haven, CT and London: Yale University Press, 2005. Eamon Duffy, *Reformation Divided: Catholics, Protestants and the Conversion of England*, London: Bloomsbury Continuum, 2017.
7 Milton, *Reformation and Identity*, p. 10. MacCulloch, *The Reformation*, pp. 485f.
8 Diarmaid MacCulloch, *The Later Reformation in England, 1547–1603*, New Haven, CT: Yale University Press, 1990, p. 100.
9 MacCulloch, *The Reformation*, pp. 377–8, 486–91. W. Bradford Littlejohn, *Richard Hooker: A Companion to His Life and Work*, Eugene, OR: Cascade, 2015.
10 Marshall, *Heretics and Believers*.
11 MacCulloch, *The Reformation*, p. 497.
12 Geoffrey Rowell, Kenneth Stevenson and Rowan Williams, eds, *Love's Redeeming Work*, Oxford: Oxford University Press, 2001.
13 John Spurr, 'Religion in Restoration England', in L. K. J. Glassey, ed., *The Reigns of Charles II and James VII and II*, London: Macmillan, 1997. N. H. Keeble, *The Restoration*, Hoboken, NJ: John Wiley, 2002.
14 Steve Pincus, *1688: The First Modern Revolution*, New Haven, CT and London: Yale University Press, 2011.

15 John Walsh, Colin Haydon and Stephen Taylor, *The Church of England, c.1689 – c.1833*, Cambridge: Cambridge University Press, 1993.

16 David Bosch, *Transforming Mission*, Maryknoll, NY: Orbis, 1991. John Flett, *The Witness of God*, Grand Rapids, MI: Eerdmans, 2010.

17 Mark Noll, *The Rise of Evangelicalism: The Age of Edwards, Whitefield and the Wesleys*, Downers Grove, IL: IVP Academic, 2010.

18 John K. Nelson, *A Blessed Company: Parishes, Parsons, and Parishioners in Anglican Virginia, 1690–1776*, Chapel Hill, NC: University of North Carolina Press, 2001.

19 Daniel O'Connor, *Three Centuries of Mission*, London: Continuum, 2000. Rowan Strong, *Anglicanism and the British Empire, c.1700–1850*, Oxford: Oxford University Press, 2007.

20 Strong, *Anglicanism and the British Empire*, pp. 112f.

21 D. Bruce Hindmarsh, *The Spirit of Early Evangelicalism: True Religion in a Modern World*, Oxford: Oxford University Press, 2018. Stephen Tomkins, *The Clapham Sect*, Oxford: Lion Hudson, 2010.

22 Linda Colley, *Britons*, New Haven, CT: Yale University Press, 1992, p. 17.

23 Colley, *Britons*, p. 18.

24 Colley, *Britons*, p. 18.

25 Tomasz Zarycki, 'An Interdisciplinary Model of Centre-Periphery Relations: A Theoretical Proposal', *Regional and Local Studies* (2007), pp. 110–30.

3

Catholicity and Contextualization

The *ecclesia anglicana* begins in England, but Anglicanism did not begin there. A precursor to the term was used as early as 1616 by a Roman Catholic critic of the English Church. Thomas Harrab complained that yet another Protestant heresy was emerging. To distinguish it from Lutheranism, Calvinism and Anabaptism, he called it 'Anglianism'.[1] This almost but not quite Anglicanism, as we have already seen, almost but not quite begins in England. In the American colonies, the story was similar. What emerged, an extension and then an adaptation of an English Church, was quite but not quite Anglicanism.

Anglicanism begins in Africa. It begins in contextualization and contestation. Anglicanism begins in critical mission theology and it begins in the processes and provocations of contextualization. Anglicanism, as contextually distinct from the Church of England and the Protestant Episcopal Church in the United States of America, emerges particularly clearly in the witness and controversies surrounding two key figures – Samuel Ajayi Crowther (1809–91) and John William Colenso (1814–83). This chapter will deal first with the expansion of 'Anglianism', arguing that this, despite the commonly held belief, should not be the point of departure for a definition and understanding of modern Anglicanism. Second, the controversies surrounding the work and witness of Crowther and Colenso will be held up as a more appropriate place to begin the definition of Anglicanism as championed in this book. Both men were engaged in disputes about the nature of Christian witness in cross-cultural settings. Such cultural and cross-cultural contestation, we argue, is foundational to the very nature of Anglicanism. Crowther, along with Henry Venn (1796–1873) of the Church Missionary Society, pointed

57

to Anglicanism beyond 'Anglianism' in contextual and contextualizing leadership. Colenso along with William Ngidi and the controversies they provoke point to a polity beyond 'Anglianism' emerging in the first Lambeth Conference. Third, this conference neither transcended an imperialist frame nor established an international Anglicanism that centred on a curia. Instead, processes of contextualization would be indicative of promise. This would suggest a particular, and always contested, form of Anglican catholicity.

The Expansion of 'Anglianism'

The Book of Common Prayer (1662) exhibits little thought for an international family of Anglicans. The only imagined liturgical setting beyond Britain is found in 'The Ministration of Baptism of such as are of riper years and able to answer for themselves'.[2] In explaining the rationale for such a service, the preface of the BCP states that it is necessary and 'may be useful for the baptizing of Natives in our Plantations, and others converted to the Faith'. Yet, in an age of European invention, discovery and broadened horizons, European Christians looked at the world in ways that previous generations could not. Europe pushed out into the world in exploration and colonization. It was within this broadening context that a renewed understanding of mission as expansion emerged. Against the tide, mission leaders like the Baptist William Carey (1761–1834) and Anglican Thomas Scott (1747–1821) read the Matthean 'Great Commission' as not only binding on the apostles but also for all subsequent followers of Jesus. The call of the Church was to expand from the centre out into the peripheries bringing good news, good medicine, good manners and good schools. Although Anglicans were not at first keen on overseas mission, the work of Anglican missionaries spread not only the gospel and Anglicanism but competing interpretations of Anglicanism to the world.[3]

Expanding the reach of Anglicanism were High Church, Broad Church, liberal, evangelical women and men grounding their vision of the gospel within a British Empire and beyond a

British Empire. Barbados, Calcutta, Mombasa, Nagasaki, Port Jackson and Rio de Janeiro all became venues for this expansion largely through the auspices of the Society for Promoting Christian Knowledge (SPCK), the Society for the Propagation of the Gospel in Foreign Parts (SPG), the Church Missionary Society (CMS), the Universities' Mission to Central Africa (UMCA) and the South American Missionary Society (SAMS). Beyond these traditions, a contextualized form of Christianity beyond empire and connected to North American mission would take root in East Asia.

While foreign Anglican agencies were not entirely responsible for the growth of the Japanese Nippon Sei Ko Kai or the Chinese Chung Hua Sheng Kuing Hui, they were vital to its genesis.[4] Prima facie, it was often an expansionist understanding of foreign mission that laid the foundation for an internationalized Anglicanism. But how would this Anglicanism beyond the realm be understood, practised and held together? In preparation for a 1908 pan-Anglican congress, the Dean of Westminster, Armitage Robinson, sought to answer the question that many continue to ask, what is Anglicanism? For Dean Robinson, the answer was clear. It is a 'portion' of the Catholic Church distinct from the Latin and Oriental 'branches'. Anglicanism, for Robinson, was Anglo-Saxon in character and what bound it together was a belief that the Anglo-Saxon race had a 'providential mission'. The purpose of the Anglican Communion is, therefore, to 'express and guide the spiritual aspirations and activities of the Anglo-Saxon race'.[5] Robinson noted that the Anglo-Saxons were related by 'various degrees of closeness' to other races and thus God might expect of them a duty of care. For the Dean, however, it was difficult to imagine a greater duty than bestowing upon them the apostolic faith, order and an opportunity to grow the Church beyond Anglo-Saxon tutelage.[6]

Writing in 1977, Alan Stephenson warned his readers against any bashful reticence in taking pride in this Anglo-Saxon or English formed Church and Communion. 'We must' he wrote 'resist this temptation'.[7] Many have taken Stephenson to heart. What in fact is 'Anglianism' has become the standard story of Anglicanism. Few would now put it in the terms Dean Robinson adopted, but the idea of Anglicanism as the offspring of an English parent persists. We argue a distinction must be made between 'Anglianism' and Anglicanism. The former is defined by the extension of, in Robinson's terms, an Anglo-Saxon Church in Britain and in American colonies. The latter refers to an international fellowship defined by contextualization that emerges in deep intercultural encounter, contestation and theology. We argue that the work of contextualization, and the attendant contestation it causes, is the heart of Anglicanism. In this section, we outline the expansion of 'Anglianism', demonstrating that it cannot serve as the point of departure for understanding Anglicanism as promise.

A desire for English religious expansion beyond the realm goes back at least to the sixteenth century. That desire and the strategizing of key churchmen would find mixed success amid the competing visions of imperialists, colonialists, mission societies and successive governments. Church expansion would at times accompany colonial expansion, be supported by the British state and eventually see the state withdraw its support. That withdrawal not only signifies British governmental expediency but also points towards an idea of Anglicanism that would resist imperialism in favour of contextualism. Indeed, expressions of international Anglican accommodation and contextualization would ultimately outgrow the Church of England and the Church of England's paternalism.

When Sir Francis Drake set out to circumnavigate the globe in 1577, he carried not only material provision but also spiritual resources. Along with a chaplain for the crew were supplies of Bibles, prayer books and Foxe's *Book of Martyrs*. Accompanying attempts at enrichment, advancement and even the possibility of imperial expansion was the worship of the church. The Virginia Company advertised itself as a means to spread Protestantism and wealth. With a desire for international expansion as a bulwark against Catholicism, an impulse present in all eras in which Anglicans exist, the preachers of the Virginia Company laid on England a moral and missiological responsibility to establish a robust Protestant base. Whatever else the English were exporting to the new world, they were exporting their church and their customs as true and necessary for salvation.[8]

James VI addressing the Virginia Company exhorted them to reach out to the indigenous people 'whereby they may be the sooner drawne to the true knowledge of God, and the Obedience of us'.[9] Thus, to the extent that one can speak of an understanding or rationale for Christian mission in this period, it was expansionist. The mission was about expanding the influence of English ways, including religious ways. The opportunity for planting the Church of England on foreign soil arose from the desire for economic expansionism of the chartered companies and the desire and strategy for doing so was inextricably linked to their priorities. Perhaps George Herbert expresses it best in his blatantly transactional theology:

> Religion stands on tip-toe in our land,
> Readie to passe to the *American* strand . . .
> My God, thou dost prepare for them a way,
> By carrying first their gold from them away:
> For gold and grace did never yet agree:
> Religion alwaies sides with povertie.
> We think we rob them, but we think amisse:
> We are more poore, and they more rich by this.[10]

Herbert's sentiments coalesced with economic expansion and, as will be seen, such sentiment was not limited to the sixteenth or seventeenth century.

Rowan Strong sees a particularly clear imperial mission rationale emerge with the SPG (founded in 1701). In the annual SPG sermons, he charts major theological themes that include a confidence that providence had gifted England with her overseas territories, that the gift of salvation she brought far outweighed any material disadvantage indigenous peoples experienced, and that her calling was to establish true religion and a just empire over against idolatrous oppressive Catholic empires. In truth, in its rejection of the sacramental logic that correlates salvation with freedom, such imperialist mission acted as a '"hegemonic instrument" for the maintenance of the power of the ruling groups in colonial North America and the West Indies'.[11]

While Herbert might have thought that the Christian gospel was compensation for plunder and theft, even this purported comfort would not be extended to all places or peoples. The slave owners, including the SPG to whom Sir Christopher Coddrington had bequeathed a plantation in Barbados in 1704, feared a faith that associated salvation with liberation. Instead, a message of submission and obedience was preached.[12] Though the Synod of Dort (1618–19) had declared that baptized slaves were to be given the rights of Christian citizens, the Church of England did not make any such declaration.[13] The Church was subordinate to the 'dominance of a landed and commercial hegemony in English society and its colonies', resulting in weak theology and weak leadership.[14] A presenting issue that illustrates this is the competition between colonialism and the search for the episcopal nature of the Church beyond Britain.

On the one hand, many colonialists seemed happy to have the spiritual comfort of Church of England chaplains. On the other hand, many colonialists were opposed to the idea of bishops upsetting the status quo in the colonies. Yet, even in revolutionary times the call for American bishops continued from some quarters. Granville Sharp's tracts *The Law of Retribution* and *Congregational Courts* (1776) had such an impact they converted some Dissenters and Presbyterians to the necessity of an American episcopate. William White's *The Case of the Protestant Episcopal Church in the USA Considered* (1782) proposed a 'superior order of ministers'. The vision for such bishops was that they would provide catholic order but would be contextualized for a more revolutionary milieu. These bishops would be presiding ministers who would continue ministry as parish clergy. Indeed, *in extremis*, White proposed episcopal consecration by three presbyters.[15]

In distinction to White, Connecticut clergy saw the necessity of a bona fide consecration to be of first importance. With no support from the English government, the loyalist

Samuel Seabury was North America's first bishop consecrated according to the Scottish Rite in 1784. The roots feeding this precursory vine were to be Jacobite.[16] However, it would not be the Jacobite nor high view of bishops that would prevail in an American Church seeking to balance its colonial settlement with catholic sentiment. In response to the impudent consecration of Seabury, General Conventions met to ensure an English character to the Church that eventually resulted in the consecration of William White and Samuel Prevost by the Archbishop of Canterbury in 1787. What emerged was quite but not quite an English Anglicanism. Decisions of General Conventions resulted in a hybridized polity fundamentally concerned with representative governance where the place of the laity was elevated and the influence of bishops curtailed. While assured of its catholicity by way of the Scottish and English line, 'bishop' would mean something distinct on 'the American strand'. The American Anglican experience and experiment would lead Britain to adopt a different approach to overseas episcopacy.[17]

The task facing the colonialist children of the Church of England became the nourishment of an American episcopalianism that could survive in revolutionary times and thrive in a post-revolutionary settlement. Such a task, both before and after the Revolution (1775–83), would mean controversy, loss of loyalist clergy and an adaptive form of an English church in the colonies. Eventually, the British Parliament made provision for bishops to be consecrated without the oath of allegiance to the crown, and in 1787 more bishops were provided for an independent America. In 1792, the Bishop of Maryland, Thomas John Claggett, became the first consecrated by American bishops. By 1840, full communion was established with the Church of England. Here was a church, beyond the crown, that remained largely 'Anglian'. The Episcopal Church might now serve an independent nation, but that nation continued to be forged by the familiar forces of white colonialism and plantation. The colonial expansion of the United States in the 1800s, as with British colonial expansion, involved key religious actors and invoked powerful theological tropes on

God's providential favour and the incorrigibility of native peoples. As continues to be seen in the racial demographics of the Episcopal Church (90 per cent white), this was a European settler church.[18] With few notable exceptions, the theologies and policies of the Episcopal Church served expansion to the widespread detriment of Native American cultures and lives.

The 1820s marked an era, especially in Britain, where the reality of denominational pluralism was being recognized. The Test and Corporation Acts were repealed and the Emancipation Act was passed, meaning nonconformists and Roman Catholics could take a greater role in civic life. By 1831, a Whig government let it be known to the SPG that they were phasing out their grant allocations to the North American Church. Revolutionary America shaped a Church suited to its context. A top-down established Church in what remained of British North America proved unnecessary as a bulwark against radicals and proved largely inept at Christian expansion. After 1840 no new government grants, apart from in India, were forthcoming to support overseas bishops and existing grants were gradually withdrawn.[19]

Echoing the situation of the Restoration almost 200 years prior, the withdrawal of state support for Anglicanism overseas meant a new era for mission. This withdrawal of the state from the Church overseas correlated with an already pre-existing vision of some Anglican missionaries. The Society for Missions in Africa and the East was founded in 1799. In 1812 it would become the Church Missionary Society. Given its evangelicalism and its voluntarism, it was well suited to an era where the state and the state church would be less prominent in mission practice.[20] Indeed, its missionaries would clash with colonial officials and imperial agenda, and with this resistance came a distinct understanding and practice of the promise of Anglicanism. As will be seen in the next section, such a call for a contextualism that supported a catholicity not imposed by Canterbury or London was well captured by the son of a founder of the CMS, Henry Venn and his colleague in mission, Samuel Ajayi Crowther.

CATHOLICITY AND CONTEXTUALIZATION

Anglicanism as Contextualization and Contestation

Crowther, baptized in 1825, was crucial to the anti-slavery work of the CMS in West Africa.[21] Crowther, himself a former slave, was a much more complex figure than either his severest critics or warmest eulogists recognized. Rescued by the British navy from a Portuguese slaving ship in 1822, he would go on to further studies in Sierra Leone and England. He was priested in 1843. In 1864 he was consecrated in Canterbury Cathedral as Bishop of 'West African countries beyond British jurisdiction'.

Crowther did not zealously seek an end to polygamy, had deep respect for the traditional religions of Africa and was at the missionary forefront of establishing the Africanness of Christianity not least through his work in translation. Because of his commitment to contextualization, some critics fretted that he had, in effect, left the faith for a heterodox syncretism thus proving that Africans were not ready to lead the Church. Such misjudgement and racism stood against the vision of both Crowther and Venn who became secretary of the CMS at the time Crowther was undertaking ordination training in London.

Venn inaugurated the 'native pastorate' predicated upon the evangelical belief that the power of Christ can transform and equip all people regardless of their race or culture. God's spirit could Africanize the Church by raising up evangelists, catechists, deacons, priests and bishops. The imposition of leaders from outside the African context was a short-term and unsatisfactory arrangement. Surely Crowther would embody just this vision of an incarnated gospel. In partnership with Venn, his gifts and leadership would put into action an Anglicanism forged in intercultural encounter. However, Venn and Crowther's vision for contextualization, inter-contextualization and the 'euthanasia' of the foreign missionary effort was not shared by missionaries on the ground. Between 1871 and 1874 controversy over the native pastorate broke out and would ultimately lead to the end of Crowther's ministry.[22]

Bishop Crowther may have been the leader of the Niger Mission, but that leadership was contested at every step and eventually undermined by the lobbying of European missionaries. In the age of social Darwinism, his accommodationist or contextualist approach to mission would be increasingly seen by foreign missionaries as laxity.[23] Crowther was keen to stress continuity between culture and gospel and was patient, some would say lenient, with fellow African missionaries. This, along with unfair accusations that he and his associates were pursuing commercial enterprise at the expense of evangelistic enterprise, would result in the CMS stepping in with disciplinary measures. In 1880, now in the post-Venn era, the CMS set up a Commission of Inquiry into the conduct of the Niger Mission. In 1890, now in the post-Berlin Conference (1884–5) era, a commission dismissed 12 of the 15 Africans working under Crowther. The bishop died in December 1891.[24] It would not be until 1951, when A. B. Akinyele became Bishop of Ibadan, that an African became a diocesan bishop again.[25]

The mistreatment, misjudgement and missed opportunity that the Crowther debacle represents was, unfortunately, multiplied by other incidents in other contexts. However, the impulse of leaders like Crowther and Venn for a deep contextualizing witness in the face of an imperial 'Anglianism' would live on. We argue that an impulse to contextualization remains both a means to fulfilling the promise of Anglicanism and a reason for controversy throughout the Communion. Crowther knew that the proclamation of God's love becomes promise when expressed in reference to local idiom, custom and concerns. In the context of imperial 'Anglianism', he discovered that this could be controversial. Despite the tragedy of the Crowther affair, here was a glimpse of Anglicanism forged in intercultural relationship beyond 'Anglianism'. Here was a contextualist approach to theology that would eventually become the Anglican way. How intercultural theology might resource the further promise of the Communion will be explored in more depth in Chapter 6. At this juncture, the further issue of polity as it arose in the Colenso case will be considered.

The same accommodationist or contextualist spirit at work in Bishop Crowther's evangelicalism was also at work in Bishop John Colenso's liberalism. This affair, with Africa as the locus once more, would provide not only a theological means towards Anglicanism (as with Crowther and Venn) but would also provide an institutional means (the Lambeth Conference) to an eventual Anglican end. The attitudes and actions of Crowther's opponents unveiled a weak theology of mission and contextualization infected by racism. In derogatory tropes against African peoples and religions, racism was not absent in the Colenso controversy. Both cases continue to have implications for critical intercultural theology and polity in the Communion. Colenso's case, considered in the context of the first Lambeth Conference, unveils the contestations around an emerging polity for an international family of churches that does not have a central authority figure. Here was an emerging polity with paternalistic tendencies that had no earthly parent. In the mid nineteenth century, many thought a developed polity – that could cross colonial, national and cultural boundaries – had no earthly hope. Before a consideration of the impact of Colenso on the Lambeth Conference and Anglican polity, we must first briefly rehearse the outline of the controversy itself. Taking his commentary on Romans and his commentary on the Pentateuch together, Colenso was seen to be guilty of a number of theological mistakes. Among his errors were his diminishment of the Scriptures, rejection of the doctrine of eternal punishment, promotion of universalism and devaluation of the sacraments. Not only were such views a cause of the crisis in polity but he directly addressed the uncertainty of 'Anglian' polity by questioning the relationship between the state and Church, between the clergy and Anglican formularies, and between the Church of England and the Church in the colonies.[26]

Bishop Robert Gray, first Bishop of Cape Town, nominated Colenso for the newly created diocese of Natal. Gray, it would appear, did not thoroughly investigate Colenso's theological views. In the same year that Colenso was consecrated, his friend and inspiration F. D. Maurice was dismissed from his teaching role at King's College, London for heterodoxy. Colenso was not to know that he, like his friend, was to face a similar fate. As a missionary, Colenso was clear that his theological work began in his exchanges with Zulu thinkers. Particularly important was the thought of William Ngidi for Colenso's evolving theology.[27] As his theology continued to develop so too did a sense of foreboding in the mind of Gray. When in 1861 Colenso published his *St. Paul's Epistle to the Romans*, from a 'missionary point of view' submitting the text to the 'ordinary rules' applied to all 'human compositions', Gray's fears were realized.[28] In 1862, when the first volume of his work *The Pentateuch and Book of Joshua Critically Examined* was published, Gray's alarm grew.

Colenso dedicated *Romans* to his friend Theophilus Shepstone, secretary for Native Affairs. He encouraged Shepstone that providence may be calling Britain to a 'great work among the Zulu' by bringing to them the blessings of 'civilisation'.[29] In *Romans*, Colenso contrasted his mission theology to theology written 'in the midst of a state of advanced civilisation and settled Christianity'.[30] Like St Paul himself, Colenso considered as his point of departure the missionary situation. For seven years an intercultural process of conversations and challenges from his 'native' interlocutors resulted in a shift in his theology. Nonetheless, Colenso, even in the face of imperialist brutality, was never able to transcend the colonialist frame.

In depicting the Zulu people, Colenso did not rise above common colonial tropes but, rather, added theological significance to them. What light the Zulus had as children or grandchildren of Abraham was all but quenched. The glimmer of that light remained in their belief in a divine creator.[31] In the context of his exegesis of Romans 9.1–13, he depicted 'Zulu and Kafirs' as the descendants of Ishmael and Esau. The 'Jewish Church of old' and English Christians were 'more highly favoured'. He made the impact of this reading plain in his application of Romans 9.13. '"England has God loved, and Africa has He hated." Yet not all English Christians are children of the Light, nor are all Africans heathen children of Satan; but those who have received most, shall have most required of them.'[32] Colenso never lost hope in the colonial project. He focused rather on criticizing particular missionary and colonial priorities and policies. He depicted missionaries as arrogant, harsh and uncharitable who often spoke with the 'most obscure and defective utterance'.[33] He, in contrast, thought of himself as entering into deeper dialogue, taking seriously the language and culture of the Zulu people he was working among. Elsewhere he had depicted such intercultural conversation and exploration as 'friendly discourse with natives of all classes' in a 'spirit of earnest, patient, research, with a full command of the native language' towards entering the 'secret chambers of light, which may be written by God's own finger there'.[34] Crucial to that work were the conversations and disputations he had with Zulu thinkers.[35] Colenso was publicly mocked for suggesting that an African convert could tutor an English missionary.

A bishop there was of Natal,
Who took a Zulu for a pal,
Said the Native 'Look 'ere,
Ain't the Pentateuch queer?'
Which converted the Lord of Natal.[36]

The idea of mutual conversion, in more recent times, has been recognized as important in understanding Christian mission. This was rarely the case in Colenso's day.

In *Romans*, he admitted to a development of his thought. In an earlier publication, on the eve of his foreign missionary work, he continued to give some credence to the notion of eternal punishment. On the missional interface, however, he had come to reject such a doctrine. While the Roman Catholic Church had fallen into error, it seemed to Colenso that a post-mortem 'remedial' or 'purifying' process was necessary because the Scriptures testified to gradations of sin and the eternal justice and love of God.[37] Aware that evangelical missionaries would view a rejection of the doctrine of eternal punishment as disincentivizing conversion, Colenso argued precisely the opposite. Instead of strengthening mission theology, vocation and strategy, an emphasis on eternal punishment drastically weakened it. He wrote, 'The conscience, healthy, though but imperfectly enlightened, does not answer to such denunciations of indiscriminate wrath . . .'[38] Any talk of love in the face of such a vengeful depiction of God seemed, Colenso submitted, anaemic. We hear the same theme in a pre-missionary sermon of 1853 when he spoke of the missionary's vocation not as the loud exposition of divine terror. The call of the missionary was to go as a 'voice of comfort and love . . . to whisper of Him, Who has been with them all along – Who has *not* left them alone . . . Whose Voice they have heard already, though they knew it not . . .'[39]

Colenso's was a mission theology of continuity and not discontinuity. Here was an emerging commitment to what we call in this study contextualization or enculturation. The work of the missionary was not 'to make all things new'; it was not to 'uproot altogether their old religion'. The task of mission was to declare in 'plainer' terms the love of God and invite the evangelized into the privileges of Christ's Church.[40] That love was centred on Jesus Christ but was not dependent on a doctrine of substitutionary atonement. The idea, avers Colenso, that Christ died instead of us is absent in the New Testament. He most certainly did not bear the punishment of our sins. Jesus died on our behalf and not in our place.[41] Christ took human nature and as 'our brother' died as all humans must. As righteous, his death was not due to the 'sinful taint' that the children of Adam inherited. We are counted as having partaken in his death. Thus, humanity is counted righteous because of him. Being righteous in God's eyes is, therefore, because of the work of Christ and not because of our own doing. Our sins 'fade away' in the light of Christ's perfect righteousness.[42] While Colenso's apparent universalism meant God's grace was available to all, this same grace was not present peculiarly in the sacraments.

Colenso detected a 'superstitious' piety at work in the Church of England that could have had negative ramifications for the growth of the Church in other cultures. Christ was no more present when eating and drinking at the Holy Table than he was 'when we are privileged to have communion with Him at any other time, and in any other manner'. Theorizing and not revelation had led the Church to 'make a distinction *in kind* between our Lord's Presence in the Holy Eucharist, and that which He vouchsafes to us, when we kneel in retirement'.[43]

As always, Colenso had the missionary situation in view. The believer privileged to live in circumstances with an abundance of priests and parishes cannot, given the love and grace of God in Christ, be somehow in a more spiritually profitable position than those who would never meet a priest or utter a word of England's liturgy. No one or no theory could 'interpose impediments of rank, or fortune, or colour, or religious opinion, between those who are in Christ'.[44] We are called to 'believe' in the Christ and not simply profess Christ and profess our baptism as some sort of 'charm upon our breasts, as if *that* would save us from His judgement'. We must 'commit ourselves entirely to Him, receive Him as our Saviour and obey Him as our Master and Lord'.[45]

As a missionary, Colenso knew such 'commitment' would always mean a grappling with faithfulness in new cultural contexts. Thus, while he called polygamy 'evil' he could not justify the importation of one version of sexual morality to another culture and context. The practice of converts abandoning their wives and choosing one at baptism he found 'unwarrantable, and opposed to the plain teaching of our Lord'. Colenso could not find 'any decisive Church authority on the subject'. On learning that Baptist missionaries in Burma decided in 1853 to admit polygamists to membership of the Church, but not to the offices of the Church, he wrote, 'this appears to me the only right and reasonable course'.[46] Colenso wrote to the Archbishop of Canterbury on the subject in 1861 asking for direction.[47] It was not until 1988 that the Lambeth Conference would adopt the position that Colenso proposed in 1855.[48] If the community will consent to receiving them, the polygamist will be received in baptism and to the Lord's table providing a promise is made not to marry again.

Colenso's questioning of the authority of the doctrinal status quo did not exclude the Church's relationship with the state and more particularly the Church's relationship with colonial policies. Things came to a head for Colenso in 1879. His earlier hopes for the blessing of Africa through colonial expansion were shattered when the British invaded Zululand. In the aftermath of the bloody invasion, Colenso preached on Micah 6.8. 'It is true that, in that dreadful disaster ... we have ourselves lost many precious lives ... But are there no griefs – no relatives that mourn their dead – in Zululand?' He asked, 'Wherein in our invasion of Zululand, have we shown that we are men who love mercy?' Colenso had been converted. No longer would he accept the colonialist frame. He moved from 'colonialist collaborator to colonialist enemy.'[49]

In early 1863 a pastoral letter from 40 English and Irish bishops, including the Archbishop of Canterbury, had urged Colenso to resign.[50] He did not. In the wake not only of *Romans* but of *The Pentateuch*, Colenso was tried and convicted of heresy by the Church in South Africa. Making an appeal to his appointment by the queen, Colenso appealed to the British courts. Colenso won the case and remained Bishop of Natal in the face of Gray appointing a new Bishop of Maritzburg to replace him.[51]

The contrasting results of the two trials transcended disagreement between mission leaders and bishops. It embodied and highlighted different visions of polity. While it may be too much to say that the Colenso case led to the first Lambeth Conference, it is true to say that it was decisive.[52] The admixture of controversies around race, intercultural theology and the reach of a colonial Church thus set the stage for the 1867 Lambeth Conference.

Anglican Catholicity: The Ongoing Pilgrimage

The Lambeth Conferences would do much for an international sense of a Church beyond England if not a Church beyond 'Anglianism'. A number of bishops and leading thinkers had been calling for some kind of episcopal, patriarchal, imperial or consultative forum for some time before 1867. Regional meetings, variously configured, were also already occurring in colonial contexts including in Australia, New Zealand, Canada and South Africa. Adding to the rationale and appeal for an international gathering was also the great success of the third Jubilee of the SPG (1851–2). During the celebrations, bishops from all over the empire – and, towards the end of the celebrations, two bishops from the United States of America – came together in celebration of Anglican mission.[53] It was, however, the Lambeth Conference that would be a fundamental sustaining focus for an internationalized Anglicanism. Archbishop Longley wrote the letter of invitation to the first conference of September 1867 for 'brotherly consultation' on 'many practical questions, the settlement of which would tend to the advancement of the kingdom of our Lord and Master Jesus Christ, and to the maintenance of greater union in our missionary work, and to increased intercommunion among ourselves'.[54]

Both Crowther and Colenso had peculiar relationships to the first conference. Crowther, who would only attend the third conference in 1888, could not attend the first conference. For some, Colenso was the cause of the 1867 conference. For Gray, the Colenso case was crucial to the rationale of the gathering and thus to an emerging polity that would signify an international Anglicanism. Bishop Tait of London had threatened to boycott the conference if Colenso was on the agenda. He was not on the official agenda, but any hope that Tait had of Colenso not being discussed at the conference was quickly dashed. Gray, of course, wanted to make sure the conference endorsed his condemnation of Colenso. Samuel Wilberforce of Oxford, Presiding Bishop John Henry Hopkins of Vermont, George Selwyn of New Zealand, Charles Wordsworth of St Andrews, John Travers Lewis of Ontario and Walter Hamilton of Salisbury were in support of such a move. Along with Tait, Alexander Ewing of Argyll and the Isles and Connop Thirlwall of St David's opposed any such international episcopal censure.[55]

This conference would pass a resolution setting out 'adaptions' and 'additions' to the 'services of the Church' according to the 'peculiar circumstances' of foreign mission. Changes beyond the 'Mother-Church' and her 'faith and doctrine' found in the 'spirit and principles of the Book of Common Prayer' would not be tolerated.[56] Thus, Colenso, in Resolution 6, was depicted as having caused deep injury and scandal to the Church. A committee would be established to ensure that the 'true faith' be 'maintained'. In a further resolution, the conference agreed with the policy to appoint a new bishop in Colenso's stead and that a 'formal instrument' establishing sound doctrine and the submission of the clergy be created by the Church of South Africa.[57] A committee set up to envisage a way for the Communion to be 'delivered from a continuance of scandal' reported that the Colonial Bishoprics Council no longer pay his stipend and his Letters Patent be cancelled. The committee adjudged the see to be 'spiritually vacant' and thus in need of a new bishop.[58]

The first Lambeth Conference was very much a colonial conference bringing together, in the words of the Archbishop of Canterbury, 'our widely scattered Colonial Churches . . .' bound together by Christian faith and 'by the ties of kindred' and a 'mother tongue'.[59] The bishops spoke of 'the Churches of our Colonial Empire and the Missionary Churches beyond them' in union with 'the Mother-Church'.[60] It was not, however, an international general synod that would promulgate binding canons. It never has been. Rather, the conference was designed for collegial fellowship and the discussion of 'matters of practical interest' and resolutions that would 'serve as safe guides to future action'.[61]

The Archbishop of Canterbury was aware that for some observers there would be disappointment that the conference did not define 'the limits of Theological Truth'. Rather, the conference was a testament to existing theological communion found in 'our priceless heritage set forth in our Liturgy and other formularies'.[62] The conference continued to respect a polity that would honour the 'independence of separate Churches' while rejecting the notion that 'any Bishop of the Church Catholic' could have 'dominion over his fellows in the Episcopate'.[63] Conversation among this all white gathering did turn to the concept of a pan-Anglican synod and even an international tribunal, to meet in England under the chairmanship of Canterbury, that could arbitrate on matters of heresy. The committee assigned the work of reviewing the functions and futures of synodical government within the Communion did recognize a need, in principle, for a 'higher Synod of the Anglican Communion' and 'united counsel in a sphere more extensive than that of a Provincial Synod'.[64]

A larger and separate committee explored the possibility of a 'spiritual tribunal'. The committee did recommend the formation of such a tribunal for the sake of unity in matters of 'Faith, and uniformity in matters of Discipline, where Doctrine may be involved'.[65] They too recognized that forming such a tribunal would have to overcome significant obstacles in law and polity.[66] At the second Lambeth Conference (1878) it was discussed again. The American Church leaders made it clear that they would not submit to such arbitration but recognized that it could be useful for the Church in the colonies.[67] Delegated to conference committees, the idea was never implemented with the bishops preferring to leave such discernment to provinces. The committee reported that, 'Every Ecclesiastical Province . . . should be held responsible for its own decisions . . . and your Committee are not prepared to recommend that there should be any one central tribunal of appeal from . . . Provincial tribunals.'[68] Only in cases where a province had not yet been founded could the conference imagine a tribunal to review discipline. Despite this, the idea of a centralized tribunal or arbiter would continue to raise its head throughout the decades.[69]

The cases of both Crowther and Colenso brought together a series of contested and controversial matters relating to empire, race, contextualization and polity. Whatever else might be deduced from the early Lambeth Conferences, it is clear that the Anglican Communion would stumble towards polities and contextualizations in international and intercultural fellowship eschewing an Anglicanism founded on a centralized patriarch or curia. This would mean, inevitably, that Anglicanism would continue to be a site of contestation. In large part, this book will argue that such processes of contestation should not be shunned. Rather, they should be seen as having missiological and theological import. That is to say, it is through such processes of contestation that Anglicans discern what it is they are to do and what it is they are to say.

Defending himself against his CMS detractors in 1889, Crowther provided a telling parable to illustrate his method within an African mission and Church. He pondered on a recently lit fire that makes a lot of smoke and in doing so gently pointed to the folly of his accusers. If 'the cook at that early stage decided to search out and pull out all the logs that smoked, the food would never be cooked'.[70] Tragically, that is what his opponents sought to do. Yet, these opponents of Crowther, and other foreign missionaries steeped in empire, exceptionalism and expansionism – especially after the Berlin Conference – would have to learn that their critical interlocutors were steeped in other ancient traditions and customs. These traditions, alongside emerging post-colonial nationalisms, would remain important not only psychically but theologically. The world Anglicanism that was emerging, distinct from 'Anglianism', was diverse. Indeed, it may be more accurate to say that it was polarized. As in Crowther's case, those who were zealous for foreign mission could also be zealous for an expansion of 'Anglianism'. In contrast, Anglicanism was emerging in inevitable contextualizations of the faith by believers who translated the gospel of Christ and the traditions of the Church of England into new tongues and new cultures.

For the vast majority of world Anglicans, the gospel of Christ would not come to them from the witness of foreigners but through the life and love of their sisters and brothers and mothers and fathers.[71] Even when the form of worship seemed strangely foreign, though often seasoned or subverted by local insights and sounds, the seemingly infinite translatability of the gospel could not be suppressed even by 'Anglian' order and missionaries.[72] Anglicanism sprang up in places beyond colonial governance or where no British colony ever existed. Angola, the Congo, Rwanda, Burundi and Nepal, for example, never possessed an English-speaking congregation but do have an Anglican Church. Along with French and Portuguese, Arabic too became the language of small but influential Anglican communities in the Middle East.[73]

English would not remain the first language of the majority of Anglicans nor the second language for many others.[74]

Deep processes of contextualization and contestation were the seedbed for Anglicanism. A key mitigating factor against a polarized Communion would have to mean, therefore, a broad commitment to contextualization. For inherent in the very message of God incarnate is an 'appeal to the indigenous milieu' where the message of salvation not only brings something new but adopts and adapts what went before.[75] John S. Mbiti puts the point plainly. Despite the disparagement of traditional religiosity – by foreign missionaries, North Atlantic clerics and academics – the God described in the Bible 'is none other than the God who is already known in the framework of our traditional African religiosity'.[76]

The ever outward-turning God turns to humanity in all its cultural embeddedness without ever baptizing one language or one culture as the primary expression of the mission of God.[77] The Church is not, then, a project of expansion from one place to another. Rather, the Church is born anew in each context.[78] Such conviction emerges not least from the experience and consequences of biblical translation. By the close of the nineteenth century, the Bible or portions of the Bible had been translated into 300 languages.[79] In turn, converts were not only involved in translation processes but could now themselves access and interpret the biblical text. Such interpretative agency began to make imported interpretations unstable and fuelled a more subversive hermeneutics. The converts could convert the intent of the evangelizers within church structures or by founding independent church structures.

The promise of Anglicanism, in contextual terms, is therefore the recognition that an ongoing commitment to the revelation of God in Jesus Christ means that all theology is contextual and practising catholicity will mean conversation, relationships and formation across contextualized differences. In sum, the notion of Anglican 'catholicity' is grounded in relationship to and in tension with a myriad of missional interfaces in a vast array of contexts. The believers that would make up the Anglican Communion beyond an 'Anglian' Communion already knew God and they knew

God could not be reduced to divine emperorship. Rather, the incarnate God was clothed in local dress and spoke good news to the victims of empire.

Recognizing the suffering of the Zulu people at the hands of the British Empire and recognizing the intercultural theology and advocacy of Colenso, the Church of the Province of Southern Africa revisited his case in 2002. A resolution from the Durban diocesan council stated that Colenso had 'sought to rethink Christian theology and the interpretation of Scripture in the light of his understanding of the Zulu people in their culture'. The council noted that Colenso and his family fought for 'the preservation of Zulu culture and autonomy, and for justice for the Zulu people'.[80] A century and a half after Bishop Crowther's consecration, the Church Mission Society held a service of 'thanksgiving and repentance'. Speaking on that day in 2014, the Revd Canon Philip Mountstephen, executive leader of CMS, spoke of 'the shame we share'. At the height of empire, young English missionaries 'effectively tried to place the shackles back' on a man who had been freed from slavery.[81] Preaching at the service in Canterbury Cathedral, Archbishop Justin Welby made the invitation to repentance clear: 'We in the Church of England need to say sorry that someone was properly and rightly consecrated Bishop and then betrayed and let down and undermined. It was wrong.'[82] 'Anglianism' it appeared would not, in the end, win out.

As the Crowther and Colenso affairs demonstrated, the process of cross-cultural conversion was never going to be one way. 'Anglianism' would need to go through a process of contestation and contextualization before Anglicanism would emerge as an intercultural and international reality.

The tradition that would become known as Anglicanism emerged in political, social and theological contestation. Anglicanism would remain a site of contestation. Too often the contestation was understood as a struggle between contextualization and catholicity or between groups that emphasized contextualization over catholicity or emphasized catholicity over contextualization. Inevitably this contestation has led to a pluralist tradition, if not a family of traditions, that would continue to be in tenuous relationship one with another. We will argue that this apparent tension between catholicity and contextualization is not a binary of opposition but is, in the final analysis, the promise of Anglicanism. Anglican theologies and practices of contextualization are not a challenge to theologies and practices of catholicity. Rather, an Anglican understanding of catholicity is a catholicity from below.

Considering Anglicanism in such terms has several benefits. It recognizes that what is at stake is more than simply 'the local option'.[83] What is at stake is international and intercultural fellowship that takes seriously an ongoing commitment to Scripture and tradition amid human experience, social location, culture and change.[84] It problematizes easy dichotomies such as 'liberal' and 'conservative'. It addresses crises not as fully fledged and fully defined issues but as processes of discernment and theology. It brings a variety of positions together not in their association with perennial Anglican partyism but in terms of missiological method. As missionaries, both Crowther and Colenso grappled with how to express the gospel faithfully in distinct contexts, cultures and languages.[85] Their approaches sought to testify to the love and grace of God through the Church and for the world. If Anglicans can hold on to this in good faith, then opportunities for deeper empathy and understanding across differences open up without any assumption that such differences would dissolve. It recognizes that the Anglican tradition always grapples with grounding the gospel in relationship to the vagaries of context. This mission or missiological story and process will be further explored in subsequent chapters. A more immediate issue emerges presently. If an intercultural Anglicanism wins out over an Anglo-Saxon Communion, what then holds the family together? Lambeth Conferences made appeal to common liturgy and formularies. However, processes of contextualization, liturgical reform and spiritual renewal and revival have created deep diversity, plurality and difference in form and practice. Against such a backdrop, the next chapter will address how Anglicans have balanced contextual adaptation with adherence to faithful norms.

Notes

1 Alec Ryrie, 'The Reformation in Anglicanism', in Mark D. Chapman, Sathianathan Clarke and Martyn Percy, eds, *The Oxford Handbook of Anglican Studies*, Oxford: Oxford University Press, 2015, p. 39.

2 See Alan M. G. Stephenson, *Anglicanism and the Lambeth Conferences*, London: SPCK, 1978, p. 8.

3 See R. S. Sugirtharajah, *Postcolonial Reconfigurations*, London: SCM Press, 2003, p. 20.

4 In Japan, converts, particularly from the 'intellectual class' and key cultural framings of private and public devotion were important in the development of the Church. In China, Chinese missionaries and Anglican evangelicals – working as missionaries of the China Inland Mission – made vital contributions to the growth of the Church. See Ward, *History*, pp. 246–56. John M. Takeda, 'The Experience of Japanese Anglicans', *Anglican and Episcopal Church History* 65 (1996), pp. 412–30. Irene Ebor, *The Jewish Bishop and the Chinese Bible*, Leiden: Brill, 1999.

5 Stephenson, *Anglicanism*, pp. 1–2.

6 Stephenson, *Anglicanism*, p. 2.

7 Stephenson, *Anglicanism*, p. 3.

8 Rowan Strong, *Anglicanism and the British Empire*, Oxford: Oxford University Press, 2007, pp. 1–9.

9 Eliga H. Gould, 'Prelude: The Christianizing of British America', in Norman Etherington, ed., *Mission and Empire*, Oxford: Oxford University Press, 2005, p. 20.

10 George Herbert, 'The Church Militant', *Christian Classics Ethereal Library*, available online at www.ccel.org/h/herbert/temple/ChurchMilitant.html [accessed 11 August 2015].

11 Strong, *Anglicanism and the British Empire*, pp. 111–17.

12 Gould, 'Prelude', p. 34. Kevin Ward, *A History of Global Anglicanism*, Cambridge: Cambridge University Press, 2006, pp. 86–8.

13 Ward, *History*, pp. 84–5.

14 Strong, *Anglicanism and the British Empire*, p. 111.

15 W. M. Jacob, *The Making of the Anglican Church Worldwide*, London: SPCK, 1997, pp. 62–4.

16 Gould, 'Prelude', p. 37.

17 Jacob, *Making*, pp. 65–72.

18 'Religious Landscape Study: Members of the Episcopal Church', *Pew Research Center*, available online at www.pewforum.org/religious-landscape-study/religious-denomination/episcopal-church/#racial-and-ethnic-composition [accessed 29 November 2018].

19 Jacob, *Making*, pp. 83–104.

20 See Strong, *Anglicanism and the British Empire*, p. 129.

21 Lamin Sanneh, 'The CMS and the African Transformation: Samuel Ajayi Crowther and the Opening of Nigeria', in Kevin Ward and Brian Stanley, eds, *The Church Missionary Society and World Christianity, 1799–1999*, Grand Rapids, MI: Eerdmans and Richmond: Curzon Press, 2000, pp. 173–97. Lamin Sanneh, *Abolitionists Abroad: American Blacks and the Making of Modern West Africa*, Cambridge, MA: Harvard University Press, 1999, pp. 139–81.

22 Ward, *History*, pp. 116–25. C. Peter Williams, *The Idea of the Self-Governing Church*, Leiden and New York: Brill, 1997. Sanneh, *Abolitionists*.

23 Herbert Spencer, *The Principles of Sociology Volume 1*, New York: D. Appleton and Company, 1895, see pp. 537–63.

24 Sanneh, 'CMS', p. 193. Lamin Sanneh, *West African Christianity: The Religious Impact*, Maryknoll, NY: Orbis, 1983, pp. 168–73.

25 Ward, *History*, p. 127. See Willie James Jennings, *The Christian Imagination: Theology and the Origins of Race* (Haven, CT: Yale University Press, 2010), pp. 150–55.

26 Jeff Guy, *The Heretic: A Study of the Life of John Willian Colenso, 1814–1883*, Pietermaritzburg: Natal University Press, 1984, p. 96.

27 Ward, *History*, p. 139.

28 J. W. Colenso, *St. Paul's Epistle to the Romans: Newly Translated, and Explained from a Missionary Point of View*, Cambridge: Macmillan and Co., 1861, p. 122.

29 Colenso, *Romans*, pp. v–vi. See Jennings, *Christian*, pp. 124–39, 161–8.

30 Colenso, *Romans*, p. v.

31 Colenso, *Romans*, p. 58.

32 Colenso, *Romans*, p. 234.

33 Colenso, *Romans*, p. 106.

34 Guy, *Heretic*, p. 77.

35 Guy, *Heretic*, pp. 64–6, 90.

36 Guy, *Heretic*, p. 133.

37 Colenso, *Romans*, pp. 196–215.

38 Colenso, *Romans*, p. 218.

39 J. W. Colenso, *Village Sermons*, Cambridge: Macmillan and Co., 1853, pp. 139–40. See John William Colenso, *Ten Weeks in Natal: A Journal of a First Tour of Visitation among the Colonists and Zulu Kafirs of Natal*, Cambridge: Macmillan & Co., 1855.

40 Colenso, *Village*, p. 141.

41 Colenso, *Romans*, p. 115.

42 Colenso, *Romans*, p. 182.

43 Colenso, *Romans*, p. 301.

44 Colenso, *Romans*, p. 97, see pp. 301–7.
45 Colenso, *Village*, p. 145.
46 Colenso, *Ten Weeks*, pp. 139–41.
47 Guy, *Heretic*, p. 74.
48 Resolution 26, 'Church and Polygamy', available onlineat www.anglicancommunion.org/resources/document-library/lambeth-conference/1988/resolution-26-church-and-polygamy?author=Lambeth+Conference&year=1988 [accessed 25 October 2018].
49 Jennings, *Christian*, p. 163.
50 Charles Gray, ed., *Life of Robert Gray: Bishop of Cape Town and Metropolitan of Africa*, Vol. II, London: Rivingtons, 1876, pp. 50–2.
51 Peter Bingham Hinchliff, *John William Colenso*, London: Nelson, 1964, pp. 172, 181. Ward, *History*, p. 140.
52 See Ward, *History*, p. 140.
53 Stephenson, *Anglicanism*, pp. 18–30.
54 Stephenson, *Anglicanism*, p. 32.
55 Stephenson, *Anglicanism*, pp. 31–43.
56 Resolution 8, Lambeth Conference, 1867, available online at www.anglicancommunion.org/media/127716/1867.pdf [accessed 26 October 2018]. Randall T. Davidson, *The Five Lambeth Conferences*, London: SPCK, 1920, pp. 86–7.
57 Resolution 8, Lambeth Conference, 1867.
58 Davidson, *Lambeth*, pp. 133–6.
59 Davidson, *Lambeth*, p. 79.
60 Davidson, *Lambeth*, pp. 99–100.
61 Davidson, *Lambeth*, p. 79.
62 Davidson, *Lambeth*, p. 81.
63 Davidson, *Lambeth*, p. 83.
64 Davidson, *Lambeth*, pp. 114–15.
65 Davidson, *Lambeth*, p. 117.
66 Davidson, *Lambeth*, pp. 117–21.
67 Stephenson, *Anglicanism*, p. 64.
68 Davidson, *Lambeth*, p. 172.
69 Stephenson, *Anglicanism*, pp. 39–43, 67. Davidson, *Lambeth*, pp. 84–6, 171–4. See *The Anglican Communion Covenant*, third edition, section 4, available online at www.anglicancommunion.org/media/100850/ridley_cambridge_covenant_english.pdf [accessed 29 October 2018].
70 Sanneh, 'CMS', pp. 188–9.
71 Kevin Ward, 'The Development of Anglicanism As a Global Communion', in Andrew Wingate, Kevin Ward, Carrie Pemberton and Wilson Sitshebo, eds, *Anglicanism: A Global Communion*, New York: Church Publishing, 1998, p. 19.

72 Lamin Sanneh, *Translating the Message: The Missionary Impact on Culture*, Maryknoll, NY: Orbis, 2004.

73 Grant LeMarquand, 'Globalization of the Anglican Communion', in Ian S. Markham et al., eds, *The Wiley-Blackwell Companion to the Anglican Communion*, Malden, MA: Wiley-Blackwell, 2013, p. 667. Dennis D. Hudson, *Protestant Origins in India: Tamil Evangelical Christians 1706–1835*, Grand Rapids, MI: Eerdmans, 2000.

74 Kevin Ward, 'Mission in the Anglican Communion', in Mark D. Chapman, Sathianathan Clarke and Martyn Percy, eds, *The Oxford Handbook of Anglican Studies*, Oxford: Oxford University Press, 2015, p. 69.

75 Lamin Sanneh, *Disciples of All Nations: Pillars of World Christianity*, New York: Oxford University Press, 2008, pp. 26–7.

76 John S. Mbiti, 'The Encounter of Christian Faith and African Religion', *Christian Century* 97:27 (1980), pp. 817–20, at p. 818.

77 Sanneh, *Disciples*, p. 27.

78 David J. Bosch, *Transforming Mission: Paradigm Shifts in Theology of Mission*, Maryknoll, NY: Orbis, 1998 [1991], p. 454.

79 Jehu J. Hanciles, *Beyond Christendom: Globalization, African Migration, and the Transformation of the West*, Maryknoll, NY: Orbis Books, 2008, p. 106.

80 Ward, *History*, pp. 139–43.

81 Philip Mounstephen, 'Crowther Talk: Canterbury Cathedral', *Church Mission Society*, available online at www.churchmissionsociety.org/our-stories/crowther-talk-canterbury-cathedral [accessed 30 November 2018].

82 Justin Welby, 'Archbishop Welby on the First Black Anglican Bishop', *Anglican Communion News Service*, available online at www.anglicannews.org/news/2014/06/archbishop-welby-on-the-first-black-anglican-bishop.aspx [accessed 22 May 2019].

83 Philip Turner, 'The End of a Church and the Triumph of Denominationalism: On How to Think About What is Happening in the Episcopal Church', in Ephraim Radner and Philip Turner, eds, *The Fate of Communion: The Agony of Anglicanism and the Future of a Global Church*, Grand Rapids, MI: Eerdmans, 2006, pp. 19–20.

84 Stephen B. Bevans, *Models of Contextual Theology*, Maryknoll, NY: Orbis, 2002, p. 15.

85 On the dangers of Anglican partyism, see Andrew Atherstone, 'Identities and Parties', in Mark D. Chapman, Sathianathan Clarke and Martyn Percy, eds, *The Oxford Handbook of Anglican Studies*, Oxford: Oxford University Press, 2015, pp. 77–91.

4

Catholicity and Communion

Missionary Bishops and Their Churches

The expansion of the Church of England beyond its place of origin awakened the first glimmers of mission by Anglicans. We have seen how profoundly Anglicanism took root in mission contexts; the growth of the Church was tangible from the seventeenth century onward in North America, and then in a variety of settings. Anglican mission gained momentum from the nineteenth century onward. Cross-cultural encounters beyond identification with empire emerged in every instance. Initially Anglican mission began in various places as chaplaincy to English expatriates without reliance upon having bishops in the field. As colonial life arose, the Church found forms of accommodation to these social circumstances. In some North American colonies, a semblance of English religious establishment developed, with Virginia becoming the most complete likeness. Even there, the Church's colonial life developed without episcopal oversight.

As we have described, the office of commissary, or administrator, arose, a noteworthy appointee being Thomas Bray late in the eighteenth century. Though Bray's tenure in Maryland was brief, his experience in North America prompted him to encourage new forms of mission. Through the creation of the Society for the Propagation of the Gospel (SPG, now USPG) and the Society for Promoting Christian Knowledge (SPCK, founded in 1698), Bray linked the Church's mission to a new emphasis on Christian education, mainly among the English populations.[1] Such education helped to secure the life of the colonial Church even among people suspicious of it. The Church's growth in New England was an alarming development to Puritan sensibilities, which resented the SPG's emphasis on the Church's tradition and its alliance with the state. Mission by the SPG focused upon building the Church, yet it was cautious about efforts to evangelize non-white, non-Christian populations. When the SPG built an emphasis upon evangelism of non-Western peoples, it had been anticipated by the Church Missionary Society (CMS), an outgrowth of the evangelical party in the Church of England. CMS missionaries made evangelism their priority without seeking bishops until there were the beginnings of church life. Thus, as mission began, bishops did not seem required for this work.

However, the circumstances of mission eventually compelled their presence. The office has been the historic centre of the Church's sacramental life and governance; in fresh ways it proved central as the Church expanded its footprint in mission. North America was the first instance. In the wake of revolution and political independence, the new Episcopal Church could not rely upon the Church of England for guidance. As its dioceses began to organize, along comparable lines but with varying priorities and at varying paces, their bishops were elected, an American innovation that would be replicated elsewhere as Anglicanism expanded. The first American bishop was Samuel Seabury of Connecticut who was consecrated by the Scottish Episcopal Church in 1784. By contrast, the first Canadian bishop, Charles Inglis of Nova Scotia, was appointed by King George III in 1787.[2] Whether in Canada or the United States, early North American bishops faced tasks that were as much organizational as they were evangelistic. Their work included the creation of ecclesiastical structures, for which American democracy became the model. William White, first Bishop of Pennsylvania, articulated the framework of the Church, modelling its General Convention after the American Congress. Later, Anglican governance would feature democratic synods and bishops generally would be elected.

The rise of synods and elections were not simply aspects of the Church's expansion beyond England. The Church's advance in mission required innovations in its structures and procedures. At stake were the Church's identity and effectiveness when shorn of the privileges of establishment and forced to build itself in circumstances new to it. This would not be the only instance of such a challenge as Anglican expansion in the nineteenth and twentieth centuries would demonstrate. The promise of Anglicanism has been a function of the Church's mission, which has required adaptable church structures, how they have been configured as well as how they have functioned in the face of unprecedented contextual challenges. Repeatedly Church debates, and conflicts, have been over the shape of church structures in mission fields.[3] Efforts to change aspects of church life have often been defended as advancing mission, while efforts to preserve aspects of church life have reflected allegiance to forms of tradition deemed crucial to the Church's identity. Such debates have arisen amid mission when the fact of disestablishment surfaced. The resulting tensions account for many of Anglicanism's fault lines.

The rise of an organizational framework for the Episcopal Church became the prelude to a wave of mission for which bishops became central. As the United States expanded westward, the Church also expanded. At first, Episcopalians were outflanked by the frontier evangelism of Baptists and Methodists. During the nineteenth century Episcopalians cultivated their own approach to mission and the Church expanded. But what did mission mean and how did bishops influence it? The experiences of early American bishops provide vivid examples. Philander Chase became the Bishop of Ohio in 1819, the first American bishop west of the Allegheny mountain range.[4] Chase perceived that the Church needed to embark on mission. Ordained in 1798, he first served in remote parts of the state of New York. There he travelled constantly to evangelize, preach and baptize, and he organized congregations in Utica and Canandaigua. Near Poughkeepsie, he also taught school. His ministry took unusual turns in 1805 when Chase moved to Louisiana to found what would become Christ Church Cathedral, and in 1811 when he became rector of Christ Church in Hartford, Connecticut which also would become a cathedral.

Continuing to feel the call of mission, he went to Ohio where his ministry included helping to found Christ Church in Cincinnati, yet another future American cathedral. Chase would preside at Ohio's first diocesan convention in 1818. Later in that year, a gathering of Ohio clergy and laity elected him as their first bishop. Consecrated in 1819 in Philadelphia, Chase returned to Ohio in a manner befitting a missionary. Along the way he stopped to evangelize, and he continued such travels for the next few years. But as bishop in a frontier diocese, other duties demanded his attention. He was responsible for expanding the Episcopal Church's life in a new area. To train future clergy and to give the Church a public role in education, Chase founded Kenyon College in 1824. Unable to raise funds for the intended college in the United States, he secured donations in England from the second Lord Kenyon and the first Lord Gambier, as well as the writer Hannah More. Kenyon College has become a leading liberal arts college.

Chase's ministry focused on evangelism and the organization of church life. In doing so, he forged connections that transcended the Church's institutional channels in order to achieve his ends. While building the Church's following and its structures, he expanded its educational role, a combination of initiatives that would become characteristic of Anglican mission. At first Kenyon was a modest institution, and Chase's leadership style was autocratic. But his approach and his results were not unique. This pattern would be apparent in the work of early American bishops, including John Henry Hobart in New York, Benjamin Bosworth Smith in Kentucky and James Hervey Otey in Tennessee. As missionaries, bishops served as evangelists, teachers and pastors. They were also organizers and institution builders. They served as pastors of pastors, raised funds and built volunteerism, providing leadership for existing congregations while encouraging the formation of new ones. Early bishops had to be innovative, adaptive and collaborative across institutional lines and even across oceans, as Chase's work illustrated.

The Anglican Church of Canada's development revealed similar patterns. In 1839, John Strachan was consecrated as the first

Bishop of Toronto, alongside Aubrey Spencer, first Bishop of Newfoundland, at Lambeth Palace, London. Already there had been bishops in Nova Scotia and Quebec. As a priest, Strachan had become a forceful leader insisting upon the Church's social and religious prerogative. He had been instrumental in founding King's College, later the University of Toronto. He had launched mission work to First Nations peoples, an important church precedent. Well into his ministry, Strachan held establishmentarian assumptions, only to find that by the 1830s the Church could no longer presume a favourable relation with the state. The Canadian situation was resembling its southern neighbour more than its mother Church. Strachan's ministry adapted to North American realities in ways that enhanced church life.[5]

The identification of the office of bishop with mission increased. In 1835 the General Convention of the Episcopal Church created the office of missionary bishop and named Jackson Kemper as the first to be consecrated.[6] By 1870 there would be 18 Episcopal missionary bishops, most serving in North America. The designation had some precedent. The examples of English mission societies loomed large, and the Episcopal Church had already declared itself to be a 'domestic and foreign missionary society'. The creation of the post of missionary bishop made this emphasis tangible. What this meant was spelled out in Kemper's consecration sermon, given by Bishop George Washington Doane of New Jersey, in Philadelphia on 25 September 1835. Noting that this was a new office and a novel occasion, Doane depicted the Church, and the expanding nation, as being sheep without a shepherd. A time of opportunity and confusion required apostolic example, the agency of one designated to model all that the faith and the Church must be. Such bishops, Doane declared, cannot wait for the Church to arise, but must take the lead in organizing it. Pervading Doane's imagery, and his notion of mission, was an emphasis on uniting the Church, and through it society, according to those 'inherent principles of union which alone can bind in one large masses of mankind . . .'[7]

Doane argued that the episcopal system of church life was ancient and thus held priority over other systems. But the superiority and truth for which he argued could not be presumed. 'If we believe that our principles as Protestant Episcopalians are most in accordance with the divine will, and therefore most for the promotion of human happiness, it is our duty to demonstrate it in action, to carry them out before the world in vigorous and efficient practice . . .'[8] By its presence and its conduct, the office of bishop should embody the Church's commitment to mission in the name of Christ. There would be variations in the Church's form and priorities, of course, because the circumstances of mission vary from one setting to another. But apostolic form had abundant precedent as the Church's mission has grown. The field of mission is the entire world. For this task, he continued, the Church's constitution has been consistent. The Church is the trustee of the gospel, and bishops are the Church's foremost trustees. The unique challenges of time and place do not mitigate the form and intention of the Church. The 'lost sheep in the vast West' required the guidance of a missionary bishop, whose ministry would bring alive the compassion of Christ. Kemper lived up to Doane's charge. Missionary bishop principally in Missouri and Indiana, his work extended to Iowa, Wisconsin, Nebraska and Kansas. In 1838, he was joined by Leonidas Polk, the second missionary bishop, whose ministry guided the Church's growth in Louisiana and nearby areas of the American South. Unlike Kemper, Polk's legacy was not admirable. A slave owner and military officer, he became a general in the Confederate forces seeking to secure the South's secession in the American Civil War.[9] When Polk died in combat in 1864, his life had been defined by moral disgrace and conflict rather than compassion and mission.

Bishops in the Field

The rise of missionary bishops in North America, and of bishops for whom building the Church loomed large, were pieces of larger developments. During the first half of the nineteenth century there were three decided turns in the shape of Anglican mission and the relation of the office of bishop to it. The first was the appearance of bishops in mission fields, a turn that reflected North American developments. The rise of the episcopate in India, begun with the consecration of Thomas Middleton as Bishop of Calcutta in 1814, signalled that North America would not prove unique. Notably, the creation of the Indian episcopate resulted from evangelical emphasis upon England's foreign duties, as these religious sensibilities viewed them. A coterie of public figures known as the Clapham Sect, linked by their evangelical commitments and gathered around the noted William Wilberforce, advocated mission and social reform in India almost as avidly as they pursued abolition of slavery in British territories. As India became more of a colonial territory than a trading outpost, the English Church expanded its evangelism and ministry there, looking beyond chaplaincy to the expatriate population. Over time, Anglicanism, and Christianity generally, took root in India as an influential minority. The Church's relation to indigenous peoples has been a mixed legacy. The Church's ministries would give Anglicanism a presence beyond the numbers of its adherents.

The arrival of bishops in what would become major centres of Anglicanism – Australia, New Zealand and South Africa – followed a similar course. Like the Canadian Church, in the South Pacific and southern Africa there had been Anglican growth without detachment from Britain and without the presence of bishops. William Broughton became Australia's archdeacon in 1829, then its first bishop in 1836. George Augustus Selwyn arrived in Auckland in 1841 as New Zealand's first bishop and Robert Gray reached Cape Town in 1847, like Selwyn and Broughton having been consecrated in England.[10] By the time of Gray's elevation to episcopal office, the number of bishops in colonial areas was growing steadily. Gray was consecrated with the first bishops of Melbourne, Adelaide and Newcastle, all in Australia. What Gray found in South Africa reflected what other overseas bishops discovered in their domains. The Church existed tenuously, consisting of far-flung congregations, with clergy of uneven quality labouring sacrificially with little oversight. A few church-related institutions, such as schools, existed as small initiatives that struggled to impact their localities. The Church required the vision and authority only its central office could provide. Like Chase in Ohio, new bishops set out on extended travels that combined mission and oversight, evangelism and organization. They built worship communities, planned for schools and gained credence with local leaders.

Democratic Governance

Just as notable, they launched democratic governance of their emerging branches of Anglicanism, following American precedent. The second turn in nineteenth-century Anglican life was the rise of synodical governance as the Church spread. The first Australian synod met in 1850, with South Africa following in 1857, and New Zealand launched its own synod in 1859.[11] The presence of bishops and the rise of synods consolidated the Church's mission in a context. Such development occurred in comparable ways from one church context to another. It was becoming possible to speak of Anglicanism as catholic, the Church expanding in varied contexts along parallel lines of development. Bishops took the lead, building the Church in new places. Early bishops faced similar challenges and displayed similar styles of leadership that required innovation and assertiveness. There were obvious differences among them and the clergy and laity they guided. The most apparent difference concerned church party affiliation, whether Low Church and evangelical, or High Church, or by the mid-century Anglo-Catholic, reflecting influences of the Oxford Movement. The differences were profound, and often matters of dispute that discouraged collegiality. The divergences of church parties influenced aspects of mission, such as how it styled worship. The modes of expressing the Church's faith, and translating it into practical expressions, varied considerably. In some settings, the Church's life reflected the dominance of one or another party. Portions of the American Midwest reflected Oxford Movement influence in ministry and worship.

By contrast, portions of African Anglicanism became evangelical in the priority they have given to conversion and the authority of the Holy Spirit. Yet other portions of Africa reflected the Oxford Movement in its worship. Anglicanism has grown in ways that could privilege contextual initiative over deference to external authority. The resulting differences could rankle and divide, but have only occasionally fuelled lasting conflict.

In the nineteenth century, Anglican conflict often centred on church party differences and on the conduct of bishops. There were occasional fears that a bishop's Oxford Movement sympathies could foreshadow efforts to impose Roman Catholic practices or even to encourage allegiance to Rome itself. The defection of American bishop Levi Silliman Ives to Rome in 1852 lent credence to this suspicion. As a result, Bishop George Washington Doane, articulator of the ideal of the missionary bishop, became suspect and faced church proceedings on three occasions in the mid nineteenth century. Leading evangelical bishops Charles McIlvaine of Ohio and William Meade of Virginia mobilized investigations into Doane's conduct of his office. The incident generated furore but ended without resolution in 1853. The uncertainty of its conclusion was fitting given the vagaries of its inception. Doane's style of church life, and the limits of his accountability to other bishops and the larger Church, seemed to be the actual issues.[12]

The fault lines that arose among Anglicans as the Church expanded reflected notable differences and the shape of church governance augured less for resolution than for perpetuation of the tensions that fostered them. The differences were real then and remain so now. Hotly contested and bitterly alienating at times, the sources of division among Anglicans, to which we will devote more attention, have never lessened the necessity of mission or the challenges that attend it. Nevertheless, in the face of mission's real dimensions, the differences of Anglican life lost some of their urgency. In mission fields all Anglicans faced similar demands requiring similar forms of response and evoking similar forms of leadership, especially by bishops.

The fact that the demands of mission proved similar was conducive to conversation and cooperation that became widespread as Anglicans built means of consultation with one another. The challenges of mission, so comparable despite contextual differences and cultural variations, shaped the development of church life. Mission entailed evangelism, teaching and ministry, building the Church as a faith community and building the common good in local society. We conclude that a de facto catholicity emerged among Anglicans. While contextual life was framed by sacramental worship and historic forms of ministry, patterns of collaboration arose among the Church's varied contexts, fuelled by conversations, discourse, even debate. The Anglican lingua franca reflected the common challenges of mission in contexts new to the Church, challenges for which there was little preparation or anticipation, challenges which faced all church parties. In the face of these realities, bishops were challenged to serve as unifiers and catalysts who spoke for their contexts while creating linkages and modelling the Church's faith and ministry in ways that could bring creative focus on mission. As much as any who have guided mission, bishops have named the challenges entailed and cast visions of church life to address them.

Mission required that Anglicans face a focal question: what does it mean to be faithfully Christian and Anglican in new settings amid the tasks of mission? A process of church development had begun, for which bishops served as linchpins. At their best, bishops in mission fields transcended party divergences, encouraged church growth and promoted local social development. Bishops encouraged steps to build society in new places, posing the Church as the social cornerstone. The Church traded on its legacy as religious establishment, bringing a sense of catalytic social responsibility to bear on issues in their contexts. To do so, bishops organized the Church, taught the faith, developed leaders, built worship and launched education, setting boundaries of belief and practice. Through these bishops in mission fields, an Anglican consensus became possible, even amid tensions that arose in church life. A focus on mission became the basis of an Anglican catholicity.

Cast on Its Own Resources

The third turn in Anglican life during the nineteenth century reflected the impact of a shift in English political life upon the Church. By the late 1820s and early 1830s, pressure for political reform coalesced in a series of decisive measures that passed Parliament, as we have noted. Catholic Emancipation (1829) and repeal of the Test and Corporation Acts (1828) removed disabilities imposed upon religious dissenters in the United Kingdom. It was no longer necessary to receive Communion in the Church of England in order to hold public office, and members of the Roman Catholic Church could sit in Parliament. The first was the Irish lawyer Daniel O'Connell, who had led a campaign against civil disabilities on religious divergence.[13]

Religious reform presaged political change. The Reform Act of 1832 widened the British franchise and addressed abuses in elections and the influence of patronage. The electoral map was redrawn to add districts in areas of population growth, and qualifications for voting became defined more regularly, reducing local idiosyncrasies. It is worth noting that a year later, in 1833, an act to abolish slavery in British possessions passed Parliament. Religious influence in British life had become more public, with accountability based on debate and a capacity to persuade on moral grounds. The established Church had to build its influence, not presume it.

In the wake of reform, defenders of the Church mobilized forcefully, especially those who prized the alliance of Church and state. In 1838, a young politician, William Ewart Gladstone, published *The State in its Relations with the Church*. Seemingly a defence of the old order, it proved to be an obituary for it and an obituary for Gladstone's adherence to Tory views.[14] In time, he would become a leading political Liberal, valuing the Church's distance from the state as the guarantee of its integrity. The Church was being revived as much by external forces as by internal initiative that acknowledged changing social realities. Bishop Charles James Blomfield of London emphasized the Church's integrity in practical terms. He felt that in a society marked by enlarging urban areas, the Church had to be in fact what it claimed to be in theory, namely, the Church of England. He resolved to bring the Church to those people and places where it was not present. A campaign to build churches in new urban areas resulted. Blomfield did not confine his efforts to London or England alone. In 1841 he helped to launch the Colonial Bishoprics Fund to provide the episcopate and to create dioceses in new colonial territories. The logic behind this provision defied acquiescence to the state or chaplaincy to colonial society. Leading figures in the Church of England, some moved by high views of the Church, some by the needs of mission fields, concluded that the Church could not rely upon the state for its mission.[15]

The Church should define its own life and exercise its own initiative. The new reality of religious diversity at home, and the inherent pluralism of mission fields, meant the Church must possess its own integrity, defined by the gospel and Christian tradition. The old alliance with the state was being revised even as the fact of religious establishment continued. By the mid nineteenth century the integrity of the Church's life required it to act independently of the state. Anglicans continued to trade on proximity to social influence as they advanced plans of mission. But they increasingly asserted the independence of their faith and ministry in doing so. Not all church leaders granted the episcopate priority in this process. Henry Venn, CMS general secretary, demonstrated the evangelical approach to mission and the episcopate's role in it. Venn believed that mission should develop new branches of the Church to which bishops then would be appointed. The Church must build itself, becoming self-supporting, making bishops not the basis of the Church's inception but of its consolidation.[16] Anglicans differed on the timing of the episcopate's appearance. However, they agreed on its necessity for mission and on the tasks that mission entailed. Consensus emerged amid contestation, a fact of the Church of England's history which was becoming characteristic of new mission areas. The office of bishop was proving emblematic of the Church's challenges as well as its promise.

In Search of Guiding Principles

The expansion of the episcopate had become a prominent aspect of Anglican mission by the middle of the nineteenth century. The episcopate did not simply follow the Church's growth; increasingly bishops launched the Church's entry into new places. But with expansion there were anomalies, that is, instances of bishops whose conduct was less than exemplary. We have noted the instance of Leonidas Polk, an American slave owner who died in combat as a Confederate general. In South Africa, several instances of controversy arose concerning bishops, one being a matter of blatant misconduct, the other a situation of heterodox theological views and, more important, refusal to abide by the Church's authority. Both cases, and another legal challenge to the South African Church's authority, exemplified two issues that have dogged Anglican life ever since: First, how have Anglicans framed their identity in ways that promised consistency given the Church's diversification across varied contexts and cultures? Second, a related issue, how have Anglicans created forms of common life that would balance cultural roots in particular contexts with tangible forms of accountability to one another? The one issue concerns the integrity of Anglican identity, the other addresses the integrity of Anglican intramural relations.

As Anglicanism grew in South Africa, moving inland from its initial base at Cape Town, more bishops were needed to consolidate new dioceses. Edward Twells was recruited from England by the Bishop of Cape Town to serve as the first Bishop of the Orange Free State, later the diocese of Bloemfontein. In 1863 Twells was consecrated in Westminster Abbey and, upon his arrival in South Africa, began an energetic episcopate. He founded a diocesan grammar school and encouraged the formation of a missionary brotherhood to advance the diocese. Twells supported Robert Gray as controversies surrounded South African Anglicans. But soon a cloud also enshrouded Twells, the most devastating of all controversies. In 1869 Twells abruptly left his diocese and resigned his episcopate. Charges of pederasty surfaced, the details kept vague in church records. Seemingly Twells remained in South Africa and died in obscurity.[17]

In the same year that Twells arrived in South Africa, John W. Colenso was deposed as Bishop of Natal. He had arrived ten years earlier, in 1853, recruited by Robert Gray from England and, like Twells later, consecrated there. Unlike Twells in other respects, Colenso possessed sensibilities shaped by the theology of F. D. Maurice. The first of the Christian Socialist voices in the Church of England, Maurice saw God's presence in every social class and culture. He advanced the Church's engagement with working-class people and fostered its critique of the ills of industrial society. Maurice posed the unprecedented idea that Christians could find enhanced images of God through constructive engagement with other world religions. Such openness to diverse experiences of the sacred and compassion for those who suffered stamped Colenso's approach to his episcopate.

As we have described, Colenso studied local cultures as he built up diocesan life. He developed particular acuity for the life of the Zulu, producing a grammar book and dictionary of their language. Moving into deeper water, Colenso wrote a qualified defence of the practice of polygamy, which was common among the Zulu. Of course, more alarming to church sensibilities, Colenso wrote critiques of the Bible, culminating in a challenge to the literal truth of miracle stories and disputing the assumption that Moses wrote the Old Testament's first five books, or Pentateuch. When challenged, he refused to resign and continued to function as an alternative to his successor in Natal, W. K. Macrorie.[18]

As if the cases of competing bishops were not enough, Gray also contended with a priest who was determined to challenge his authority. At the first South African synod, five parishes had refused to send delegates. When a second synod was called in 1861, one priest refused to attend or to commend it to his parishioners. William Long had been a colonial chaplain who was ordained as a priest by Gray. Until the matter of synods arose, Long had seemingly been a loyal and faithful parish priest. But the rise of synods provoked his ire. He maintained that such synods constituted an affront to the authority of the Church of England. It is likely that Long associated synods with his bishop's sympathies for the Oxford Movement, while Long professed greater allegiance to the Reformation, as he saw it. Bishop Gray convened a church court, which declared Long suspended, though his salary was not withdrawn. Long appealed, eventually to the Privy Council in London where true authority resided in his view. Long was reinstated, a momentary challenge to Gray's authority and that of the South African Church's synods.

Gray was not deterred, and a preponderance of opinion in the Church supported him. As the South African Church grew, and its synod matured, the practical fact of autonomy from the Church of England was evident. The South African Church was forced upon its own initiative and resources, and it evolved its own means of authority. In 1870 it was formally constituted as the Church of the Province of South Africa, the culmination of Gray's episcopate. Seemingly he had triumphed in spite of monumental challenges. But the string of challenges had not run out. Long's suspicions of Tractarian assertions and synodical authority were shared sufficiently to evoke a movement of protest. Though Gray died in 1872, some parishes persisted in their refusal to participate in the Church he had nurtured. These congregations remained scattered, but their number grew somewhat as new gatherings arose, sharing the sense of defending Reformation principles and the true Church of England. After periodic court battles, a rival Church calling itself the Church of England in South Africa arose late in the nineteenth century. At times it launched legal challenges to the dominant Church of the Province, later renamed the Anglican Church of South Africa. In 1936, the breakaway group failed in its effort to claim church property in Cape Town. Less contentious at other times, there have been consultations between the two bodies, claiming the same heritage though framing it quite differently. Aided at times by the diocese of Sydney in the Australian Church, the Church of England in South Africa created a congregationally based structure with one bishop shepherding what are now estimated at 100,000 members. In 2013 it renamed itself as the Reformed Evangelical Anglican Church of South Africa and claimed alliance with various Reformed churches beyond the ken of Anglicanism.[19]

Overall there were few reported instances of clerical misconduct and insubordination among Anglicans in mission fields. These were not the issues besetting church growth. It was sadly ironic that glaring circumstances arose in the South African Church and overshadowed Gray's legacy as the first bishop there. The preponderance of clergy, as well as bishops, in South Africa and elsewhere, served responsibly and even sacrificially. As trouble arose over the opinions of Colenso, for example, Charles Frederick Mackenzie was consecrated in 1861 as missionary bishop to build the Church in the region near Lake Nyasa, now Malawi. Only 36 years old, Mackenzie left Cape Town where he had been commissioned with an initial support group to create the Church in an area drawn to English awareness by the work of David Livingstone. His pleas for mission inspired the creation of the Universities' Mission to Central Africa (UMCA) and Mackenzie was selected as the founding bishop.

The new initiative was eagerly anticipated in England, but not without discomfort for some. Despite the popular support that Livingstone rallied, there were already two Church of England mission agencies, the CMS and the SPG. Further, the new UMCA embraced Anglo-Catholic principles, affirming the Oxford Movement's legacy and thus giving priority to the roles of bishops in launching mission. A Cambridge graduate, Mackenzie had served in mission under Colenso but was not tainted by the scandal that was developing. His choice seemed fitting, but, in 1862, only a year after his consecration, Mackenzie died. He and much of his party were stricken with fever when they reached the vicinity of Lake Nyasa. In the face of this tragedy, the UMCA persisted. William George Tozer succeeded Mackenzie in 1863, serving for ten years before stints as bishop in Jamaica and Belize, the latter as founding bishop. In Africa, Tozer created a second base of UMCA operations in Zanzibar where education and opposition to slavery marked the Church's work. In time, especially under Edward Steere who followed Tozer, the UMCA revived its mission work in the region of Lake Nyasa, firmly planting the Church.[20]

What can we conclude about the mission of the Church by the second half of the nineteenth century? The dynamics in southern Africa proved representative of Anglicanism's expanding mission presence. Amid rare instances of tension, and rarer reported instances of misconduct, mission advanced in multiple contexts on every continent. The Church had accepted its distance from the state in colonial circumstances. Bishops functioned as entrepreneurs who raised resources of personnel and funding, created congregations and nurtured church-related institutions. Missionary societies supplied much that was needed and constituted the earliest networks linking Anglicans to one another. The Church was developing along comparable lines that were largely recognizable from one context to another. It built modes of governance where authority was shared by bishops and synods. An incipient catholicity was emerging.

But the fact of divergence in Anglican life was apparent in English perspective. The Church that was so assuredly English in its origins was becoming something else. The nature of this entity, increasingly known as Anglican and not simply English, was unclear. Worse, it was variegated and beset by tensions. Two missionary societies, representing different approaches, worked independently of each other and were facing the more focused efforts of the UMCA and the Cambridge Mission to Delhi, founded in 1877. The later merger of the UMCA into the SPG (in 1965) and the Cambridge Mission into the SPG (in 1968) did not fully clarify the picture. Two realities stamped Anglican mission initiative beyond sheer growth. The first was the historic and continuing divergence among church parties. As mission grew, more than styles of worship or the priority given to the episcopate were at stake. Anglicans differed over the extent to which they intended to evangelize, or to integrate with, and hence accept to some degree, the culture of a given context. No one approach dominated Anglican mission. The impulse to convert was apparent and continued. But as mission became enculturated, conversion gained nuance. The emphasis upon founding schools, and often medical clinics and social service agencies as well, expanded the Church's ethos and its impact.

Rightly, there has been much consideration of the Church's relation to empire. But that relation did not consist simply of reinforcing colonial authority. The encounter between mission and context reflected an encounter of cultures, and not simply English life writ large. The Church brought its own culture, one often at variance with colonial strictures. The development of mission centred on encouraging recognition of the Christian faith, including conversion, while building the contextual viability and role of the Church as an institution as well as a religious fellowship. We have suggested how this unfolded as mission began. Now we emphasize that the process was uneven, being marked by different approaches and outcomes among Anglicans from one context to another. Anglicanism's fabric was mottled; its variety suggested discordance; paradoxically its growth proved troubling. As the Church grew, its consistency in approach and uniformity in outcome were unclear. In what sense could Anglicanism be called catholic?

The question was not abstract; it arose as a practical exigency. The Church's expansion framed the issue but could not resolve it. More than religious conformity of a certain sort, catholicity generally means comprehensive, broad, having universal character. With its expansion, Anglicanism matched part of that definition. But what was its character? In terms of uniformity and adherence to primal Christian tradition, the Anglican situation was less clear. Challenges to biblical interpretation and belief accompanied varieties of practice and relations to indigenous cultures. There were instances of disregard for episcopal and synodical authority in emerging branches of the Church. Anglicanism appeared to be an ill-coordinated collection of churches functioning comparably in varied contexts but without consultation. An impetus to address divergences and to clarify catholicity arose among some bishops. Already there had been calls for consultations linking the Church of England and emerging provinces. In the 1850s, bishops John Henry Hopkins of Vermont and William Whittingham of Maryland issued such calls. Francis Fulford of Montreal picked up the theme and played a catalytic role. English-born with Oxford Movement sympathies, Fulford had arrived in Montreal in 1850 as its first diocesan bishop. He held a high view of the Church's worship and offices, and of its autonomy from the state. He organized his diocese's first synods, seeking a broad base of authority. Fulford sensed what Anglican catholicity could mean as the Church's unwieldy development continued.

By 1865 all Canadian bishops supported the idea of a gathering of bishops. When Fulford preached at Christ Church, Oxford, in 1866 he promoted the idea of a 'Pan-Anglican synod'. A colleague, John Travers Lewis of Ontario, urged the idea upon C. T. Longley, Archbishop of Canterbury, who then consulted English bishops. Notably, he also consulted the revived English Convocations of Canterbury and York. Thus, as we have described, Longley invited 151 bishops to meet at Lambeth Palace in 1867. In September of that year, 76 attended four days of discussion. The focal points were not surprising: synodical authority and the case of Colenso's refusal to abandon his views or his see in Natal. These foci anticipated a raft of future Anglican tensions and discussions. The tenor of discussion in 1867 offers lasting insights.[21]

What precedent did the first Lambeth Conference set? It fostered the idea of the Anglican world as a communion of churches, 'a self-constituted, spiritual subjection, by their consent to yield obedience to the decision of some higher synod'.[22] Lambeth created a forum in which bishops could explore unity amid diversity, giving voice to new instances of mission, Christian life and church experience. Lambeth stopped short of emulating the synods emerging at diocesan and provincial levels. Rather, it became a site for consultation, and even contestation, as diverse priorities and styles surfaced amid contextual Anglican life. Lambeth passed resolutions that were deemed advisory but presumed to honour the decisions of provincial synods. As Sachs has noted elsewhere, the first Lambeth Conference urged the creation of a 'voluntary spiritual Tribunal' with representation from each Anglican province that would seek resolution of disagreements to promote unity of faith and to achieve 'uniformity in matters of Discipline'.[23]

Lambeth intended to model the Anglican ideal of the *via media*. Thus George Selwyn, preaching before the Episcopal Church's General Convention in 1871, sought a middle ground between uniform doctrinal adherence and the autonomy of individual provinces.[24] We find that Lambeth has sought to move tensions away from the divisive impulses that fuel them. Unity in the Church requires building a fellowship of bishops. From its inception the Lambeth Conference envisioned a communion of churches animated by common beliefs, practices and commitment to mission. Such a communion could not be forced but must emerge consensually.

Lambeth Conferences have faced stubborn questions, especially about the Church's relations with its host cultures. Polygamy became one of the most frequently addressed topics for decades, lying at the intersection of morality and culture. After decades of discussion and division, something of a consensus was reached in 1988. A practising polygamist could be baptized and confirmed as Anglican so long as he promised not to enter future polygamous relations.[25] Existing spouses and children should receive adequate care. Matters of colonialism, war, social inequality and morality have also pervaded discussions. Uncertainty about the Church's uniformity, often reflecting fears about threats to its unity, have surfaced. A major affirmation of the pillars of Anglican life, the Chicago–Lambeth Quadrilateral, was adopted by the Lambeth Conference of 1888.[26] Its persistence reflected the Anglican pattern of commendation rather than compulsion. Church authority resides in provincial and diocesan synods. The adoption of the Quadrilateral and of other resolutions by Lambeth Conferences reflects the spread of consensus rather than fiat. A certain view of unity pervades Anglicanism. It is catholicity from below, marked by consultation, deliberation and contestation. In such processes, bishops play pivotal roles, framing issues and guiding their consideration. The basis of communion is consensus framed by mission, achieved by staying at the table even amid threats of division. Communion becomes possible to the extent that the Church's bishops embody it.

Building Mutuality in Theory and Practice

The first Lambeth Conference awakened the ideal of communion. It began to emerge though it has never been complete, and its shape has frequently been contested. In a sense the catholicity of Anglicanism was realized more readily. Catholicity became visible in the historic forms of worship and ministry that marked church life. The spread of Anglicanism further animated the claim to being catholic. Anglicanism steadily became one of the most widely dispersed of all religious traditions. As it did, the roles of bishops gained prominence that befit their office. As we have explained, different church parties allotted different roles to bishops as mission began in a new context. But all agreed on the pivotal roles bishops must play. Episcopal leadership, sacramental worship and even synods that harkened to ancient councils confirmed Anglicanism's catholicity as a growing consensus of opinion acknowledged.

It was also striking that the Church grew along comparable lines in disparate locales. With diminished reliance upon the state outside England, Anglicans adapted and even affirmed the erosion of formal connection. Cast upon their own resources, they could grasp their own, religious identity. The fact of catholicity, reinforced at Lambeth Conferences, canonized by the Quadrilateral, had been articulated in theory. But what did it mean in practice? The question must be asked because Anglicans found they did not always function in the same ways, even as they embraced catholic principles. Authority could be exercised differently in pursuit of diverse, at times contrasting, priorities of church life. Styles of worship differed. The roles of synods could be enhanced or diminished in one place versus another. The catholic marks of the Church could mask variations in practice, an issue the Colenso matter made plain. Colenso functioned as bishop, but in ways that raised probing questions about the unity of faith and practice. Even as Anglicanism's catholicity became apparent, the prospect of communion became clouded. The ideals of Anglican life proved as disparate in practice as they appeared compatible in theory.

In part the pursuit of communion reflects Anglicanism's growth, which has occurred contextually. With little means of coordination among the Church's branches and reduction of establishment as a basis of identity, Anglicanism was becoming a disparate set of churches with discomforting variations even as they resembled one another and claimed the same heritage. Thus, more than growth, communion arose as an effort to secure unity amid variety. It has been an ideal of Anglican life, as well as a practical necessity. Reflecting our sense of the relation between catholicity and communion, Ephraim Radner has observed that before 1930 the fact of communion among Anglicans had been an informal if 'relatively consistently ordered set of experienced and identifiable realities'. In 1930, the Lambeth Conference adopted a statement of the meaning of communion as:

> The Anglican Communion is a fellowship, within the one Holy Catholic and Apostolic Church, of those duly constituted dioceses, provinces or regional Churches in communion with the See of Canterbury, which have the following characteristics in common:
>
> a they uphold and propagate the Catholic and Apostolic faith and order as they are generally set forth in the Book of Common Prayer as authorized in their several Churches;
>
> b they are particular or national Churches, and, as such, promote within each of their territories a national expression of Christian faith, life and worship; and
>
> c they are bound together not by a central legislative and executive authority, but by mutual loyalty

sustained through the common counsel of the bishops in conference.[27]

Radner adds that the Lambeth Conference of 1930 also affirmed that Anglicans could be in communion with other churches, meaning that communion was not simply descriptive of inter-Anglican relations. Rather, communion was posed as a feature of Anglicanism that might build a broad swathe of relations among Christians who uphold catholic marks of church life.[28]

The ideal of communion did not arise *ex nihilo*. Radner traces the 'semantic origin' of the concept. In part, it is an image of a group sharing the Eucharist, and then a larger ecclesial fellowship. American bishop William White spoke of an ethos, and Parliament, in 1840, noted that it extends across national boundaries. Similarly, 'Anglican' as a term began to mean more than English. As Radner puts it, 'Anglican' began to migrate to a larger set of churches, marked by catholicity but unfolding through ethos and the intentions of mission with contextual contours. Variety among Anglicans was based partly on preference, especially that of the Church's parties, a reality that became transmuted in the twentieth century by such terms as 'conservative' and 'liberal', later 'orthodox' and 'progressive'. Anglicanism as a religious tradition proved expansive and energetic in one context after another. Its expanse bespoke an inclusive and comprehensive body, marked by similar priorities and forms of expression. But as a Church, rather than simply a religious tradition, its variety seemed dominant over its unity. Thus, the pursuit of communion became intense, even urgent. It could not be advanced in theory without being located in fact.

But what sort of unity did 'communion' imply? The resolution of 1930 bespoke the mind of the Church's bishops: 'mutual loyalty sustained by the common counsel of the bishops in conference', a bond 'exercised not by a central legislative and executive authority'. In turn, 'mutuality' suggests being in relation as a means of working together and learning from one another.[29] Mutuality is a sharing of a feeling and

CATHOLICITY AND COMMUNION

then a commitment. It becomes a journey together, a connection with one another centred on exchange and the cultivation of mutual respect. Variety and even divergence are presumed; times of fragmentation and suspicion are inevitable, as befits any relation, such as that of a family, especially a large one. But walking together on a common journey in pursuit of understanding, cooperation, trust and reciprocity prove to be the hallmarks of mutuality, as least in the abstract. Such a journey has characterized the Anglican intention of being in communion. The pursuit of this intention can be seen in the unfolding of Lambeth Conferences. Lambeth Conferences have embodied the intention of realizing mutuality among Anglicans while both adhering to the Church's catholic features and honouring its contextual variations. Anglicans have sought a balance between faithfulness to Christian tradition and adaptations of it in light of the contextual demands of mission.

But given Anglicanism's diversification as it grew, Lambeth Conferences steadily adopted an emphasis on the Church's unity as essential to its mission. Unity has been a two-sided coin. On the one hand, unity has meant achieving a common mind and speaking with a common voice among the Church's bishops. In doing so, the hope has been that the bishops will set a tone for Anglican life, indeed a quality that can only be nurtured, not legally construed or enforced. By doing so, Anglicans, and especially their bishops, have intended to demonstrate the possibility of unity among all Christians. At times, a prominent swathe of Anglican opinion has located the Church's identity and mission in terms of its ability to join those of differing confessions, honouring the variety of Christian expressions while building common purpose among them. Doing so has meant that Anglicans must validate such an approach to unity among themselves, a task that has been daunting at all times, and particularly challenging at others.

Unity cannot be created in the abstract. Its pursuit has been shaped by issues that have demanded the Church's response. Invariably such issues have reflected the Church's intended relation to culture, with Anglicans attempting to configure their life both faithfully and adaptively. The resolutions of Lambeth

Conferences reveal energetic debates as the Church's bishops have been compelled by social and political forces to address the meaning of faith in challenging situations. As one reviews Lambeth debates and resolutions, it is intriguing to consider what issues have commanded the attention of bishops and to consider how such would be the case. In the process of identifying pivotal issues, and mulling appropriate responses to them, one glimpses something of a theological and pastoral method. It is framed by determination to speak in a manner that, while being faithful, also proves to be distinctively Anglican. In other words, Anglican bishops gathered at Lambeth have consistently attempted not to legislate, nor to create doctrinal barriers, defining those who are in and those who are out. Instead, they have considered the shape of a faith tradition, Anglicanism, in light of its unique possibilities and challenges.

We cannot give a detailed review of Lambeth Conference resolutions and their outcomes; rather, we seek to characterize how they have been clustered and what they have meant in terms of efforts to realize one or another sense of Anglican promise. Of course, one could argue, given the absence of legislative enforcement, that resolutions have sketchy results at best. On vexing social issues of war, unrest, political change, colonialism and decolonization, economic disparity and the like, the Church's voice could appear drowned out by larger forces it could barely sway. Yet the tenor of the Church's voice, and the ways in which it has sought a common mind, as well as wider influence, prove striking. From 1948 to 2008, the foci of resolutions adopted by the Lambeth Conferences have been apparent. After World War Two, Anglican bishops were intent on emphasizing the disparity between the Church and the world, an emphasis that has become apparent across Anglican life. Themes of Christian vocation and unity gained importance and were seen in the context of mission. But unlike calls for mission early in the twentieth century, Anglican bishops later in the century were quicker to identify and embrace adaptive expressions of church life. The rise of union churches in South Asia is an example. Adaptive expressions of church life were welcomed in light of changing social and political circumstances in diverse contexts. The adaptation of the Church became a focus of Lambeth Conference discussions.[30]

Lambeth resolutions also began to focus on the theme of cultural identity. The bishops became alert to the range of identities church leaders and councils must assess. By the late twentieth century, Anglican bishops envisioned commitment to an essence of the Christian faith while granting that there were varied, valid expressions of it. But as the end of the twentieth century neared, there were fears that the Church's allowance for variation had gone too far, that there had been breaches of core faith commitments and church practices. The issues that arose and the divides that resulted have become intensely familiar: the ordination of women to the priesthood and episcopate, and the acceptance of openly gay persons in all aspects of church life. Discussed both at Lambeth Conferences and beyond, at provincial levels and by inter-Anglican bodies, these vexing issues have defied ready resolution. Though various means to address them have been proposed, the tensions are unresolved.

Our assessment of Lambeth Conferences and their resolutions leads to three conclusions. First, that the Lambeth Conferences, and the roles played by bishops in Anglican life, have moved towards considering specific forms of response to tensions in church life, especially given the fracture of relations and rise of alternative church structures that have occurred. This does not mean that tensions have been resolved. Passage of a resolution could mask unresolved issues, though searches for common ground can be identified. Second, Lambeth Conferences have focused on the Church's identity when external cultural forces have shaken it, as has often been the case. Anglicans have become more liable to division because of disputes over sensitive issues of faith and ministry. Ironically many Anglicans agree that the Church now appears uncertain of its faith deposit and faces severe threats from external forces. Where Anglicans have consistently disagreed has been over the proper means, the actual steps to be taken, amid church crises. Our crises have arisen over the relation of faith to culture, and how Anglicans have attempted to manage that relation.

However, we believe that crisis and Kairos have coexisted, that through contestation the Church has engaged both the gospel and social challenges. We note, third, that the urgency of inter-Anglican gatherings increased in the later twentieth century as the search for ways to secure communion intensified. The creation of the Anglican Consultative Council (ACC) in 1968 with an executive officer embodied this search.

Colin Podmore has described the rise of inter-Anglican structures of Communion, especially of the 'Instruments of Communion' – Lambeth Conferences, ACC and Primates' Meetings. Several Archbishops of Canterbury, notably Geoffrey Fisher (in office 1945–61), grasped the need for new steps towards Anglican unity and encouraged expanded forms of consultation and collaboration. Building on the precedent of the Pan-Anglican Congress of 1908, Anglican congresses were held in Minneapolis (1954) and Toronto (1963) with the intention of shaping the Church's mission amid political conflict and social change. At each congress, clergy and laity, as well as bishops, participated in discussions and heard lectures focused on mission, the Church's relation to culture and initiatives designed to address realities of contextual life. Those in attendance gathered for large-scale worship services designed to build community and motivate determination to apply what they had learned in their own settings. The overarching purpose was to cultivate Anglicanism's unity amid its increasing diversity. The question of unity focused on one theme: Communion. What did it mean to be the Anglican Communion? What did it mean to be in communion? What role did large-scale gatherings play? More pressing, how could communion be achieved given the disparity of Anglican contextual realities? More strategically, what role could the Church's bishops play in securing communion?[31]

The Anglican Congress of 1963 at Toronto arrived at an image of communion that linked its intentions with its outcomes, its international bodies with its local expressions. Jesse Zink credits this achievement to the adoption of 'Mutual Responsibility and Interdependence' (MRI), a document which proposed a new vision of Anglicans in relation to one another and to mission. Further, Zink credits Bishop Stephen Bayne, first executive officer of the Anglican Communion, with cultivating the view of mission and being in communion that pervaded the document. Bayne's perspective was compelling. He understood the cultural dominance that accompanied mission as well as the disparities of church parties that clouded it. By the 1960s, Zink adds, the fact of Anglicanism's spread and growth beyond its sources required redress of relations. The result was the congress of 1963 and the document that became its hallmark, MRI.[32]

Though brief, MRI had the immediate impact of conveying that Anglicanism was turning a corner. The nature of being in communion was recast and, Bayne hoped, characterized by a new spirit. Zink observes that Bayne's role in the actual drafting of the document was unclear, but his influence shaped it and ensured its prominence after the congress adjourned. MRI focused on mission, seen now as God's mission and not simply programmes launched by the Church. As such, mission could become faithful, contextual and shared on a new basis of fellowship. The MRI statement called for increased support for mission towards certain ends:

1 Training of clerical and lay leadership, through existing or new centres and enlarged provision for travel and scholarship aid, conference and retreat centres, centres for literature and the allied communication arts;
2 Construction of churches and other buildings in new areas of Christian responsibility;
3 A beginning on the great needs of new provinces, if they are to be rescued from the humiliation of beggary and given the means to make their freedom real . . . .[33]

Particular attention should be given to 'manpower', especially the training of new priests to meet a shortage. The document also encouraged 'the whole process of inter-Anglican consultation', which 'has deepened markedly in recent years'. Such consultations should extend to all levels of the Church, including partnerships among provinces and dioceses. The creation of diocesan partnerships has been a lasting result of the MRI statement. Further, MRI encouraged the provinces of the Anglican Communion to consider their own 'obedience to mission', including 'study of (their) structures, of (their) theology of mission, and of (their) priorities in decision'. 'We need to ask whether our structures are appropriate to our world and the church as it is, and if not, how they should be changed'.[34] The various Anglican provinces should return to the question of being in communion and consider the meaning of both giving and receiving from one another, in pursuit of 'full communion'. Each province must rediscover the meaning of being the Church, a process which entails development of new channels of communication. MRI envisioned a rebirth of the Anglican Communion on a 'more equitable basis'. At the time this seemed breath-taking.[35]

But Ephraim Radner views MRI's results, and Bayne's input, critically, however appealing its intentions. Bayne gave away crucial ground by declaring that the Book of Common Prayer no longer united Anglicans, though various developments justified the observation. From Radner's perspective, Bayne and MRI intended to advance the new spirit that must be the means of communion as 'national diversity' and 'local churches' arose. Yet, 'local churches subsequently drifted between unfocused mediocrity in formation, or towards particular political concerns and cultural inventions unassimilable within the larger Communion's theological grammar'. Despite the intentions of partnership in mission, mission and communion became contested, and 'common threads in the Communion' began to unravel. In a later generation, the distressed state of communion was detailed by the Virginia Report and then the Windsor Report, the latter eliciting 'To Set Our Hope on Christ', the American response.[36] The notion of the Church as being in communion was being challenged by circumstances which tore its fabric. The notion of being in communion had been focused on the bishops and on structures designed to build unity. But Anglicanism was being turned upside down. The ostensible centres of church life were eroded by the increasing variety and influence of its one-time peripheries.

Contextual developments were outpacing, and at times confronting, the Church's capacity to create a framework of communion that was both faithfully comprehensive and locally validating.

From a different perspective, Radner's critique is echoed by William Danaher. Taking Canadian church life as his basis, Danaher argues that MRI perpetuated old imperialist and centrist assumptions in Anglican life. Using the work of Benedict Anderson and Charles Taylor, Danaher speaks of 'social imaginaries', that is, how MRI reimagined Anglican life and how this vision was implemented. He concludes that, in Canadian experience, the implementation of MRI, for all its intention of mission partnerships and horizontal relations, perpetuated old assumptions about power, process and control. The initiative remained with church life and institutions in what now is called the Global North. An implication that ran throughout Anglican initiatives after World War Two, congresses as well as Lambeth Conferences, was a centralized process that reflected Global North conception and execution. The theological headiness of being in communion was relegated to familiar institutional channels. Yet, Danaher observes, citing the work of Max Warren, the process did introduce contestation. Thus 'the emergent social imaginary, Warren articulated, was now predicated on contestation', which he depicted as '"irreconcilable" conflicts between "philosophies of religion", and between diverse accounts of "what constitutes the good life"'. Warren turned to a vision of mutuality amid contestation. His concern has become the predominant concern of Anglican life, of its emphasis on mission, of its search for communion.[37]

What can Anglican catholicity mean in the midst of Anglican contestation? In this chapter we have deepened a sense of the paradox surrounding Anglican identity: as Anglicanism grew, it became varied in ways which posed different expressions of being Christian and being the Church. From one context to another, the same hallmarks of Anglican identity were seen in different fashion, often bespeaking diverse relations between faith and culture. Bishops proved to be key measures of this trend, seeking to balance Christian faithfulness with rootedness in their contexts. However, their ways of performing such a balancing act varied, at times beyond what church leaders elsewhere considered permissible. Bishops took the lead in seeking mutuality among Anglicans in an expanding faith tradition. But what did being in communion actually mean? The pivotal issue for Anglicans became the coherence of their faith and fellowship as the twentieth century proceeded. We now turn to consider the question of Anglican coherence.

Notes

1 Daniel O'Connor, ed., *Three Centuries of Mission*, New York: Continuum, 2000, pp. 15ff.

2 David Hein and Gardiner H. Shattuck, Jr., *The Episcopalians*, Westport, CT: Praeger, 2004, pp. 45–6, 53–7, 230–1. Curtis Fahey, *In His Name*, Ottawa: Carleton University Press, 1991, p. 6.

3 'Mission fields' is a historic term that could be read as uncritical identification of the Church's intention with the colonial world. The term occurs in the writings of recent authors on mission, including Dana Robert in her book *Christian Mission*, Oxford: Wiley-Blackwell, 2009. Our use of the term 'mission fields' is informed, first, by the usage of Lamin Sanneh in his book *Translating the Message*, Maryknoll, NY: Orbis, 2009. There the term appears in the sense of an anthropological 'field'. We are informed by the work of Pierre Bourdieu, especially his book *The Field of Cultural Production*, New York, NY: Columbia University Press, 1993. There, 'field' denotes social and cultural settings within which struggles for meaning and identity occur, often between social actors who do not share economic and power resources equally. Bourdieu is alert to such categories as hierarchy, class and cultural norms, which inform our work.

4 Charles R. Henery, *Yankee Bishops*, New York: Peter Lang, 2015, pp. 30, 61f.

5 Fahey, *In His Name*, pp. 55ff.

6 Hein and Shattuck, *The Episcopalians*, pp. 69f.

7 George Washington Doane, *The Missionary Bishop*, Burlington, NJ: Powell Missionary Press, 1835, p. 14.

8 Doane, *The Missionary Bishop*, p. 14.

9 Hein and Shattuck, *The Episcopalians*, pp. 77f.

10 Rowan Strong, *Anglicanism and the British Empire*, Oxford: Oxford University Press, 2007, pp. 230–41, 248–55, 273–80. William L. Sachs, *The Transformation of Anglicanism*, Cambridge: Cambridge University Press, 2002, pp. 197–204.

11 Sachs, *The Transformation of Anglicanism*, pp. 190–201.

12 *The Record of the Proceedings of the Court of Bishops Assembled for the Trial of the Rt. Rev. George Washington Doane, D.D., LL.D*, New York: Stanford and Swords, 1852.

13 Boyd Hilton, *A Mad, Bad, & Dangerous People*, Oxford: Oxford University Press, 2006, pp. 379–84, 384–91.

14 Hilton, *A Mad, Bad, & Dangerous People*, p. 485. Strong, *Anglicanism and the British Empire*, pp. 207–10. W. E. Gladstone, *The State in its Relations with the Church*, London: J. Murray, 1838.

15 Hilton, *A Mad, Bad, & Dangerous People*, p. 526. Ephraim Radner, 'The Anglican Communion and Anglicanism', in Jeremy Morris, ed., *Global Western Anglicanism, c. 1910–present, Volume IV, The Oxford History of Anglicanism*, Oxford: Oxford University Press, 2017, p. 314.

16 Jeffrey Cox, 'The Dialectics of Empire, Race, and Diocese', in William L. Sachs, ed., *Global Anglicanism, c. 1910–2000, Volume V, The Oxford History of Anglicanism*, Oxford: Oxford University Press, 2018, pp. 27–8. T. E. Yates, *Venn and Victorian Bishops Abroad*, London: SPCK, 1978.

17 William L. Sachs, *Homosexuality and the Crisis of Anglicanism*, Cambridge: Cambridge University Press, 2009.

18 Jeff Guy, *The Heretic: A Study of the Life of John William Colenso*, Pietermaritzburg: Natal University Press, 1984.

19 Herbert Hammond, 'The Church of England in South Africa and the Anglican Communion', *Churchman* 102 (1988), pp. 251–5. The Church's history is recounted on its website: www.reachsa.org.za.

20 A. E. M. Anderson-Morshead, *The History of the Universities' Mission to Central Africa*, Volume One, London: UMCA, 1955.

21 Alan M. G. Stephenson, *Anglicanism and the Lambeth Conferences*, London: SPCK, 1978. Randall T. Davidson, *The Five Lambeth Conferences*, London: SPCK, 1920.

22 William Redmond Curtis, *The Lambeth Conferences*, New York: Columbia University Press, 1942, p. 152.

23 Sachs, *The Transformation of Anglicanism*, p. 203.

24 *The Sermon Delivered By The Rt. Rev. George Augustus Selwyn, D.D., D.C.L., Lord Bishop of Lichfield Before a General Convention of the Protestant Episcopal Church in the United States of America, Held in Baltimore, Maryland, October 4–26, A.D. 1871*, Hartford, CT: The Church Press, 1871.

25 Kevin Ward, *A History of Global Anglicanism*, Cambridge: Cambridge University Press, 2006, p. 306.

26 Mark D. Chapman, 'William Reed Huntington, American Catholicity and the Chicago-Lambeth Quadrilateral', in Paul Avis and Benjamin M. Guyer, eds, *The Lambeth Conference*, London: Bloomsbury, 2017, pp. 84–106.

27 *The Lambeth Conference 1930*, London: SPCK, 1930, Resolution 49, p. 55.

28 Ephraim Radner, 'The Anglican Communion and Anglicanism', in Jeremy Morris, ed., *Global Western Anglicanism, c. 1910–present, Volume IV, The Oxford History of Anglicanism*, Oxford: Oxford University Press, 2017, pp. 303–28.

29 *The Lambeth Conference. Resolutions Archive from 1930*, available online at www.anglicancommunion.org/media/127734/1930.pdf [last accessed 16 June 2019].

30 *The Lambeth Conference. Resolutions Archive from 1948*, available online at www.anglicancommunion.org/media/127737/1948.pdf [last accessed 16 June 2019].

31 Colin Podmore, 'The Development of the Instruments of Communion', in Jeremy Morris, ed., *Global Western Anglicanism, c. 1910–present, Volume IV, The Oxford History of Anglicanism*, Oxford: Oxford University Press, 2017, pp. 271–302.

32 Jesse Zink, 'Changing World, Changing Church: Stephen Bayne and "Mutual Responsibility and Interdependence"', *Anglican Theological Review* 93:2 (Spring 2011), pp. 243–62.

33 'Mutual Responsibility and Interdependence in the Body of Christ', Toronto Anglican Congress, 1963. Available online at http://anglicanhistory.org/canada/toronto_mutual1963.html [last accessed 16 June 2019].

34 'Mutual Responsibility and Interdependence in the Body of Christ', cited in Zink, 'Changing World, Changing Church'.

35 'Mutual Responsibility and Interdependence in the Body of Christ'.

36 Radner, 'The Anglican Communion and Anglicanism', p. 319.

37 William J. Danaher, 'Beyond Imagination: "Mutual Responsibility and Interdependence in the Body of Christ" (1963) and the Reinvention of Canadian Anglicanism', *Anglican Theological Review* 93:2 (Spring 2011), pp. 219–41.

5

Testing Anglican Coherence

A Disputed Identity

In the spring of 1922, Henry St George Tucker concluded that he must resign as Bishop of Kyoto and leave Japan. A difficult personal decision, it came with no prompting other than his own conscience. A missionary of the Episcopal Church to Japan for over 20 years, he felt at home there. He had married Mary Lillian Warnock, also a missionary in Japan, and their two sons were born there. As priest and teacher, he had advanced in church life, becoming president of St Paul's College, now Rikkyo University, in 1903. A major campus building still bears his name, Tucker Hall. In 1911 the Episcopal Church's House of Bishops chose him to be Bishop of Kyoto, and by all accounts Tucker thrived in the episcopate in Japan. But by 1922 he had decided to resign. He and his family promptly returned to Virginia.[1]

Tucker subsequently served as Bishop of Virginia (1927–44) and presiding bishop of the Episcopal Church (1938–46). But in writing his memoir, Tucker spoke exclusively of his service in Japan. The years of mission were formative and, he suggested, the time of his greatest contribution to the Church. So, his readiness to depart could seem puzzling but for the principle that motivated his resignation. The time had come, Tucker concluded, for the Japanese Church to have Japanese leadership. For Tucker, the promise associated with mission was the creation of an independent, self-supporting branch of the Anglican world in Japan.

His vision was not an isolated one that was unique to his ministry. Since the mid nineteenth century and the career of Henry Venn as secretary of the Church Missionary Society, the widely acknowledged goal of Anglican mission had been the creation of indigenous churches. Tucker's initiative reflected this stated intention. Indigenous leadership lay at the heart of the promise of Anglican mission. As he described in his memoir, Tucker determined that church facilities were adequate and well maintained by lay and ordained leaders in his diocese who were prepared to direct their own affairs. He was pleased with the quality of parish vestries and noted the rise of lay leadership at the grassroots as a point of pride. With the creation of an Osaka diocese, and the election of a Japanese bishop for it, his own office should be held by a Japanese person.[2] Without hesitation, and with a momentous sense of his decision, Tucker left.

As natural as this step seemed, and as gracious as Tucker proved in taking it, before the era of decolonization forced the issue of indigenous leadership, few missionary bishops readily ceded control to indigenous successors and returned home. Indeed, by the time of Tucker's resignation, there were few indigenous bishops to whom leadership could be transitioned. The Japanese Church appeared more advanced, but the difference was only a matter of degree. Overall control of the Japanese Church remained in missionary hands beyond the ken of local vestries and some parish clergy. The senior bishop of the Japanese Church, John McKim, was an American who served for 42 years. He took steps that led to the consecrations of the first Japanese bishops: Joseph Motoda and John Naide. But the preponderant stance of missionary leaders in Japan and elsewhere made it plain that Tucker's act was a pioneering one. Indigenous forms of Anglicanism were arising in various contexts, but transitions to independent, self-supporting forms of Anglican life lagged. The difference between ideal and reality was stark.

In Chapter 4 we described how a vision of communion arose among Anglicans and was fostered by such bishops and leaders of mission as Stephen Bayne and Max Warren. We spoke of the ideal of mutuality and of steps proposed by Lambeth Conferences to advance it. We noted what Ephraim Radner has called the drift of local churches that has tested the ideal of being in communion and the inevitable disparities of church life from one context to another. However certain dynamics proved relatively consistent across Anglican life. In particular, the late colonial era was marked by varieties of contextual challenge to control from outside. Anglican identity became more disputed than it was clarified. Tucker's resignation raised more questions than it answered. Anglican life became less coherent as the Church grew from the late nineteenth to the early twenty-first century. In this chapter we describe how the Anglican world fragmented amid challenges to its promise while the numbers of its adherents grew markedly.

What sort of coherence in church life was intended, and how did the vision of indigenous Anglican branches advance the intention? There would be little dispute among Anglican leaders, before Tucker's time in Japan or after his departure, that the goal of mission was the creation of indigenous churches. But the appropriate means of realizing this goal would be disputed and the dispute deepened as the colonial world faded. Contextual realities intruded upon the process of becoming an indigenous Church even as the steps towards securing it seemed apparent. New tensions beset the Church amid the shadow of colonialism. The promise of Anglicanism has been tied to one or another post-colonial theological, social and political development by various observers. But the issue of being indigenous in disparate settings, forging an identity that is grounded in context yet transcends locality, has been an elusive goal. The end of colonialism pressed the issue more than resolving it.

As Anglicans have grappled with the meaning of being indigenous, similar issues and patterns of local response have arisen. In effect, Anglican identity has developed through contestation, with recurring tensions between consistent ideals of worship and ministry in church life and seemingly disparate, contextual approaches to their expression. But contextual disparities have often been belied by comparable practices of mission, as we shall see. Thus, the promise of Anglicanism lies less in what marks of church life Anglicans have prized than in how they have worked to secure them in varied circumstances. That challenge proved difficult enough in England and the British Isles; even there the Church's worship and ministry continued to be contested. Nevertheless, bolstered by its establishment status, Anglicanism achieved broad consensus about its religious identity and relation to culture.

When Anglicans were forced to define their faith and their Church in new cultural circumstances, the challenges were multiplied. It could not be presumed that establishment status in the metropole ensured religious affinities in colonial settings, even among expatriates. Among peoples without prior experience of the faith and the Church, mission became the focus of Anglican life and the creation of indigenous churches became mission's intention. On the basis of Christian belief and Anglican practice, missionaries from Britain and North America encouraged churches marked by evangelism and ministry, which, as they saw it, uplifted local peoples. Education and social service programmes became means to this end. In their eyes the missionaries held a sacred trust, which most approached conscientiously. But few would grasp the extent to which they misunderstood the realities they faced in contexts new to them and the priority of devolving control to local peoples. Many foreign missionaries and the agencies they represented presumed that mission required their control. They came to proclaim the gospel and to plant the church; but, certain of their cultural superiority, most were reluctant to turn over authority and leave. The mission churches somehow never seemed to measure up to European norms. Even with steady growth, those who were converted were never quite ready to be in charge. Tucker's conclusion that he must leave Japan was rare. Most missionaries who came from overseas could not imagine fledgling churches without them. Even if they were not overtly racist, their view of the contexts in which they ministered could be patronizing.

The ideals of Anglican mission and the outcomes of mission life could differ markedly. As a result, the coherence of Anglican identity has been tested by the Church's encounters with particular cultures. Repeatedly, contextual realities have confronted Anglican ideals of faith and ministry and eroded missionary presumptions of control. The promise of Anglicanism has been as reliant upon patterns of contextual adaptation as it has upon a historic, comprehensive vision of the Church. But have forms of contextual adaptation predisposed Anglicans towards the sort of 'drift' that Ephraim Radner has decried? We shall explain that variations in Anglican life arose as indigenous peoples began to contest missionary control, in both passive and aggressive ways in diverse cultural contexts. The issue of coherence in Anglican life reflects in part the reality of efforts to control mission churches by authority from outside, glossing over cultural realities to which the Church should adapt. We are mindful of this question of the coherence of Anglican identity and of the nature of faithful adaptation to contextual realities.

Some forms of adaptation were integral to the intention of mission and could be presumed. For example, in the early stages of their work, missionaries inevitably faced tasks of translation. In China, Samuel Isaac Joseph Schereschewsky, sometime bishop in Shanghai and long-term missionary, dedicated much of his career to translation of the Bible into Mandarin, achieving his goal by the end of the nineteenth century, and dying a few years later, in 1906. Various Anglican missionaries have worked to translate the Book of Common Prayer into particular cultural settings. That task has entailed more than idiomatic alteration; questions of how to conduct worship have arisen, often requiring the search for common ground between the culture that created the Prayer Book and the culture that would embrace it. Thus, in the early twentieth century, Frank Weston, Bishop of Zanzibar, worked to translate the Book of Common Prayer in more than one sense. The 'Zanzibar Rite', his blend of practices familiar to his East African locale with the historic Prayer Book, evoked much discussion. Weston could hardly be charged with syncretism. Earlier he had accused several Anglican bishops in his region of being overly familiar with non-Anglican mission gatherings, thus seeming to dilute the purity of faith to which he aspired. He was a contentious figure intent on foisting his Anglo-Catholic sensibilities upon the nascent Church on Zanzibar and in East Africa. But Weston was alert to the need for the Church's adaptation to circumstances that were new to it. By the time of his death in 1923, he had made a lasting statement about the need for Anglican adaptability.[3]

In addition to Bible study and worship, Anglican mission has emphasized education in the tenets of the Christian faith as well as formal education. In his study of church life in Buganda in the mid twentieth century, John V. Taylor depicted rural Anglican mission stations where worship, work and education were integrated into daily routine.[4] The result was the rise of a Christian ethos that embodied the goal of mission as one of growth into Christian faith and community. Even in places where Christians faced a dominant religion and conversion proved problematic, the Anglican presence took root, often gaining cultural legitimacy because of schools and colleges created by the Church. Richard Jones has described Anglican educational institutions in Muslim-majority societies where the Church's emphasis on mission must be subtle, but where educational contributions have been valued and the Church's witness has been recognized. The spread of Anglicanism has depended heavily upon formation for the Church and for public life. Thus, Church-inspired educational institutions have been key expressions of mission. As Lamin Sanneh observes in his study of West African religion, missionaries envisioned the transformation of tribal life into modern societies. Church-led education would raise up a class of people who would guide social and educational development in their contexts. The Church would help to create new nations and their leaders, grounding social life in faith and ministry. If Anglicans thus participated in the larger vision of colonialism, they justified it by the assumption that, at some point, Africans would assume control in Church and society, once they had proven worthy according to the norms of their missionary patrons. Henry Venn envisioned a Church that someday might be as much African as it would be Anglican along British lines.[5] But Venn, like Tucker later, held a minority sentiment that other leaders of mission would dispute. Even as Anglicans built faith, fellowship and service, they tended to retain control, not devolve it. The conduct of mission could beg the question of becoming indigenous rather than resolve it.

As we described in Chapter 3, the experience of Samuel Crowther in West Africa reflected the prospect of Anglicanism becoming indigenous while tending to thwart itself in the process. Henry Venn had imagined that Crowther's ministry would extend the scope of Anglican mission. Venn envisioned that the 'native pastorate' network of congregations would grow, especially with Crowther's guidance and further mission initiatives. As Lamin Sanneh observes, the end of control from beyond could be foreseen, at least in theory.[6] But Venn's death in 1873 removed one of the foremost architects of indigenous Anglican life. At the same time, white missionary suspicion of African religions and leadership grew. They intended to retain control, and often their views were racially biased. The potential for conflict increased as separatist religious sentiment emerged. Anglicanism became one source of the rise of independent West African churches. When white missionaries launched a vendetta against Bishop Crowther, restricting his activities until his death in 1891, the inclination for independent, African-led movements grew and initiatives towards a genuinely West African Anglicanism intensified.

Intent upon reinforcing their control of church life, white missionaries largely failed to grasp the extent to which their presentations of Anglican Christianity were conditioned by British and North American cultures. Nor were missionaries always sensitive to the implications of their stance, to the religious and social messages they were sending. They tended to compound this inclination by their emphasis on maintaining control, their readiness to find fault with local patterns of life and the racism to which some of them succumbed. Few granted that in mission settings the Church must adapt, drawing fresh distinctions in practice between its form and its content. Core aspects of Christian belief and practice must be expressed in altered form, allowing contextual variations while being alert to the threat of syncretism. Leadership must be developed along such lines, then shared, then devolved. Even though this was not consistently realized in practice, in remarkable ways, Anglicanism gained religious footing in disparate contexts, African ones proving to be some of the most vibrant. Anglicanism displayed a prodigious religious generativity, giving rise to influential forms of worship and ministry. This creative instinct stamped Anglicanism as a faith tradition more than the institutional order which missionaries felt they must guard. A crucial distinction in Anglican life arose at the grassroots in the settings to which the Church was being translated: Anglicanism is a faith tradition of universal compass first, local peoples in effect began to argue, and an institution of Western management second.

This disparity became pronounced and led to striking religious and social consequences which continue to stamp Anglican life, in contexts that have been mission fields as well as in England and the other places where mission originated. Anglicanism as a tradition encouraging a Christian way of life was diverging from the institutional bearers of that tradition. In mission fields, from the late nineteenth century on, this divergence became apparent as independent movements and alternative mission priorities arose in various contexts. As much as the fruit of missionary devolution, what has been termed 'the euthanasia of mission', indigenous Anglican life could arise spontaneously in new forms of fellowship and spirituality, bearing the hallmarks of Anglican faith and community.[7] The realities of contextual cultures and spiritualities could seem to be intrusions upon missionary control. But contextual forces have shaped life in Anglican mission sites just as contextual realities shaped the rise of the Church of England.

The most striking of such contextual forces in Africa, during the colonial era and beyond, were separatist religious movements led by charismatic figures who fostered dynamic forms of faith community beyond the influence of intended missionary handovers of control. The case of James Johnson, Samuel Crowther's contemporary and successor, illustrates the point. As E. A. Ayandele explains, before being marginalized Samuel Crowther had attempted to strike a mediating position between

African sensibilities and missionary concerns. Crowther initially looked askance as a young man named James Johnson advanced in church life. The two men revealed quite different temperaments. Crowther was inclined to be conciliatory, while Johnson was assertive. Born in Sierra Leone, he became spokesman for the native pastorate, gaining the ear of CMS leadership in Africa and England. In his role, Johnson spoke directly of the path to an indigenous Church, one that would be as much African as Anglican. In his view, Africa should be evangelized by Africans who would incorporate faithfully aspects of historic African practice into church life. The African Church would adopt vernacular languages and have its own music. Traditional Anglican liturgy and ministry resonated with African precepts. In turn, Christianity and the Church could become the basis of a new, African nationhood. Johnson thus anticipated a new generation of African leaders, many groomed by the Church, for whom Christian faith became formative of a new *polis*. His career remained within church life, but he tested the limits of missionary control and of Anglicanism itself. He served as pastor of the innovative Breadfruit congregation in Lagos from 1880, then as bishop in the Niger delta until his death in 1917. He never cut his ties with the CMS but functioned with an alternative vision of the Church, which would fuel recurring challenges to missionary assumptions.[8]

Johnson was not the only example of the phenomenon we wish to cite, and Africa was not the only continent where the intention of creating an indigenous Church would surface such dynamics. We are speaking of the fact that indigenous Anglican life could develop, even erupt, in ways that transcended Western, institutional preoccupations and control. The promise of Anglicanism could not always be plotted or managed, and the striking vision of Henry Venn could not be realized readily. Thus, in India, the career of V. S. Azariah offered something of a parallel to that of James Johnson. Susan Billington Harper describes Azariah as 'the most successful leader of grassroots movements of conversion to Christianity in South Asia during the early twentieth century'.[9] The reference to 'grassroots' and the timing of Azariah's career, especially his episcopate from 1912 until his death in 1945, are striking. Like Johnson, Azariah saw a resonance between Christian faith and local culture. Azariah did not grant culture unquestioned authority; he confronted culturally instilled patterns of discrimination. Notably he directed his ministry to lower caste and untouchable persons, as well as minority groups in general. Education was the key to their social transformation, he believed. In turn, Christianity was ideally situated to model the nation that India could become. The Indian Church must be Indian in its form, its priorities and its leadership. The tenor of Anglicanism made such a transition possible. Anglicanism created a religious ethos within which new visions of community and leadership could arise.

Like Crowther and Johnson, Azariah faced missionary opposition as his vision grew and as he became a prospective bishop. Like them, he seemed to defy what the mission agencies and pan-Protestant groups such as the YMCA intended, and his vision challenged Western control of mission. Not all missionaries aligned against Azariah, for Bishop Henry Whitehead of Madras proved to be a supporter. This was not surprising because Whitehead had positioned himself as a bridge-builder between the Church and culture as well as between the missionaries and emerging leaders. He published studies of local patterns of Indian religious life and of how education in India might advance its social prospects. Attuned to contextual life as well as missionary hopes, Whitehead resonated with Azariah's approach. The promise of indigenous Anglicanism advanced when missionary and contextual perceptions aligned. But such resonance could be more the exception than the rule. The examples of Whitehead and Tucker proved far too rare.

Clearly the promise of Anglicanism has hinged on its ability to create indigenous church life bearing faithful Christian witness in historic Anglican guise, that is, the Book of Common Prayer, the threefold ministries of bishops, priests and deacons, and being in communion with Canterbury. We are describing instances of conflict that sapped the Church and weakened Anglican promise. We are also suggesting that such conflict has recurred to the present from its origin in missionary situations. Even as the Church developed institutional structures in various situations, the ideal of mutuality, of a Church whose intention and outcome would prove coherent, became problematic. How can we explain this cloud over Anglican life? What have been the tensions that have enshrouded Anglican promise? The pursuit of an indigenous Anglicanism in mission settings proved to be a vivid and elusive goal. Emerging congregations, schools and social service programmes could defy foreign missionary expectations for how they would arise and what forms they might take. On the other hand, missionaries could frustrate converts and latent forms of church life with insistence upon control. Further, the question of who could speak for indigenous Anglican churches was becoming acute. What was reported by British and North American missionaries could differ from what indigenous voices were beginning to say. An indigenous Anglicanism was being realized, but not clearly or simply, or with consistent regard for those who should have been its genuine voices. Through Western eyes, its advance could prove unpredictable, even troubling. Through indigenous eyes, there was a struggle to articulate and to direct their own faith communities. The result has been that Anglican growth acquired inherent tensions. Being in communion became an elusive goal as indigenous forms of Anglican life blossomed.

Inherent Tensions

We have depicted efforts to create indigenous forms of Christian belief and practice as an essential aspect of Anglicanism's promise. Using select illustrations from disparate contexts, we have suggested the breadth of this intention. It should also be clear that in terms of sheer growth, it seemed that this intention advanced and that the promise of Anglicanism could be envisioned. From the missionary perspective, the path towards an indigenous Church was an obvious one, at least in theory. The translation of the faith into settings new to it included the creation of congregations and Church-run educational and social service programmes. Mission focused upon development of the Christian faith in institutional form. The capstone of mission would be the transition to indigenous leadership equipped to run Church institutions as well as to proclaim the faith. Here missionaries often hesitated and contextual realities inevitably intruded. Tension arose as questions surfaced about indigenous leadership.

A story larger than that of creating religious institutions was unfolding, one which defied missionary assumptions about the Church and their prerogative in controlling it. An indigenous Anglicanism could not be realized easily or conclusively. But in the twentieth century that is precisely what Anglican mission intended, hastened by the end of colonialism. The result was a dialogical process by which Anglicans sought cultural footing in contexts that were new to them. Previously Sachs has proposed the term 'enculturation' to depict the dynamism of Christian mission. Broadly speaking, 'enculturation' refers to the search by Anglicans, as well as other Christians, for contextual balance between the formative influences of local culture upon the Church and steps to ensure the integrity of Christian identity and Anglican tradition. That some such balance was required came as no surprise to most missionaries, nor to converts who gave life to Anglicanism's expansion. It was how fledgling Anglican enclaves advanced, where the proper balance between Church and culture was found, that both enlivened church life and tested missionary flexibility. The question of how indigenous leadership would arise and authority would be transferred became acute. But leadership was not the only issue around which tensions would surface. As Anglican worship formed a new kind of religious ethos, the question of how contextual forms of spirituality might inform church life also became acute.

One Anglican missionary effort to relate to habitual male and female initiation rites in a portion of East Africa illustrates how delicate a balance the Church's enculturation could prove to be. For the sake of the Church's identity, Anglicans sought contextual grounding while being both faithful and distinctive in their mission. The promise of Anglicanism lay in being different yet bringing wholeness to the lives of converts in ways that were faithful to the Church's deposit of tradition. Anglicanism could become a meeting place that was not simply indigenous but intercultural. Efforts to realize this promise in the sites where mission was unfolding resulted in tensions around spirituality, as it did around indigenous leadership. Inherent tensions surround leadership and spirituality in Anglican life. Thus, Anne Marie Stoner-Eby investigates the efforts of Vincent Lucas, Anglican bishop of what is now south-eastern Tanzania, to create Christian forms of traditional initiation rites for women and men. Lucas, bishop from 1926 to 1944, began work on this project when he was bishop-elect, a sign that this was a priority in his ministry. Stoner-Eby comments that Lucas has been applauded for an adaptive approach. He viewed mission as uplifting African cultures, not eradicating them. His initiative had the far-reaching effect of encouraging missionaries to take their host cultures seriously and adapt church life to them. But this proves to be only part of the story.[10]

The question of adaptation became widely discussed in missionary circles. Lucas did not persuade all missionaries that adaptation rather than wholesale cultural transformation was the desired course. It must be emphasized that Lucas's approach was not isolated; there are numerous instances of Anglicans taking one or another adaptive approach as their convictions and the contours of a context allowed. But Lucas proved to be an especially vigorous advocate of adaptation, focusing his insistence upon efforts to make familiar initiation rites genuinely Christian. Suspected of syncretism by some, he persisted, and he was not alone. Earlier and nearby, Frank Weston, Bishop of Zanzibar, had proposed a form of worship that incorporated African aspects he deemed complementary. A swathe of missionary efforts focused upon a synthetic approach that would adapt Christian practice without diluting it. The promise of Anglicanism could be seen as mission grounded in mutual religious and cultural appreciation.

Missionary readiness to understand and to adapt must be noted and applauded. But the story of Anglican adaptation to host cultures cannot be told in a one-sided way. We cannot focus simply upon what missionaries thought and initiated. To do so is to retain assumptions of Western prerogative and superiority. Instead, Stoner-Eby tells the full story of Bishop Lucas and the instance of African initiation rites. As genuine as his intention was, and as persistent as his advocacy proved to be, Lucas could not have formulated or pursued his vision without the initiative and persistence of African Anglican clergy. Stoner-Eby notes that from the inception of mission in what is now Tanzania by the UMCA (Universities' Mission to Central Africa), Anglican advance was dependent upon cooperation with local, tribal chiefs. The veneer of colonial rule could not obscure the reality that church life had to rely upon local authority and wisdom figures.[11] The adaptation of Anglicanism to a myriad of contexts has been more the result of local guidance than of missionary insistence. Processes of discourse, that is, discussion and debate, arose between the bearers and the recipients of Christian mission in diverse contexts.

We have made repeated use of the term 'context', seeking to emphasize it as the focus of Anglican life. Our usage depicts the growth of Anglicanism across a variety of cultural settings. In another sense, our usage also emphasizes our conviction that Anglican life finds its natural locus at the grassroots, in local life, rather than in the deliberations of leadership circles that presume to direct the Church. Forms of interaction between the forms of belief and practice brought by foreign missionaries and cultural patterns in various contexts revealed the possibilities and shortcomings of how Anglicans have sought to realize their promise. Confusion arose over what was universally true about Christian faith and consistently inherent in Anglican identity, versus what was distinct about particular contexts and could be adapted to church life. As we explore the development of mission, we find that the growth of the Church, as local fellowship and as wider institution, enhanced the meaning of 'context'.

In effect, the Church became a context on its own, a reality which we can also depict as 'ethos'. In their own ways, at times synchronous at times disparate, missionaries and converts shared this sense of promise. They could agree that the Church should be engaged constructively with the world around it. But the Church must also be distinctive in its foundations, its intentions and its achievements. Theoretically there was widespread agreement on these points; but the persistent challenge was how to realize this ideal amid particular cultural realities. The Church could not function in isolation from the settings where it attempted to become rooted and to grow. In turn, its function relied upon processes of discourse within itself and with its local environments, about the proper relation of faith and culture.

In East Africa, Bishop Lucas grasped this reality. He also understood that the Church intended to be distinctive, and to some extent he understood that the path towards critical balance between a distinctive identity and cultural adaptation was dialogical. But African clergy and lay leaders were the ones who first took initiative to promote Christian versions of initiation rites. Their motives were as ethereal as they were venal, Stoner-Eby states. By fostering the Church's adaptation, African men in Anglican orders enhanced both the Church and their role in it. If the Church gained cultural credibility, the stature of its African clergy would be further enhanced. Despite repeated demonstrations of loyalty to the Church, the situation of African clergy and lay leaders could be tenuous given missionary proclivity to control. An adaptive approach to worship and spirituality held great promise, though missionaries and Africans construed it differently.

Lucas has been celebrated for his emphasis on adaptation, but the idea of a Christian initiation rite originally was not his. Twenty years before, there had been discussion among some African figures in the Church. Their own explorations were not unique; there were Islamicized versions of habitual initiation rites, for example. The efforts were to prove more synthetic than syncretistic, that is, alert to the danger of diluting religious conviction for the sake of cultural accommodation. But the larger point must not be lost: Bishop Lucas tapped an idea and a dialogical process that had African precedent. He became an advocate, but not the originator, of an adaptive approach to Anglican mission. Repeatedly, innovation in mission has rested on adaptation. Repeatedly also, the process of adaptation, and of creating the Church as a distinctive context amid varied cultural contexts, has required discourse about the proper relation of the Church to its cultural settings. Consensus in practice about the Church's relation to culture has been the most critical and most elusive aspect of Anglicanism's promise.

At times, consensus about the proper form of this relation has been found. The Church and culture in one or another context have been in creative, mutual relation. When there has been an adaptive spirit, and discourse that promoted the sharing of intentions between missionaries and emerging Anglican churches, Anglicanism has taken root in religiously and culturally redemptive ways. But finding such consensus has proven challenging when contextually based religious movements have arisen. As we have described, some such movements have reflected the impetus of powerful personalities such as James Johnson. V. Y. Mudimbe and Kwame Anthony Appiah have also considered the influences of Edward Blyden and Alexander Crummell in West Africa.[12] For them, Anglicanism became a fecund source of vision for faith community and for redeemed society. Christianity broadly, and Anglicanism especially, revealed a capacity to shape leadership that encouraged indigenous faith and life. The birth of African nationalism had religious overtones that could reconstrue the Church's relation to politics from what foreign missionaries deemed appropriate. Similarly, the rise of indigenous Anglicanism occurred amid political tensions and social realities that thwarted control from beyond.

If leadership was one source of tension in mission fields, the other was spirituality. The case of African initiation rites which we have just considered had counterparts elsewhere among Anglicans in the sense of the cooperation that was possible. But the capacity of church leaders, both English and African, could be outpaced by dramatic spiritual developments. Such was the case of the East Africa Revival, a sudden eruption of grassroots spiritual experience that defied the confines of religious institutions and left a lasting imprint upon Anglican life.

TESTING ANGLICAN COHERENCE

As Derek Peterson describes it, the Revival was a movement of Christian conversion 'that began in an Anglican mission station in northern Rwanda in the mid-1930s and spread throughout eastern and central Africa during the 1940s and 1950s'.[13] Its impact can be felt to the present, and its influence spread beyond Anglicans, and beyond religious life per se into social and even political currents across several countries. The Revival was a movement of personal transformation that was prominent among young people, especially young women. It was not strictly Anglican, encompassing Lutherans and Presbyterians as well. It clearly was not the result of institutional religious programmes or leaders; in fact, it was decried and opposed by most who held religious authority. It was a spontaneous moral and spiritual revolution that was grounded in charismatic experience leaving a lasting imprint on Anglicanism. Ironically, its imprint stressed order when, in the eyes of missionaries, it was just the opposite.[14]

Peterson cites the eruption of religious fervour at an Anglican girls' school in 1936 as the onset of the Revival. At Gahini in northern Rwanda, an Anglican missionary, Dora Skipper, awoke in the middle of the night to hear various girls yelling, sobbing and displaying vivid emotional and ecstatic states, many shaking and writhing. Skipper and other missionaries tried to quieten the girls. Their instincts were compassionate, but their perplexity was clear. The outbursts not only continued, they spread to churches and then into communities at large. The outbursts centred on personal convictions of sin, guilt and the need for God's forgiveness and redemption. Demonstrative behaviours illustrated the extent of deep distress, a depth of pain that would transcend personal life and become distress at the state of society. To missionaries such as Skipper, it was insanity. To the girls, and then others who shared their pain, it was spiritual longing in search of moral discipline. This became clear as girls at the school began to return items they said they had stolen. In most cases, the infraction, if there had been one, was minor. But to the girls, and then other persons elsewhere, it was illustrative. Their lives had been casual, in religious and moral terms. They had awakened to the reality of their plight and their dependence upon God. They had to make tangible restitution, emblematic of their transformation, of having overcome sin by God's grace.[15]

The missionaries were as astonished at this religious logic as they were at the vigour of the girls' outbursts. Terror at the prospect of eternal judgement was translating into moral rigour. Seeming disorder was creating a new and vigorous order, personally and socially. Peterson traces this religious framework to the appearance of the classic book, *Pilgrim's Progress*, in the region. Several years before the Revival began, an Anglican missionary at Gahini had translated the work and it had gained immediate popularity. It seemed to embody the religious perceptions of young people especially. What the book conveyed, and what Revival participants likely heard, was that one could break free of one's sinful past, finding God's grace directly, conclusively, immediately. It was not quite the message missionaries conveyed. They portrayed the Christian faith as steady nurture guided by missionaries and clergy, especially bishops. The missionary faith was characterized by decorum, reflection and, above all, order as the Church framed it.

Instead, the Revival surfaced uncontrollably, inexplicably, vehemently transgressing the bounds of missionary religion. The Revival erupted among people who held, and largely retained, Anglican identity, just as it surfaced in Lutheran and Presbyterian circles. But the Revival fostered new hallmarks of religious life and identity, personally and socially. It laid out new criteria of being faithful and of expressing that faith. Peterson concludes that fear of the eschaton, of sin and disorder spilling beyond familiar efforts at control, including missionary religion, was the Revival's source. Certainly, this became the message of popular revivalists who arose to guide the movement. The fact of popular leaders appearing, without the sanction of religious authorities, further troubled such figures as George Chambers, Anglican bishop in Tanganyika, who launched an investigation of the Revival in 1940. Chambers described what he took to be madness, wholesale defiance of Christian norms and authorities. But his efforts at control, and those of other institutional leaders, had little impact. The Revival became something of a leaven in the religious life of eastern Africa. Peterson notes that, decades later, Yoweri Museveni launched his opposition to Ugandan president Milton Obote as a call to moral and social reform. As a child, Museveni had been touched by the Revival. Seemingly its ideals shaped his political trajectory. Clearly his call reflected a familiar ideal, which had transcended church life and missionary control.[16]

It could be argued that the Revival embodied Anglican promise. The Church's message, if not exactly the Church itself, had prompted spiritual exertions and religious convictions beyond what the originators of mission envisioned. Even Henry Venn of the CMS a century before had not imagined such energies as expressions of the self-supporting Anglican churches he intended. The outcome of mission in this sense bespoke the fears of missionaries such as Bishop Chambers and deepened their resolve to control religious life. But the Revival proved to be but one instance of a pervasive reality in the fields of Anglican mission: what missionaries proclaimed and what converts heard were not always the same. Mission conveyed the essentials of the Christian faith and the framework of the Church. But how the faith was lived and how the Church functioned could differ markedly from the religious life of the metropole. Further, Christianity in emerging nations could take on social meanings that could not be anticipated from afar. Such realities made converts in mission settings no less devoutly Christian or truly Anglican. It gave them admirably heightened religious and moral sensibilities, to the extent later that there would be talk of reverse mission, African Christians providing distinctive models of faith in the lands where mission originated. The depth of faith that emerged invigorated Anglican ideals and helps us to understand the dynamism of Anglican growth across Africa and elsewhere. But the reality that what was preached and what was heard could differ enshrined divergence into Anglican life. A basis for conflict and even division had been implanted.

The East Africa Revival was a dramatic instance of a widespread phenomenon in the dynamics of mission. Those to whom the Christian faith was presented, typically interpreted and applied it in ways that made sense of their cultural contexts. Thus, in his study of the impact of Christianity, in particular the Bible, upon the Yoruba people of what now is Nigeria, J. D. Y. Peel found that this foreign text was readily embraced. But it was seen through Yoruba eyes and lived in Yoruba ways. Conveying the faith did not mean continuing to clothe it in the garb of Western predilections. A comparable process to the one that occurred among the Yoruba arose in context after context with Anglican identity becoming enculturated as much according to local, cultural frames of reference as according to the dictates of missionaries from afar.[17]

Thus also, as John Karanja describes, mission stations among the Kikuyu in Kenya became sites where family conflicts could be addressed. Such an expression of the faith was not planned by missionaries but embraced as the extent of local need became apparent. The Church developed as it both fostered ideals of faith and applied them to daily life. More expansively, Lamin Sanneh has asked 'whose religion is Christianity?'[18] He is apt to speak of the indigenous discovery of Christianity rather than the Christian discovery of indigenous societies. Ultimately that which missionaries could not control was the very expansion of the faith which they had intended. Anglicanism became something other than what was found in the British Isles, or in the first phase of colonialism and empire, where the English language held sway. Among other peoples, in other contexts, the Church surpassed the expectations of its erstwhile leaders, in terms of the extent of its growth, and in terms of the paths towards growth it would take. As a result, Anglicans became a people of paradox: one of the largest expressions of Christianity in the world, yet seemingly subject to the 'drift of local churches' away from a coherent centre of faith and life. Did Anglicanism prove to be incoherent, that is, disjointed and incomprehensible in its expressions across varied cultural contexts? We must consider whether Anglican life represents the stranglehold of fate more than the realization of promise.

It is indisputable that the emergence of Anglicanism was intertwined with the reality of colonialism. Even where the Church developed outside the wide arc of British colonial control, such as in Japan, Anglican mission arrived as a faith and a religious institution that were obviously Western. The extent to which Anglicans proved subject to the dynamics of colonialism and the colonial legacy is a pivotal issue. We cannot consider the search for indigenous new forms of Anglicanism apart from the shadow of colonial influence under which mission unfolded in various locales. But the nature of colonialism and of the Anglican relation to it must not be presumed. Though British colonialism possessed a consistent character when viewed from afar, and through its formalities, the realities were contextually nuanced. Arguably, informal relations predominated over formal ones in terms of how people and institutions functioned on the ground. The Church could represent a significant variation of colonial political and economic patterns. The promise of Anglicanism has rested upon the intention to be both indigenous and distinctive.

But the relation of missionaries to British authority cannot be viewed simply as religious intentions versus colonial realities. Missionary intentions could be compromised by the dynamics of colonial rule. Already we have alluded to a missionary propensity to control church life in their domains and to the gradual pace of developing indigenous leadership, which seemed to point to a reluctance to surrender control. In the face of charismatic and critical local leaders, or eruptions of spirit-filled and independent religion, missionary opposition usually proved resolute. Such intransigence endorsed colonial authority rather than confronted it. Was the course of Anglican development so marked by allegiance to colonial life that Anglicanism's promise was jeopardized? How did a sense of promise emerge even as Anglicans functioned within the confines of colonialism? How could Anglicans move beyond the strictures of the colonial world and towards the larger, distinctive religious identity some could glimpse? Although the nature of British colonialism seems apparent, the reality proved complex. Importantly, the manner in which the Church participated in the colonial world was nuanced in ways that only recently have gained clarity. Anglicans often tried to distance themselves from colonial influence, if only to distinguish the Church's intention. But, in their own way, Anglicans shared in the impulse to assert control over cultures and peoples. How was this impulse made manifest?

Anthropologist Peter Pels depicts colonialism as processes of struggle and negotiation grounded in dichotomies that characterized the thinking of the colonizing powers.[19] That is, when we consider the intentions of those who embodied imperialism, we find that they rationalized their presence in Africa and Asia as processes by which they could modernize the peoples they encountered. To explain this motivation in no way excuses them for the impact of their activities upon various peoples and cultures. The result was that colonialism produced ruptures between a prior way of life and the life that was deemed better by those who asserted control. The processes associated with colonialism embodied disruptive steps designed to introduce a presumably better way of life, which in fact consistently disenfranchised and diminished the peoples forced to endure the European onslaught. As one example, achieving the ends of imperialism required securing a common language between colonizer and colonized. This was advanced, first, by acts of translation. Language became an early focus of colonialism, embodied in education, which was not a process that proved innocent or objective. Language also framed governance, exchange and social relations in ways that were convenient for the colonizers. Knowledge of local languages became a basis for their subversion.

More than control was involved. The British rationalization for their presence, namely, to bring civilization to benighted areas of the world, seldom proved benign. The disparity between ideal and reality, between intention and outcome, was stark. Bringing their civilization to complex encounters with other cultures, the British became intent on transforming those they encountered in ways that glossed over local sensitivities. In this regard, missionaries and the Church could prove compliant. After all, translation was a key aspect of the missionary task. Further, conversion followed by nurture in the faith represented a profound rupture in personal lives and social relations. Further still, the Church could be taken as a social rival, modelling a different kind of society. In effect, the Church could embody the dichotomies colonialism fostered. Contextual life and culture would be found wanting, and Western influences would urge people to advance towards better lives. One culture was bad and should be overcome; the other was good and should be appropriated.

The relationship between missionary strategies and colonial intentions was more than incidental. The colonial Church not only overlapped with patterns of governance, it participated in the outlook that framed colonialism generally. Thus, missionaries shared the emphasis on dichotomies that was prevalent in colonial life. As a result, missionaries translated the faith and church life for the sake of transforming lives and communities. Conversion meant more than assent; it launched participation in the life of the Church, characterized by both ritual practices and response to authority that were framed by Western, especially English, precedent. But did the goal of conversion result in efforts at religious and cultural proselytism? Can it be said that the task of translation was free of cultural and religious bias? Robert Yelle has observed that missionaries of various confessions differed over the role Indian language and culture could play. For some Protestant missionaries, such as William Carey, translation became an adaptive process of seeking a viable meeting ground between English language and culture and Indian patterns. Other missionaries, such as Alexander Duff, saw Indian ways as beyond redemption. These exponents of Christianity chose the colonial emphasis upon Anglicizing India over the Orientalist fascination with Indian ways.[20]

Yelle's distinction is an important reminder that colonialism in practice was far from monolithic. Colonialism wore varied faces and the representatives of colonial influence, including missionaries, approached the peoples and cultures they met in different ways. Bearers of dichotomy, intent on remaking the contexts where they laboured, the stewards of British colonialism nevertheless differed among themselves, in the application of their ideals more than in the ideals themselves. Thus, as Pels stresses, colonialism was a constantly contested relation, disadvantaging but not consistently disabling subject peoples.

Ironically, colonialism's emphasis on dichotomy had contextual counterparts that were inherent in the relations that arose between the colonizer and the colonized.

We have noted that the Yoruba people of Nigeria read and heard the Bible in ways that accorded with their cultural predilections. Similarly, as Yelle describes, the use of language in India reflected cultural and ultimately religious difference. He finds that English usage, especially that of missionaries as translators, bore the hallmarks of a Protestant approach to Scripture. The purpose of language was to convey meaning which was understood literally.[21] By the time of colonialism's rise, the Protestant world had informed the European Enlightenment with its use of reason and regard for the plain meaning of texts. In that sense, language was valued as a mode of conveyance. A different emphasis pervaded Indian life, one which Yelle traces to Hindu texts and their use. Language was less the conveyance of information and more the vehicle of ritual performance, especially patterns of social relations. Sacred texts were more regarded for the relations they enshrined than for the intention they might impose. The distinction was not a perfect one, just as the dichotomous thinking of colonial authorities could be understood in terms of relations. But, on balance, the English tendency to focus on meaning met a countervailing Indian focus on social expression.

Thus, English emphasis on translation left room for Indians to read and apply in their own way, as was the case among the Yoruba. When missionaries in India challenged social practices, the resistance proved resolute and blunted much of missionary intention. One of the early Anglican bishops in Calcutta, Daniel Wilson, consecrated in 1832, reversed the approach of his predecessor, Reginald Heber, in regard to the caste system. Wilson's arrival coincided with the rise of Anglicizing intention and the lessening of the Orientalist influence over colonial policy. The Church not only created dichotomies between English and Indian ways, it encountered cultural and religious distinctions that it could neither direct nor surmount.

However, the colonial project could not have advanced without the aid of what has been called 'native agency'. It may not be too much to say that in South Asia, or Africa, there were indigenous people who were complicit with colonial authority. The larger reality is that indigenous peoples and cultures felt compelled to adapt to the reality of colonial influence and sought meeting grounds where Western influence was accommodated to contextual life. It proved to be an unfinished project, one which bespoke the struggle, negotiation and discourse that various commentators identify with colonial relations. As a result, 'colonial discourse thus did not develop in an intellectual vacuum, defined solely by the exigencies of the colonial state'.[22] To be sure, as V. Y. Mudimbe presents, African categories were transformed by both direct and indirect patterns of Western influence, as was the case in India. The colonial presence, including that of the Church, fostered notions of what Africa was supposed to be and what Western guidance intended to build.[23] But, as Kwame Anthony Appiah has described, Africans were not always ready to surrender their cultural ways to British preferences. Indeed, the British frame of reference posed cultural categories that were unrepresentative, notably the notion of being African, or Indian for that matter. Such constructs reflected generalizations intended to facilitate British control of colonial relations. The result was that the colonizers' presence could prove so invasive that they altered the places where they settled. Hybridized cultures became prominent aspects of colonialism and evidence of complex patterns of discourse.[24]

Discourse was central to colonial relations. That is, how people spoke and engaged with one another, formally and informally, embodied their intentions, even when conflicted, across all social relations. At stake was a multifaceted search for viable social order that might join the values and mores of the differing worlds whose encounter characterized colonialism. Such order could be neither strictly colonial nor purely reflexive for any setting. Nor, we argue, could order arise solely through adaptive steps. The search for order in light of Western influence brought frequent instances of contestation, as we have suggested and as we shall explore further. That is, whose values and whose notion of order would prevail? The discourse that characterized colonial life included patterns of protest against European intentions as well as absorption of them.

Helen Tiffin describes how European influence was challenged in the colonial era and as part of rebuilding as colonialism declined. Discourse, and counter-discourse as she poses it, prove central. European accounts are countered by post-colonial ones that revise reporting of events, reinterpret experiences and reframe ideals. In Tiffin's analysis, for example, the colonial era produced forms of essentialism, that is, of an intention to define what it meant to be part of particular nationalities and races. Instead she proposes challenges to the colonial perspective, which lingers well after the institutional façade of colonialism has diminished. The focus turns to activity and relation, to what people do and how they cooperate, rather than an essential relation. The mode of speech, as much as its content, denotes the nature of human relations, whether they are coerced or prove to be authentic and untrammelled.[25]

Among Anglicans, analogous dynamics have been apparent. As the Church's mission became an adjunct to the colonial world, comparable patterns of discourse and counter-discourse surfaced. As an institution, the Church was not always distinguishable from colonial control. The resistance of some missionaries to securing indigenous Anglican life and leadership bespoke the colonial era's dichotomy between modern and primitive, capable and incapable. On the other hand, the appearance of local leaders and novel patterns of spirituality among Anglicans could be seen as forms of counter-discourse. In various contexts, Anglicanism became something other than what missionary oversight intended, by means that missionary authority could not control.

As a result, it is tempting to depict Anglicanism as irreparably fractured. The spectre of discourse and counter-discourse seems to account for tensions between the Global South and Global North. It is further tempting to see Anglican life as characterized more by fate than by promise. That is, Anglicanism can seem caught between its colonial associations and avowed resistance to them. Trapped by its entanglements with British life and culture, Anglicanism both grew and fragmented. As its grassroots life blossomed, its international, institutional ties lost momentum and even split. Is it the fate of Anglicanism to be both vibrant and conflicted? Or, in some sense, have Anglicans charted different means of both fostering indigenous life and working together across their contextual identities and other divides?

For all the importance of efforts to define and to regularize Anglican life, as we shall consider, the nature and promise of Anglicanism must be understood in two basic ways: first, Anglicanism's centre of gravity always proves to be contextual. It is a localized catholicity, with its emphasis as much on mission and ministry in particular places as on adherence to historic marks of faith tradition and church life. Second, there is an unfinished fluidity, even a restless uncertainty, about Anglican life. In one context after another, there is a dynamism that arises locally and seeks fresh combinations of adherence to tradition and lively embodiments of the Christian life. Thus, for all its genuine institutional character, Anglicanism is more of a faith tradition in the process of realization than an institution whose priority is its own preservation.

Anglicanism grew in various mission fields as some missionaries and the adherents they gathered would grasp what Anglicanism promised. Becoming grounded in Anglican forms of worship, ministry and governance, converts saw lively, novel possibilities for them, often beyond the vision or the grasp of most missionaries. The Church, as faithful fellowship more than institution, could only become indigenous by indigenous means under the sway of indigenous influences. It was a dialectic of discourse and counter-discourse, and at points it has signalled conflict and the forestalling of promise. Division over human sexuality has been an especially protracted and unresolved fracture. The reality of fate more than promise, of division more than unity, seems to characterize Anglicanism's reality, past and present.

But ongoing contestation, discourse and counter-discourse, need not be the end of the Anglican story. When we consider Anglicanism as faith tradition, viewing its life and prospects contextually, during and beyond colonial times, the outline of promise emerges. Discourse of a different sort lay at the heart of what Anglicanism could become – a discourse that united contrasted with that which divided. We can only cite a few examples among the scores of instances where those who brought the Christian faith and those who received it discovered patterns of mutual benefit. As Elizabeth Prevost concluded, mission communities were shaped not only by intention and organization from afar, but by 'grassroots control of the Christian message, institutions, and personnel . . .'[26] She explains that while 'indigenization' has become a contested concept because of its association with external control, it was a term that captured missionary intention and, in a different sense, that which resulted. Anglicanism took contextual root through mutual exchange of ideas and intentions, by mutual forms of adaptation and nurture. Those who went to evangelize were themselves converted, as she describes. The missionaries absorbed cultural insights from those to whom they preached. A wideness of faith and personal recognition advanced. Philanthropy expanded, and compassion deepened. The local character of Anglican life was enriched by the growth of mission and relation that deepened faith and enhanced the idea of being the Church together in particular places.[27] This intercultural character may be the true story of Anglicanism, not the rise of hierarchies and international networks.

One example of this dynamic arose in the midst of Anglican mission in Egypt in the twentieth century. In her analysis, Catriona Laing argues that several missionaries, notably Constance Padwick, changed the nature of mission in this predominantly Muslim setting. With her colleagues, Douglas Thornton and William Temple Gairdner, Padwick encouraged a shift in the intention of mission from proselytism to witness. That is, Anglican strategy moved from outright conversion to cooperation and mutual appreciation. As Gairdner had observed at the time of the World Missionary Conference in Edinburgh in 1910, non-Christian religions 'must be approached with very real sympathy and respect'. It seemed that there could be 'traces of the gospel' in other religions and these could become apparent 'through careful relationship building'. The basis for mutual regard and even collaboration across religious divides was being laid.[28] Gairdner advanced this intention in 1922 when he 'encouraged his colleagues to develop a relationship of mutual support and collaboration'.[29] Evangelization of the 'non-Christian population' remained 'the primary aim'. But cooperation with Copts and other Christians in Egypt gained equal emphasis. In addition, the creation of a Christian literature in Egypt became a prominent means of giving the evangelical message. A new emphasis on discourse, as open-ended as it was purposive, framed Anglican life there. Thornton and Gairdner envisioned public debate about belief and devotion. Written in Arabic, a new missionary magazine, *Orient and Occident*, posed itself as a religious public square from 1910 to 1922.

As Laing explains, Constance Padwick extended this work into explorations of the meeting points of Christian and Muslim spirituality. She had first arrived in Egypt in 1916 to assist in the development of children's literature. In the process, she learned the ways of Egypt's rural population, drafting a study of folklore. She later worked at *Orient and Occident* as well as on various literary projects. She was a missionary and, perhaps more than some, a deeply and broadly contemplative person. The result was her intense dedication to understanding Islamic devotion. This pursuit became her signal contribution. In 1961, Padwick published *Muslim Devotions: A Study of Prayer-Manuals in Common Use*. She emphasized the need for 'more accurate understanding and engagement with the lived religion of Islam' through 'identifying what she called "kinships" between Islam and Christianity'.[30] She located such kinships in 'the devotional practices of "ordinary" Muslims and Christians'. She was convinced that kinship between the faiths was the foundation for Christian conversion. Islam would find its fulfilment in Christianity because of the singular reality of Jesus Christ. Later she acknowledged that few in the Muslim world saw such a path or pursued it.

But Padwick encouraged Anglican mission in two ways, both of which have been widely emulated. First, Padwick significantly advanced the means by which Anglicans could engage different faiths and cultures respectfully. The search for common devotional ground spoke to the reality by which people of faith live. In the Muslim world, for example, Anglican intention has been embodied by the likes of Kenneth Cragg, who credited her with much of his inspiration for understanding Islam and encouraging dialogue with Muslims. Second, her turn to an emphasis on Christian presence as a minority faith acknowledged that Anglican mission must proceed by acts of witness as well as evangelism. The primacy of education, medical care and social service in Anglican mission echoes Padwick's experience and her conclusions.[31]

Even where Anglicans became consigned to minority status, which proved the case in most mission fields, their witness granted forms of influence that evangelism alone could not. With the end of colonialism, such an approach to mission gave Anglicans recognition and integrity apart from their convoluted ties to colonial presence. Again, the historical record abounds with instances from every field of mission endeavour. In each case, a generative combination of cross-cultural appreciation and Christian compassion appears. John Yieh's study of Anglican social service ministries in East Asia offers one such perspective.[32] He depicts a variety of schools, hospitals and service institutions across the region in the twentieth century. The work of Bishop Ronald Hall in Hong Kong before and after World War Two offers a striking instance of leadership. He launched programmes to care for orphans, the homeless and refugees amid war and reconstruction. In the post-war era, Hall used his seat on the Hong Kong Social Welfare Council as well as his episcopacy to advance social services. Church and state collaborated in response to human need. As Yieh observes, Hall took his inspiration from the Christian socialism of F. D. Maurice in Victorian England. His was an example of missionary intention that grasped social realities and adapted church life to them in search of ways to care. The result was to uplift the Christian faith and the Church, not to diminish them. The Church became indigenous in fact through constructive discourse and appreciative collaboration.

Henry St George Tucker's instinct to cede control of the Church and to leave Japan was the right one. He had built church life and realized that his tenure had to conclude. The story of how the Church became indigenous in Japan and elsewhere proved complex, contested and unfinished. There remains heated debate about the course of Anglicanism's development and even the appropriate terms to depict it. Difference and division frame every history of Anglican life, and the relation of the Church as an institution to its contextual manifestations is a contested topic. There is no denying the fact of divergence, nor the seeming entrenchment of contestation. Through the colonial era and beyond, the meaning of being Anglican has been disputed, twenty-first-century fractures over sexuality being an especially wrenching example. But through the maze of uncertainties and conflicts, Anglicans found ways to foster discourse, build collaboration and cultivate the Church's mission. Anglicans have learned ways of working together amid difference. This reality has become a central feature of Anglicanism's promise.

Notes

1 Henry St George Tucker, *Exploring the Silent Shore of Memory*, Richmond, VA: Whittet & Shepperson, 1951.

2 Tucker, *Exploring the Silent Shore*, pp. 251f., 287.

3 H. Maynard Smith, *Frank, Bishop of Zanzibar*, London: SPCK, 1926. Frank Weston, *The Fullness of Christ*, London: Longmans, Green, 1916.

4 John V. Taylor, *The Growth of the Church in Buganda*, London: SCM Press, 1958.

5 Lamin Sanneh, *West African Christianity*, Maryknoll, NY: Orbis, 1996.

6 Sanneh, *West African Christianity*, pp. 75f.

7 Jehu Hanciles, *Euthanasia of Mission*, Westport, CT: Praeger, 2002.

8 E. A. Ayandele, *The Missionary Impact on Modern Nigeria, 1842–1914*, London: Longmans, 1966.

9 Susan Billington Harper, *In the Shadow of the Mahatma*, Grand Rapids, MI: Eerdmans, 2000.

10 Anne Marie Stoner-Eby, 'African Clergy, Bishop Lucas, and the Christianizing of Local Initiation Rites: Revisiting: The Masasi Case', *Journal of Religion in Africa* 38:2 (2008), pp. 171–208.

11 Stoner-Eby, 'African Clergy', p. 174.
12 V. Y. Mudimbe, *The Invention of Africa*, Bloomington, IN: Indiana University Press, 1988. Kwame Anthony Appiah, *In My Father's House*, Oxford: Oxford University Press, 1993.
13 Derek R. Peterson, 'The East Africa Revival', in William L. Sachs, ed., *Global Anglicanism, c.1910–2000, The Oxford History of Anglicanism, Volume V*, Oxford: Oxford University Press, 2018, pp. 211–31, at p. 211.
14 Peterson, 'The East Africa Revival'.
15 Peterson, 'The East Africa Revival', p. 218.
16 Peterson, 'The East Africa Revival', p. 230.
17 J. D. Y. Peel, *Religious Encounter and the Making of the Yoruba*, Bloomington, IN: Indiana University Press, 2000.
18 John Karanja, 'The Cultural Origins of the Anglican Church in Kenya', in William L. Sachs, ed., *Global Anglicanism, c. 1910–2000, The Oxford History of Anglicanism, Volume V*, Oxford: Oxford University Press, 2018, pp. 171–95. Lamin Sanneh, *Whose Religion is Christianity?* Grand Rapids, MI: Eerdmans, 2003.
19 P. J. Pels, 'After Objectivity: An Historical Approach to the Intersubjective in Ethnography', *Journal of Ethnographic Theory* 4:1 (2014), pp. 211–36.
20 Robert A. Yelle, *The Language of Disenchantment*, Oxford: Oxford University Press, 2013.
21 Yelle, *Language of Disenchantment*, p. 37.
22 Raf Gelders and S. N. Balagangadhara, 'Rethinking Orientalism: Colonialism and the Study of Indian Traditions', *History of Religions* 51:2 (2011), p. 106.
23 Mudimbe, *The Invention of Africa*, pp. 44f.
24 Appiah, *In My Father's House*, pp. 107f.
25 Helen Tiffin, 'Post-Colonial Literatures and Counter-Discourse', *Kunapipi* 9:3 (1987), pp. 17–34.
26 Elizabeth E. Prevost, 'Anglican Mission in Twentieth-Century Africa', in William L. Sachs, ed., *Global Anglicanism, c.1910–2000, The Oxford History of Anglicanism, Volume V*, Oxford: Oxford University Press, 2018, pp. 232–57, at p. 232.
27 Prevost, 'Anglican Mission in Twentieth-Century Africa'.
28 Catriona Laing, 'Anglican Mission Amongst Muslims', in William L. Sachs, ed., *Global Anglicanism, c.1910–2000, The Oxford History of Anglicanism, Volume V*, Oxford: Oxford University Press, 2018, pp. 367–90.
29 Laing, 'Anglican Mission Amongst Muslims', p. 377.
30 Laing, 'Anglican Mission Amongst Muslims', p. 381.
31 Laing, 'Anglican Mission Amongst Muslims', p. 387.

32 John Y. H. Yieh, 'Anglican Social Ministries in East Asia', in William L. Sachs, ed., *Global Anglicanism, c.1910–2000, The Oxford History of Anglicanism, Volume V*, Oxford: Oxford University Press, 2018, pp. 417–38. David M. Paton, *R. O.: The Life and Times of Bishop Ronald Hall of Hong Kong*, Hong Kong: The Hong Kong Diocesan Association, 1985.

6

Renewing Communion in Mission

Up until now we have been telling the story of Anglican promise through historical witness and counter-witness. In this chapter, we seek to further discern the promise of Anglicanism by exploring what it might mean to understand Anglicanism as a movement of mission.[1] A variety of assumptions about mission and mission models proliferated before even the first colonial bishop was consecrated. The Church of England's impulse towards 'Anglianism' revealed an early tradition that was reluctant to evangelize people beyond Anglo-Saxon and 'kindred races'. It was an emerging Christian tradition for an emerging nation. To the extent that such a reforming project can be considered contextual, it was a contextualization that was contested from within and without. It was contested in discourse and bloodshed. It was contested in assemblies and on battlefields. It was contested in martyrdom and in regicide. Reforming Catholicism for the British was a deadly serious matter. It had eternal consequences, and it had temporal and international implications. The internationalizing of 'Anglianism' related both to colonialisms and missions. It was an emerging tradition for an emerging empire.

Alongside this birth narrative, we have been telling another birth narrative conceived and contested in translation, in contextualizing theology and liturgy, in service and in education, in intercultural dispute and fellowship, and on peripheries unwilling to be subservient to powerful centres. We argue that this mission narrative is the heart of Anglicanism's history and Anglicanism's promise. In this chapter, an explicitly missional or missiological perspective for the future promise of Anglicanism will be submitted in two main moves with a third move being made in the next chapter. First, major criticisms of Anglican mission practice within the broad context of the modern missionary movement will be identified. Second, in light of such criticism, a definition of Anglican contextualization as theological method will be outlined. In the next chapter, a critical missiology with an emphasis on what we will call inter-contextualization as descriptive of Anglican practice and promise will be submitted.

Criticisms of Mission Practice

In light of Anglican promise partially fulfilled and partially forestalled, a direct appeal to 'mission' cannot ignore the criticisms already identified in this study relating to mission theology and practice. Particular criticisms about expansion, acculturation and sectarianism found within the modern missionary movement cannot be avoided in relation to Anglican missions. We will face such criticism squarely, not to disparage mission or missionaries, but rather to clear the way for a constructive missiological move that will further elucidate what might be expected in a renewal of Anglican promise.

First, as we have already seen, Anglican mission practice is criticized for being part of and giving licence to violent imperialism and colonialism. Individual mission leaders like Crowther, Colenso, Taylor or Allen may have to some extent mitigated or modified such dominant expansionist discourse. However, what is in view here is that Anglicans were largely impotent in offering a critical view of colonialism and imperialism itself. The criticism unveils direct theological association and justification for Christian mission via colonial and imperial circumstances and categories and unveils explicitly theological justification for imperialism.

Despite early 'Anglian' expansion related to the British state, a key feature of the modern missionary movement would be its growth not through direct state sponsorship but through voluntary associations moving beyond 'the realm' to contextualized pluralities in multivocal and multidirectional witness. The stories of Colenso and Crowther speak to this shift with

Colenso appealing, successfully, to the state and Crowther appealing, unsuccessfully, to the CMS.

Arguably, it was 1792 that marked the beginning of the modern missionary movement with William Carey's *An Inquiry into the Obligations of Christians to Use Means for the Conversion of the Heathens* and the foundation of the Particular Baptist Society for the Propagation of the Gospel Amongst the Heathen. Carey was greatly influenced by Anglican Thomas Scott who, with others, would found the Church Missionary Society in 1799.[2]

Like the Baptists, the CMS would not depend on state sponsorship nor restrict their activities to British territory. That is not to say that, in an era of unprecedented territorial expansion by the West, missionary leaders did not take a view on imperialism or colonialism. The dominant position was that in God's providence a Christian empire was either a means to God's work or, with godly reform, an opportunity for God's work. For Carey, the trading companies of his age meant that 'providence seems in a manner to invite us to the trial'.[3] Because of exploration and commerce it appeared that the 'ignorance, or cruelty' of the 'barbarians' lay unveiled to all Christian people.[4] Just as the ships of Tarshish brought people to the name of the one true God (Isa. 60.9) so too might the trading ships of Carey's day do likewise. He writes, '*navigation*, especially that which is *commercial*, shall be one great mean [sic] of carrying on the work of God'.[5] The tenacity and bravery of traders and explorers stood as an example to the church whose 'truest interest lies in the exaltation of the Messiah's kingdom' and whose 'charter' is expansive and 'the returns promised infinitely superior to all the gains of the most lucrative of ventures'.[6] Such theological thinking on mission was done explicitly within the frame of the extension of Western commerce and imperial expansion. Given their establishment status in England, it should be no surprise that voluntarist Anglicans in the CMS could provide even stronger imperial theology than that penned by Baptists.

In the 1899 preface to Volume 1 of Eugene Stock's famous history of the CMS, Sir John H. Kennaway spoke of the 'absorbing' and 'marvellous' way in which God had led 'the expansion of England'.[7] Despite this, Stock laments the torpor of the state in appointing bishops beyond the English realm. 'England had been colonizing for two hundred years before the Church of England sent a bishop beyond the seas.'[8] He does not blame the Church or English bishops for this but the state and particularly 'the successive Ministries that raised endless political obstacles'.[9]

For Stock, the modern Anglican missionary movement begins 13 years prior to the founding of the CMS when, in 1786, Parliament passed legislation that made ordination without the oath of allegiance to the British monarch possible. This allowed for the consecration of William White and Samuel Provoost for the American Church in February 1787 and the consecration of Ulsterman Charles Inglis for Nova Scotia six months later.[10] The innovations of the modern missionary movement are often seen in its voluntary, associational, entrepreneurial and lay nature. Stock consistently kept the salvation of souls at the centre of his definition of mission while at the same time eulogizing the work of mission that 'promoted civilization . . . facilitated colonization . . . furthered geographical discovery' and opened doors for commerce, science, amendment of national life and strengthened family life.[11]

Alfred Barry saw England's exceptionalism extended to her national Church.[12] The 'mission of England' to the world was not only to 'enrich it by her commerce, and girdle it with her dominion' but it was also to 'hold up the Lord Jesus Christ to all the nations'.[13] Such missional expansion, argued Barry, would result in a catholicity not simply in 'idea and promise' but also in fact.[14] As colonial expansion birthed a commonwealth of 'daughter-nations' centred on the 'Motherland', so too it would birth an Anglican Communion of self-governing churches centred on the See of Canterbury.[15]

In a later age, as the British Empire fell and new nations emerged, this expansionist confidence of Anglican mission as an attendant blessing of imperialism and a blessing in its own right would come to be questioned. Nonetheless, Max Warren (general secretary of the CMS, 1942–62) writing as late as the

1950s, saw particular significance in the waning of the British Empire and British pre-eminence. In such circumstances, Warren proposed a 'theology of imperialism' in the context of a lecture series at the Virginia Seminary in the USA. In effect, he was handing over the imperial Anglican baton to the US American Church as he reflected on how providence favoured empire, how a sense of vocation is served within empire, how order is brought about by empire and how believers have a sense of a greater good because of empire.[16] While the theology of such leaders in this period must be weighed against historical circumstances and the limitations of context, it must also be recognized that clear imperial theological rhetoric was part of the modern Anglican missionary movement right into the twentieth century. As will be seen, in the next section, European mission leaders and theologians do not have the final say. The Communion writes back.

In this study we emphasize the contextualizations that are embraced by a broad international Anglican family as the heart of the tradition. This promise is hard won. It is achieved amid a range of circumstances some of which are dishonourable because 'Anglicanism' or 'Episcopalianism' really meant an 'Anglianism' that demanded some kind of alignment with foreign thought, ritual and governance. The story of Anglicanism is contextualization, but it is also the story of misplaced practices of acculturation and attempts at assimilation. In the United States of America, the Church cooperated with administrations that sought to 'civilize' Native Americans by way of 'the Bible and the plow'. Such a policy would ultimately lead to shameful practices that included the forcible removal of children to residential schools. 'Civilization' meant assimilation, and classroom education became a means to acculturation that denied the 'identity and value . . . of indigenous people'.[17] Such tragedy can be multiplied in various contexts in the Communion, and opposition to such thought and practice would be common in positions that sought to displace expansionist theologies of mission.

Expansionist theologies attended British colonial expansion and the opportunities that European exploration and colonialism afforded. When Anglicans did reach out beyond garrisons and beyond Anglo-Saxon identities, their approach was often couched in attitudes of cultural and racial superiority. Elizabeth Isichei captures the essence of acculturation when she writes, 'It has been suggested that both mission and imperialism rest on the same postulate: the superiority of one's own culture to that of the other.'[18] This second criticism is that an Anglican theology of mission has expanded conversion to mean (whether implicitly suggested or explicitly stated) not only submission to Christ but assimilation into a foreign culture. In a variety of contexts this is borne out. For example, Timoteo D. Gener points to Euro-American colonization and a lack of 'rootedness' in Asian cultures as the 'major factor', despite significant and growing numbers, for Christianity's persistent 'minority status'.[19]

In China, the first Anglican priests in the nineteenth century were associated with the British East India Company and the first missionaries of the Episcopal Church from the United States, arriving in 1835, faced so much hostility that they sought refuge in Singapore. American imperialist ambition under President William McKinley (1843–1901), who testified to specific leading by the Almighty, included attempts to 'civilize and Christianize' the Philippines.[20] At the close of the nineteenth century, Episcopalian missionaries arrived first as chaplains to the invading American force. The first missionary bishop, Charles Henry Brent, was 'an enthusiastic supporter of American imperialist adventures'.[21] Alongside Anglicans whose mission was to support foreign forces, European migrant communities and ethnic pride, there were figures like Lydia Mary Fay (1804–78), William James Boone (1811–64) and Samuel I. J. Schereschewsky (1831–1906) who exhibited deep learning and respect for host cultures in Asia. This enabled them to produce first drafts of scriptural and liturgical translations.

In 1844, Boone became the first Anglican bishop in China.[22] He, along with missionary graduates of the Virginia Seminary, contributed to translation work and set up medical and educational centres. The Americans were prepared to promote indigenous leadership more quickly than British mission leaders, and in 1863 Boone ordained the first Chinese priest, Huang Guangcai. Fay too was a gifted linguist and educator, founding Duane Hall, which became foundational for the creation of Shanghai's St John's University. Schereschewsky, also intimately associated with St John's, was crucial in the translation of the Bible and the Book of Common Prayer into Chinese.[23] In Japan, the missionary bishop most associated with the Church was Channing Moore Williams who, arriving in 1859, stayed for 50 years. As in other contexts, missionaries founded key medical and educational institutions. In distinction to the situation in China, missionaries in Japan cooperated and agreed on a common Prayer Book for Japan.[24] In 1889, Bishop John Corfe (1843–1921) was consecrated missionary Bishop of Korea. He emphasized deep language and cultural study both for missionaries and would-be converts. It is possible that such a demand for a high level of literacy, especially in rural areas, hindered the growth of the Church. The first Korean Anglicans were not baptized until 1897.[25]

In Latin America, Anglicanism arrived with diplomats and merchants under British treaty agreements that allowed for their presence but not for proselytism. Anglicans were first present in Brazil under such circumstances from 1810. Thus, because of the inclination of leaders and parishioners, and because of legal codes that embedded the supremacy of Roman Catholicism, Anglicans formed communities that guarded both a sense of English liturgy and English ethnicity.[26] By 1819 the first Protestant church was built in Latin America by Anglicans in Rio de Janeiro followed by, as freedom of worship expanded, churches planted in Venezuela, Chile, Uruguay, Costa Rica and Peru. By the middle of the twentieth century there were significant centres of Anglican English-speaking worship particularly in the Southern Cone. Right into the twentieth century, David Rock adjudges Anglicanism in Latin America to be largely 'an ethnically exclusive institution serving the interests of the British commercial and investment economies'.[27]

In the wake of the American Civil War, African American mission effort would bring James Theodore Holly to Haiti in

1861. Unlike European settlers, African American missions reached out with the gospel mitigating the 'foreignness' of the Church. Despite much suffering the Church grew, and Holly became its first bishop in 1876.[28] In contrast, even into the 1920s the Bishop of the Falkland Islands continued to display attitudes of white supremacy on the part of British Anglicans in the region. He regretted that South Americans did not meet nor could ever match the British in terms of morality, character, race or 'the superiority of our civilization'.[29] Visiting a missionary community in Paraguay, he wondered 'How far were these dull minds capable of understanding?'[30]

Capturing the intent of missionary acculturation on that continent least honoured by the modern missionary movement, Teresia Mbari Hinga depicts foreign missionary work as 'cleansing African minds of the effects of their "primitivity," "ignorance," and "superstition"'.[31] At the 1910 Edinburgh conference Africa was largely marginalized not least because in missionary circles there was much debate on whether or not African peoples had 'religion'.[32] 'Civilization' would be visited on Africa as foundational to Christian proclamation.[33] Holding to such a presupposition was to believe that 'Jesus has to destroy the core of . . . indigenous religious teachings and practices . . . in order to effectively extend the benefits of his work to the people'.[34] Mbiti, considered by some to be the father of published African Christian theology, speaks of a 'bulldozer mentality' among foreign missionaries who aimed at sweeping aside African traditional philosophies, practices, and rituals.[35]

Victor I. Ezigbo complicates the picture by identifying African theologians who also promoted a thoroughgoing discontinuity between culture and gospel. Controversially, he assesses such contextualization as a translation of foreign expansionist theologies of mission predicated on an acceptance that Western missionaries 'embodied the universal ideals of humanity'.[36] Ezigbo calls this internalizing the 'deconstructionist presupposition' and associates it with, among others, Yusufu Turaki, Tokunboh Adeyemo and Byang Kato. For such theologians, Christ 'liberates' people from their 'fears, superstitions, and satanic entanglements that permeate their indigenous religions'.[37] Ultimately, this kind of mission theology creates cultural hierarchies with cultures more or less capable of revealing truth and more or less capable of carrying the gospel. Such thinking divides communities.

Third, the modern Anglican missionary movement is criticized for being a destabilizing force that creates, solidifies or exacerbates sectarianism. This criticism arises in response to a mission theology that distinguishes and ranks those who have participated in the reception of the gospel above those who have not. Such criticism was owned by colonialists, contextualists and nationalists.

The *colonialist* criticism was predicated upon the desire for profit. The policy of the British East India Company, founded in 1600, forbade its chaplains from proselytizing or strategizing for Anglican establishment in India.[38] The company directors feared that acculturation would lead to destabilizing disputes and, like Portugal, Britain's empire and its profits would fall. However, in the aftermath of Britain's 1783 loss of 13 North American colonies, a 'second' British Empire was emerging 'suffused' and influenced by Anglican leaders. Between 1790 and 1830 the Church of England played an 'integral part in a renewed government confidence and push for empire'.[39] During this period young evangelicals became chaplains to the company with a desire not only to pastor Europeans but to evangelize Indians. Eventually, not least because of the lobbying force of evangelicals, the company's charter was amended in 1813 to make foreign missionary activity legal and to establish Anglicanism in India in the guise of a Bishop of Calcutta and three archdeacons (in Calcutta, Madras and Bombay).

Missionaries of both High Church and Low Church persuasion in this period viewed the world as divided between heathenism against God and faithfulness to God. Subordinate to Christianity was Islam because it promoted a false prophet. Further distanced from divine truth was Hinduism because it was adjudged to be 'idolatrous', 'primitive' or 'degenerate'.[40] Thus, foreign missionaries were to bring to such contexts truth and civility. But this 'gift' often seemed to be lacking. Like

Herbert before him, Claudius Buchanan (1766–1815) recognized that Britain had extracted great wealth from her colonies and in return had granted little blessing. 'Is it said that we give protection to the inhabitants, and administer equal laws? This is necessary for obtaining our wealth. But what do we give in return?' He saw a conservative impulse to refrain from evangelizing Indians as standing in contrast to Christian principles. Providence has laid before Britain a great opportunity. The Indian people, he averred, 'yield submissively to our mild sway, reverence our principles, and acknowledge our dominion to be a blessing'. In return, England owed it to India to establish her Church among the people and instruct them in the Christian faith from which further and deeper 'civil', 'moral', and spiritual blessing will flow.[41] Such expansionist mission theology pitting 'paganism' against 'Christianity' did not have any real practical import in India until the 1820s when the governor-generalship was taken over by evangelical Lord William Bentinck.[42]

The destabilizing force that the company initially feared came to pass with Christian missionary resolve for reform in the face of practices such as widow burning (*sati*). The resolve and outrage was well captured by Buchanan: 'Moloch has many a tower in the province of Bengal'.[43] Along with social reformers, including Raja Ram Mohan Roy (1772–1833), *sati* was abolished in 1829 causing a 'storm of opposition' to erupt among the very elites upon whom the Raj depended:

> Over thirty thousand Calcutta gentry (*bhadralok*) signed a 'Sacred Petition' protesting against the violation of their ancient 'religious freedoms' and interference in their 'eternally hallowed and time-honored tradition' of burning widows.[44]

Unlike Bishop Reginald Heber (1783–1826), of hymn-writing fame, who saw correlations between the caste system and the class system in Britain and North America, Bishop Daniel Wilson (1778–1858) acted to ban the caste system in 1833. Amid Anglican attacks on *sati*, on the company's patronage of Hindu ceremonies and ceremonial sites, and on the caste system, the Raj was unable to satisfy the competing demands of Christians, Hindus and Muslims. The violent instability it so wanted to avoid, by pacifying all religious communities, came to pass and reached its apex with the eruption of the Great Rebellion of 1857–8 that brought the rule of the company to a bloody end. Robert Eric Frykenberg notes that among the first to be killed was an Oxford Movement SPG missionary-chaplain well known for his public and vehement condemnations of idolatry. With the governance of India moving from company to crown in 1858, Anglican leadership in India became much more circumspect. George Edward Lynch Cotton (Bishop of Calcutta, 1858–66) declared two objectives for the Church: understanding the religions of India and dealing fairly with non-Anglican Christians.[45]

Distinct from the colonialist objection, a *contextualist* objection against unnecessary sectarianism and instability centred on theological analysis across both denominational and religious lines. As demonstrated by Bishop Cotton, a more contextualist approach that sought to avoid the confrontational and degrading approach of Christian proselytism was thought possible. Leading figures of the 1870s, including scholars like F. Max Müller and Anglican B. F. Westcott, argued for a shift in mission theology. They discerned God's call to the Church not so much as proselytism in India or the Christianization of India but in faithful witness and in deep mutual understanding and learning that could lead to cooperative service for India across religious and denominational differences. This ethos would be generative for groups such as the Cambridge University Missionary Brotherhood and would be seen in the leadership of people like C. F. Andrews and Sushil Kumar Rudra.[46]

While Westcott could still speak about 'conquering' India for Christianity, he also considered the very idea of a transplanted Western Christianity to be a hollow 'triumph' that would 'be in the end a loss to Christendom'.[47] As with the 'Judaizers' of the early Church, 'We must take to heart the lessons of the first age, lest we unconsciously repeat the fatal mistake ... and offer as permanent that which is accidental and transitory'.[48]

The theological tenor of such a move was not to face off against different religions, condemning them as anti-Christian or demonic, but to consider them as traditions and communities that had received some degree of divine revelation. The task of mission dialogue was, then, to find 'points of contact' that would invite non-Christian adherents to consider Jesus Christ as the one who fulfils all religious hopes and human longings. Though this 'theology of fulfilment' was most associated with the work of Scottish missionary J. N. Farquhar, it came to represent a variety of contested views.[49]

For Farquhar, the Christian commitment to the incarnation 'wonderfully crowns the ideas of Hinduism'.[50] Farquhar, as with other 'liberals' of the period, remained committed to the supremacy of the Christian faith, saw the presence of empire as a good and decried the deleterious effects of 'idolatrous' religion on society (not least seen in the caste system and *sati*). The 'multitudinous superstitions' of India 'affect the Hindu mind and character most deleteriously'.[51] Yet, for every ritual practice that scandalized foreigners – including sacrifice to 'village gods' and even 'ritual suicide' – Farquhar could point to a 'true religious instinct' at work.[52] He wrote: 'on every single one of them some glint of the spiritual world shines'.[53] On the 'Hindu system' itself, he adjudged that it had proven itself through the centuries as a 'really living religion'. Many had committed to it in thought and practice and it had 'controlled their thinking and their social and family life. Hinduism had produced a characteristic morality' and its 'religious energy' had 'expressed itself in a very great and varied literature . . . architecture, sculpture, painting, and music'. The 'survival of the race', Farquhar submitted, was 'largely due to the nature of the social and family organization of Hinduism.'[54] There are, then, in Farquhar's theology of fulfilment both dialogic and dialectical impulses. The truth of Christianity and the person and work of Christ remain central and pre-eminent. As important as finding similarities between the 'great religions' (he had in view 'higher' Hinduism, Buddhism, Christianity and Islam), there was also the necessary work of discovering where discontinuities and contradictions existed.[55]

It was especially this dialectical tendency and the ultimate necessity that Indians be converted to Christianity that sustained criticism of foreign missions and foreign churches. Ananda K. Coomaraswamy (1877–1947) opposed Christian mission education in India based on an analysis of dominant missionary discourse in the early twentieth century. Through ignorance, misrepresentation and a narrow comparative approach that only saw ritual and religion defined in light of Christian theology, he found missionary attitudes wanting. Reviewing missionary rhetoric and literature of the time, he concluded that they mistook for evil what was strange to them; they universalized the worst cases of behaviour making it true of the whole society or religion; and then romanticized their own religion, ignoring the failings and valorizing the successes of their institutions and culture.[56] 'There is no part of the Christian code of ethics more consistently ignored in missionary circles, than the commandment, "Thou shalt not bear false witness against thy neighbour."'[57]

Taking the long sweep of mission history into consideration disrupts any easy appeal to contextualization as the promise of Anglicanism. With the emergence of a reformed Catholicism in sixteenth-century England, contextualization is not a straightforwardly innocent category, nor does it signify an impeachable exercise of power. In England, key radical, conservative and moderating figures and eras make for a complex story. Processes of contextual reform, counter-reform, settlement and hegemony ebbed and flowed with the rise and fall of monarchs, prelates, politicians, aristocrats, clergy, scholars and opportunists. Thus, to say that at the heart of Anglicanism is an impulse towards contextualization may be to say very little and fall short of a hopeful understanding of promise. In the next section, a constructive, though more unstable, definition of contextualization will be sought as we move towards the future promise of Anglicanism.

Contextualizations in Communion

Contextualization can be understood as a process of expressing the gospel in relation to and in dialogue with cultural resources present in a given context. Such a definition can veil a multitude of historical and theological controversies. Some of these issues have already been highlighted in this chapter and in previous chapters of this book. Anglicans were very much part of the modern missionary movement, and the criticisms of expansionism, acculturation and sectarianism apply to the practice of mission along a range of theological opinions and convictions at work since the late eighteenth century. However, a very real danger in the criticisms of the first section is that the agency of foreign missionaries is exaggerated. As we have seen, those who engaged Anglican missionaries in Asia, Latin America and Africa did so critically and, very often did not accept their imported rhetoric or ministries that purported to be 'good news'. While this gives us a much more unstable definition of contextualization, it better reflects the historical complexities and contemporary controversies within the Communion. Anglican contextualization, in contrast to expansionism, acculturation and sectarianism, means translation, resistance and hybridization.

First, in contrast to expansionism, contextualization is translation. Expansionism emerged in the early period of the history of the Church of England and, as we have seen, continued into the modern missionary movement associated not only with English but also American expansion. Translation in such a frame meant transplantation. It was, in Sanneh's terms, 'cultural deification'.[58] However, even in ethnocentric expressions of expansionism, it was not possible to make the boundaries between a foreign English Church and wider society impervious. If that Church did turn towards proselytism with hegemonic intent to transplant English ways for societies and spiritualities beyond Britain, the interchange between evangelists and would-be converts was never one way.[59] On what might be termed the 'experiential interface' a range of exchanges, interpretations, accommodations and adaptations were made.[60]

Sanneh argues that even if expansionist or acculturationist attitudes were present in the intent and rhetoric of foreign missionaries, this was 'somewhat peripheral' on outcomes on the interface.[61] While Sanneh overstates the case, it is not too much to say that on any given interface actors were changed and new concepts, actions and attitudes could emerge.[62] Transformation took place in the to and fro of the experiential interface. This was inevitable given the necessities of daily life, exchange and interaction. For John Karanja, it was this very adaptability to negotiate, compromise and modify beliefs and practices that signified the indigenous character of African Anglicanism. He has particularly in view the Kikuyu Anglican Church in Kenya. Kikuyu culture was decentralized, adaptive and open to new perspectives and change. Karanja notes this was especially the case when the Kikuyu faced crises. Conversions to Anglicanism, beginning in the early twentieth century, were not about deliverance from guilt and the need for forgiveness – fundamental assumptions at work in foreign missionary theology – as much as they were about healing and power to overcome crises. Karanja cites examples of healing and of 'rain-making' associated with the ministry of Christian missionaries as crucial to Kikuyu conversions.[63] This adaptability and pragmatism on the existential interface helps explain the conversion even of privileged actors in society like traditional healers. This adaptability, even amid controversies on age-related ritual (*ituika*) and female circumcision in the 1920s, encouraged many Kikuyu to become Anglican. Adaptable and skilled negotiators among Kikuyu leaders, converts, missionaries and foreign mission leaders translated Christian presence and community, forging a new identity – Kikuyu Anglicanism.[64] Given the social, cultural, political and religious dynamics at work on this central Kenyan interface, transformation was inevitable. But this does not tell the whole story. Transformation on such interfaces was inevitable, but it also took place because of theological intent.

As has been seen in this chapter, missionaries were intentionally committed to the translatability of the gospel. The interfaces then were not simply experiential, they were missional. A 'missional interface' signified exchange and interaction predicated upon a particular theological commitment and in the service of a particular theological commitment. This interface does not simply signify the experience of proximity. It was experience and exchange because of a commitment to translatability. A theology of translation 'makes the bold, fundamental assertion that the recipient culture is the authentic destination of God's salvific promise . . .'[65] Frykenberg identifies a range of influential, and sometimes celebrated, Indian figures committed to this principle even if their relationship with the Church was often 'conflicted'.[66]

Krishna Mohan Banerjea (1813–85) came from a strict and pious Hindu family. During his college years, he became associated with a radical group (Young Bengal) that opposed Hindu orthodoxy. The radicalism of the group meant that he had to leave home, provoking a time of searching and stress that eventually led him to conversion and baptism in 1832. He would be baptized by one tradition, Presbyterianism, and soon move to another, Anglicanism. Alongside his scholarship and competency in ten languages, he was an evangelist, statesman, historian, social reformer and civil rights leader.

As a Christian apologist, his theological work demonstrated continuities with foreign missionary thinking, but his translation of the hope of the gospel depended on a deeper appreciation and love of cultural and national identity. Whatever else his contribution signifies, it signifies an attempt to prove the indigeneity of Christianity by making it the fulfilment of the ancestral culture of India. As an Indian theologian, he was a pioneer in his attempts to correlate the gospel with the witness of ancient Hindu texts. Without giving to the ancient writings (the Vedas) the authority of the biblical text, he does handle them in a manner that makes them 'functionally equivalent' to the Old Testament.[67] From deep readings of Hindu culture and literature, he came to the belief that a 'primitive revelation' from God existed. 'The minds of our ancestors,' he wrote, 'were universally imbued with notions of a Revelation . . .'[68] Unfortunately, as time passed this unwritten revelation dimmed and became mixed and distorted by error. Echoes of that revelation pointing forward to its fulfilment remained and could be found in the ancient forms of Hinduism. Beginning with the Vedas, he argued that Hinduism most likely began with a monotheistic vision of divinity. Human relationship with the divine centred on the generative potency of sacrifice. Through sacrifice the world was created and sustained; sacrifice brought strength against enemies; sacrifice delivered adherents from the effects of sin. However, because of the creeping distortions and forgetfulness of humans the 'origin and object . . . as a figure or type of a self-sacrificing Saviour' was lost.[69] This was particularly tragic because the texts provided the ideal of *Prajapati* or a 'self-sacrificing divine figure' that foreshadowed the work of Christ. Banerjea was the first to make the argument that the *Prajapti* prefigured Christ.[70]

> Christian evangelists when they draw our attention to the claims of Gospel truth do not utter things which can be called *strange* to Indian ears. Salvation from sin by the death of a Saviour, who was God and man himself, was a conception which had administered consolation to our ancient *Rishis*, and may yet, in a higher form, and to a greater degree, do the same to all India.[71]

For Banerjea, Christianity can be translated as Hinduism. That is to say, the Christian faith is 'essentially "Vedic doctrine in its legitimately developed form . . .", no person can be a true Hindu without being a true Christian'.[72] While it would be Brahmabandav Upadhyay who popularized the term 'Hindu Christian', it was first coined by Banerjea.

Maulvie 'Imad ud-din Lahiz (1830–1900) – from a noteworthy scholarly and Islamic background – was baptized in 1866, became a deacon in 1868 and became a CMS missionary. Before his conversion, he was an important Muslim leader and apologist. After his conversion, he became a noted Christian apologist critiquing Islam and defending the Bible. Elwood M. Wherry described his style as 'plain and terse', 'dogmatic' and carried out in 'a controversial spirit'.[73] This is no understatement. Among the themes of his apologetics – always focused on the supremacy of Christianity over other religions – Lahiz dealt controversially and confrontationally with revelation, inspiration, miracles, reason, the Qur'an as witness to the veracity of the Bible, true prophethood and its absence in the life of

Muhammad, the divinity of Christ and the doctrine of the Trinity.[74] These examples of contextualization as translation evidenced a degree of continuity with foreign missionary theologies of fulfilment. However, the deep contextual translation in dialogue with ancient traditions and texts in a context of a rising nationalism also demonstrated fundamental discontinuities. For these thinkers the pre-Christian sources prepared the way for the gospel, but they also shed new light on the gospel and identities that would resist colonial over-lordship. In sum, this deep practice of translation acted to thwart the ongoing viability of an expansionist or imperialist Anglicanism.

Second, contextualization is resistance to acculturation.[75] Such resistance relates both to critical resistance and to political resistance. The critical challenge came in the form of locally instituted churches and communions that took location and continuity with local traditions and local leadership as the theological and ecclesiological point of departure.[76] In Sanneh's terms, such 'critical evaluation' can be seen both as the logical terminus of processes of vernacularization and the departure point for a thoroughgoing contextualization of the faith.[77] Resisters did indeed leave Anglicanism but many remained. Sometimes in dialogue with foreign missionaries (famously seen in the collaboration between C. F. Andrews and Mahatma Gandhi),[78] but more often than not in opposition to foreign missionaries, resisters sought to unveil acculturation and discern the presence of Christ's Spirit deep within indigenous tradition and experience. For Sadhu Sundar Singh (1889–1929) what was needed was 'the Water of Life'. What was not needed was the 'European cup'.[79]

As Warren was mooting a theology of imperialism, published theology from the Global South was aiming at disrupting the curricula and caricatures of expansionist Anglicanism. In the context of a collapsing empire, and in an era of independence, theologians and leaders from the peripheries were challenging the centre. In the African Christian heartlands, such contestatory activity was often associated with so-called Zionism and African instituted churches. However, Isichei rightly notes that the differences between such movements and resistance in the missionary churches were more apparent than real.[80]

Resistance was working at an even deeper level in contextualizations. Protest and resistance did not simply amount to a theological account of gospel and culture in the face of assumptions that the Christian faith somehow existed above culture. Contextualization as resistance was also the voice of contextual theologians asking theological questions about their own cultures and cultural practices. This is seen clearly in the development of feminist and womanist theologies that refused to accept the stasis not only of imported culture but the stasis of their own culture. Quoting Jean-Marc Ela, Hinga argues that contextualization as resistance is not anti-Westernism nor is it conserving so-called traditional custom and ritual. It is an assertion of 'dignity' for Africans and for all people. It is *'the deeds of historical subjects*, who transform themselves as they transform the world in which they live'.[81] Ezigbo too argues that contextualization is at one and the same time a demonstration that the gospel has capacity for answering particular questions that particular communities have while, at the same time, resisting the temptation to reduce Christianity to membership of that community. The risen Christ speaks both grace and judgement into each culture.[82] From his own context and experience, Ezigbo writes: '[Jesus] does not merely provide answers to the questions African Christians are asking . . . Jesus also critiques and redirects these questions.'[83] To illustrate this, he points to the controversial issue of barrenness in African societies. Mbiti is rightly accused of further embedding 'traditional' and patriarchal views of women when he reports that a woman's 'failure' to bear children is 'worse than genocide'.[84] Ezigbo resists such interpretations.[85]

The view on barrenness as incompleteness and curse has to be rethought in the light of the gospel witness. Jesus does not simply baptize the view that barrenness means incompleteness. Rather, contextualization means a rethinking of the issue. For Jesus values and affirms the humanity of all on the basis of their created nature and not on their ability to have children (Matt. 6.25–34). The gospel does not 'merely satisfy the religious and spiritual aspirations' inscribed in a community's traditions and culture.

Jesus . . . reorients the aspirations in a manner that allows his vision of humanity to shape and transform African Christians' questions and religious aspirations. Christians need to know that being a follower of Jesus requires committing to his vision of humanity in which God, and not human achievements or inabilities, determines human significance and worth.[86]

Mercy Amba Oduyoye states this well when she questions the Mbitian presentation of childbearing as the way to immortality. Does immortality in African theology have anything to do with God?[87] Like Hinga and Oduyoye, Ezigbo warns against stasis in spiritual and theological discernment. To be God's church for God's world means to be constantly 'on the way' discerning, across differences, and working out, in disagreement as well as agreement, how the gospel is to be faithfully and contextually received. Contextualization, in other words, is also resistance.

Resistance to acculturation, as already seen in the Indian context, could have political ramifications. A critical theology and political agitation are intimately linked not least because theology always involved exercises of power in a community and communion of discernment and contestation. The 'promise of vernacular ascendancy' for Sanneh 'galvanized the national resolve' and thus helped fuel 'movements for local autonomy'.[88] The translatability of the message not only displaced transplantation as a goal of mission, in some cases it ultimately uprooted foreign dominance and rule. Mbiti recognizes that a more independent hermeneutic had effects on nascent nationalism. Revolutionaries were hearing God's word through Moses to the Pharaoh afresh, 'let my people go!'[89]

The Kenyan liberation leader Jomo Kenyatta (1897–1978), who in 1963 would become the nation's first president, in his scholarship was aiming at reconciling the traditions of his people with the teaching of the Bible.[90] Such practical theology would play a key role in the genesis of the independence movement where the intersection of a contextualizing Christianity could consolidate local and national identities. While the Anglican Church was pragmatic and phlegmatic, the mission churches that took a stand against circumcision lost large numbers and provoked a radicalization among young Kenyans (particularly among the Kikuyu).[91] This radicalization led to the revolutionary Mau Mau movement (1952–60), which fed into an independence movement. Traced back to Kenyatta and the circumcision crisis, it is not an exaggeration to say that the genesis of Kenyan independence included resistant theology. This, along with the experience of 100,000 Kenyans in World War Two, a rise in European settlers and more land alienation added further cause to radicalization. Mau Mau was brutally suppressed. It is possible that anything between 100,000 and 300,000 people died, including 26,000 children.[92] The Kikuyu Old Testament had been published a year before the movement began. At the outset, members of the movement saw themselves as seeking liberation from an Egyptian (British) bondage. The quest for liberation began with secret 'oathing ceremonies', which for many foreign missionaries confirmed that Mau Mau was anti-Christian and confirmed that Africans always had a propensity to slip back into 'paganism'. Dedan Kimathi, one of the key leaders, a baptized Anglican, saw himself as an Old Testament type prophet. When he was eventually captured among his personal effects was such a Kikuyu Old Testament.[93]

Few European Anglicans supported the African nationalist movements of the 1950s and 1960s. As we have seen, the theological discourse that had identified the British Empire as a providential means towards the greater good of humanity was not entirely absent and certainly most preferred to see the empire as benign.[94] Given such an imperial discourse, it is unsurprising that missionaries feared the coming of an independent Kenya. For it would be a very real and practical challenge to a theology that saw Western expansionism as central to the activity of divine providence in history. Independence, it was feared, would result in the breakdown of social cohesion as a result of a virulent nationalism or because a vacuum would be created for other ideologies. Communism in particular was feared. History proved missionary paternalism and hesitancy in the face of a desire for independence wrong.

The church saw rapid growth after independence along with the emergence of church leaders who took a stand against 'one-partyism' in the 1980s and 'third-termism' in the 1990s.[95] Contextualization as resistance, therefore, not only takes place within broader issues of social history and political history, but theological contextualization may also help shape social and political developments. Contextualization as contestation rejects the assumption that the values, ideas and institutions of Western societies will always dominate the world over against, for example, networks or alliances from the majority world.[96] This is not to say that practices of contextualizations further embed sectarianisms where provinces define themselves over against other provinces and African theologians define themselves over against American theologians. Rather, the final characteristic of contextualization must also be kept in view.

Third, contextualization means hybridization. Further exacerbating division in communities and emerging nations was the Anglican involvement in the importation of denominationalism and churchmanship in the context of European colonialism. Reflecting colonial policies, 'zones of influence' were divided up not only between church traditions but, in some places, witnesses to High Church Anglicanism and evangelical Anglicanism divided up tracts of land for the implantation of their missional insights and blind spots. By the fourth decade of the nineteenth century, against the backdrop of rationalism and liberalism, denominationalism was widespread and despite apparent ecumenical gains practical cooperation and schemes for church unity became difficult.[97] It is no surprise that as movements for independence gained ground, theologians in India and Africa and elsewhere not only critiqued denominationalism but were involved in projects for church unions sometimes in the face of opposition by Anglicans. As will be seen presently, one way of interpreting such contextualizations is through the lens of hybridization in opposition to sectarianism.

No foreign missionary, much to the chagrin of some, was ever omnipotent. Even the most hegemonic intent expressed by foreign missionaries and church leaders took place on an existential interface frustrated and contested by converts, would-be converts and those who consistently resisted. Given this interface, characterized by translation and contestation, it was inevitable that a pluralist or hybridized or third space between a foreign Church and a local community would open up. This interface or zone conceptually exists between a (foreign) missionizing presence and a particular community. The interface is characterized by a range of possible theological and cultural postures determined by a proximity either to a local community or a foreign missionizing presence. Because of a closeness to the foreignness of the mission pole, hegemonic attitudes associated with, for example, expansionism were often expressed. But on the missional interface were others that had moved closer to the community and, thus, further away from expansionist, acculturationist and sectarian conceptions of mission presence. Though seldom acknowledged in the missionary literature, this included the capacity for a journey across the interface in conversion to the worldview of the receiving community that ultimately subverted the very categories of reception and conversion. The missionary was received and converted by those he or she sought to convert. The interface, of course, should not be seen as a space only occupied by foreign actors. Others, from a receiving host community (who often subverted notions of reception and conversion) inhabited the interface with a capacity to accede to expansionist, acculturationist or sectarian attitudes.

Brahmabandav Upadhyay (1861–1907), born into a Brahmin family, was baptized in the Anglican Church in 1891. Though he did not esteem Anglicanism long he is considered, at least by some, to be the founder of Indian Christian theology. He was received into the Roman Catholic Church seven months after his baptism and would eventually consider himself a Hindu Christian. The Catholic Church was not associated with British colonialism in the way that Anglicanism was and it had a more open posture towards Hinduism and both of these factors would be important until the end of his life.[98] Upadhyay's witness opposed the 'confrontational attitude' towards Hinduism that dominated missionary discourse in the nineteenth century.⁹⁹ However, he would go beyond translation and resistance and move to hybridization. He argued that Hindu scriptures were analogous to the Hebrew Scriptures for they were the way in which Indians accessed, understood or received the Christian gospel. He rejected the idea that so-called Western classical theological statements, including Chalcedon, were fixed. Contextualizing such thought did not mean transplanting Greek or Latin categories. Rather, what was demanded to overcome a sectarianism that would deify particular cultures and languages was indigenized theology. For Upadhyay, this did not mean less than the primacy of indigenous language and thought relativizing Western philosophical conceptions, which, in turn, opened up wider theological insights both for India and the church catholic.

He came to the view that the highest expression of Hindu thought (which to his mind was eighth-century *advaita* Vedāntism) was distinct from and superior to the Aristotelian foundation to Thomism (which to his mind was the highest expression of Christian thought). On a range of theological issues – including creation *ex nihilo*, divine transcendence and incarnation – Upadhyay argued that this (Vedāntic) philosophy could redefine and renew Christian theological claims. Further, this Indian philosophical tradition – associated with one of the great Indian philosophers, Śaṅkara (*c*.788–820) – could be renewed by the dialogue. In such renewal, he rejected the overly Christian influenced understandings of 'religion' at work in early comparative studies. Drawing on contextual categories, Hinduism was for him a cultural expression and way of thinking (*Hindutva*). If Christianity was to be at home in India, he argued that Hinduism must be 'vigorously' defended by Christian thinkers.¹⁰⁰ Julius Lipner sums up Upadhyay's contribution:

> Upadhyay was arguing not that *advaitic* insights were the most appropriate cultural base for Hindus to appreciate the validity of Catholic doctrine while Thomism performed a similar function for the west, but that *advaita* offered *per se* the best approach to supernatural verities.¹⁰¹

He sought to work out a hybridizing that could still claim to be in some sort of continuity with the wisdom of India and the orthodoxy of the Church. Alongside his theological work, he practised Hindu worship (*pūjā*) and ritual. This was not without controversy. For example, amid his Hindu worship and his facilitation of others to participate in Hindu rites, he submitted to a ritual repentance (*prāyaścitta*) for mixing with foreigners. Not long after his 1903 return from a visit to Europe, Upadhyay became an influential and caustic voice against the British presence in India. By 1907 he was being charged with sedition. Despite the Church banning his books in 1900 and 1901 and despite his nationalistic fervour in later years – where he emphasized the importance of popular Hinduism – he did not think that his hybridizing work took him beyond Catholic truth.[102] In the final analysis, what these forerunners may ultimately witness to is the very subversion of binary categories such as contextual versus catholic.

When contestations within Anglicanism are simplified into binaries of liberal and conservative or North versus South then not only is the analysis and prognosis remote from history and lived experience but any prescription predicated on such prognosis remains far from healing the body Anglican. Indeed, with such analysis and prognosis it will be stricken further by promises of purity it never possessed and can never possess this side of the Lord's return. Should then evensong cease in Nairobi? Should the cathedral in Lusaka, modelled on an English cathedral, be demolished? Should bishops divest themselves of garb from another time and place for more contextually relevant dress? Should bishops no longer visit the University of Kent for Lambeth Conferences and instead congregate in warmer climes? Not necessarily. For the key to an understanding of contextualization and what in the next chapter we will call inter-contextualization is agency, contestation and a rejection of stasis.

Zambian Anglicans are at liberty to continue to honour imported architecture, reject imported architecture and/or reinterpret imported architecture. Kenyan liturgists are at liberty to pluralize worship by honouring the 1662 Prayer Book. We do not, however, consider such markers to be key attributes of what it means to be Anglican. Such customs are held lightly and are contested in different generations and in different locations. Even if it were possible to live passively in cultural, ecclesiastical, theological and missiological stasis, this would not constitute Anglican identity. If it were possible, such stasis might honour the contextualization and contestation of English contextualization. The promise of Anglicanism does not, however, lie in an Elizabethan equilibrium. It lies in a vision for deeper contextualization, that is to say, for a catholicity continually birthed in inter-contextuality.

To fetishize the insights of Tudor, Elizabethan, Jacobian, Carolinian, Restoration or Victorian theology, mission, or ethics is to give in to a vision of a particular people at a particular time as the universal standard for Anglican theology. Lest we forget, this is the very thing that pioneering theologians and mission leaders from the Global South have been rejecting before and since the inception of the modern missionary movement.

When controversial issues (like circumcision, barrenness, polygamy, homosexuality) become not just contested issues of contextualization and inter-contextualization but the measure of what it means to be Anglican, then we concede the contextual ground won by witnesses of world mission, world Christianity and world Anglicanism. There is deep irony here. For in the midst of such controversy too easily the disputes are framed as Global North versus Global South or imperialist Anglicanism versus grassroots Anglicanism. The picture is much more historically, methodologically and culturally complex. Ever there is danger of deifying particular periods of history, particular scholars, particular Lambeth resolutions, particular mission models or particularly situated ethics. This is to give in to a vision of these people and this wisdom at this time as the embodiment and incarnation of divine will for all humans. Anglicanism is catholicity from below. Its promise is its ongoing openness to contestation in inter-contextual presence and fellowship. How that work can be furthered is the subject of the next chapter.

Notes

1 See Robert Heaney, 'Missiology and ministry', in Martyn Percy, Ian S. Markham, Emma Percy and Francesca Po eds, *The Study of Ministry*, London: SPCK, 2019, pp. 279–91.
2 Eugene Stock, *History of the Church Missionary Society: Its Environment, its Men, and its Work: Vol. I*, London: Church Missionary Society, 1899, pp. 59–80.
3 William Carey, *An Inquiry into the Obligations of Christians, to Use Means for the Conversion of the Heathens*. Leicester: Ann Ireland, 1792, p. 67.
4 Carey, *Inquiry*, pp. 67–8.
5 Carey, *Inquiry*, p. 68.
6 Carey, *Inquiry*, p. 82.
7 John H. Kennaway, 'Preface', in Stock, *History Vol. I*, p. v.
8 Stock, *History Vol. I*, p. 404.
9 Stock, *History Vol. I*, p. 404.
10 Stock, *History Vol. I*, pp. 57–8, 405–6.
11 Stock, *History Vol. I*, pp. xiv, 16–28. See Brent Sirota, *The Christian Monitors: The Church of England and the Age of Benevolence, 1680–1730*, New Haven, CT: Yale University Press, 2014, pp. 256–60.
12 Alfred Barry, *The Ecclesiastical Expansion of England in the Growth of the Anglican Communion: The Hulsean Lectures for 1894–95*, London: Macmillan, 1895, p. 211.
13 Barry, *Ecclesiastical Expansion*, p. 160.
14 Barry, *Ecclesiastical Expansion*, p. 6.
15 Barry, *Ecclesiastical Expansion*, pp. 54–5.
16 M. A. C. Warren, *Caesar The Beloved Enemy: Three Studies in the Relation of Church and State*, London: SCM Press, 1955.
17 L. Daniel Hawk and Richard L. Twiss, 'From Good: "The Only Good Indian is a Dead Indian" To Better: "Kill the Indian Save the Man" to Best: "Old Things Pass Away and All Things become White!"', in Kay Higuera Smith, Jayachitra Lalitha and L. Daniel Hawk, eds, *Evangelical Postcolonial Conversations: Global Awakenings in Theology and Praxis*, Downers Grove, IL: IVP Academic, 2014, p. 57.
18 Elizabeth Isichei, *A History of Christianity in Africa: From Antiquity to the Present*, London: SPCK, 1995, p. 92.
19 Timoteo D. Gener, 'Christologies in Asia: Trends and Reflections', in Gene L. Green, Stephen T. Pardue and K. K. Yeo, eds, *Jesus without*

Borders: *Christology in the Majority World*, Grand Rapids, MI: Eerdmans, 2014, p. 63.

20 Quentin R. Skrabec, *William McKinley: Apostle of Protectionism*, New York: Algora Press, 2008, pp. 158–64. See Anthony J. Eksterowicz and Glenn P. Hastedt, *Presidents and War*, New York: Nove Science Publishers, 2010, pp. 126–8.

21 Carol Engelhardt Herringer, 'Anglicanism beyond the British Empire, 1829–1910', in Rowan Strong, ed., *The Oxford History of Anglicanism, Volume III: Partisan Anglicanism and Its Global Expansion, 1829–c.1914*, Oxford: Oxford University Press, 2017, p. 84.

22 Philip L. Wickeri, 'Anglicanism in China and East Asia, 1819–1912', in Rowan Strong, ed., *The Oxford History of Anglicanism, Volume III: Partisan Anglicanism and its Global Expansion, 1829–c.1914*, Oxford: Oxford University Press, 2017, p. 321.

23 Wickeri, 'Anglicanism', pp. 320–3.

24 Herringer, 'Anglicanism', pp. 69–91.

25 Wickeri, 'Anglicanism', pp. 332–3.

26 David Rock, 'Anglicanism in Latin America, 1810–1918', in Rowan Strong, ed., *The Oxford History of Anglicanism, Volume III: Partisan Anglicanism and its Global Expansion, 1829– c.1914*, Oxford: Oxford University Press, 2017, pp. 366–87.

27 Rock, 'Anglicanism', p. 387.

28 Ondina E. González and Justo L. González, *Christianity in Latin America: A History*, Cambridge: Cambridge University Press, 2008, pp. 190–200. John Lynch, *New Worlds: A Religious History of Latin America*, New Haven, CT: Yale University Press, 2012, p. 185.

29 Edward Every, *Twenty-Five Years in America*, London, 1929, pp. 42, 119. Cited by Rock, 'Anglicanism', p. 385.

30 Rock, 'Anglicanism', p. 385.

31 Teresia Mbari Hinga, *African, Christian, Feminist: The Enduring Search for What Matters*, Maryknoll, NY: Orbis, 2017, p. 62.

32 Brian Stanley, *The World Missionary Conference: Edinburgh 1910*, Grand Rapids, MI: Eerdmans, 2009, pp. 235–45.

33 Hinga, *African, Christian, Feminist*, p. 62. Stanley, *World Missionary Conference*, pp. 245–7.

34 Victor I. Ezigbo, *Re-Imagining African Christologies: Conversing with the Interpretations and Appropriations of Jesus Christ in African Christianity*, Eugene, OR: Pickwick, 2010, p. 36.

35 John S. Mbiti, 'Confessing Christ in a Multi-Faith Context, with two Examples from Africa', *Metanoia* 4:3–4 (1994), pp. 138–45.

36 Victor Ezigbo, 'Jesus as God's Communicative and Hermeneutical Act: African Christians on the Person and Significance of Jesus Christ', in Gene L. Green, Stephen T. Pardue and K. K. Yeo, eds, *Jesus Without*

Borders: Christology in the Majority World, Grand Rapids, MI: Eerdmans, 2014, pp. 45–6.

37 Ezigbo, *Re-Imagining African Christologies*, pp. 35–42.

38 See Daniel O'Connor, *The Chaplains of the East India Company, 1601–1858*, London: Continuum, 2012, p. 42.

39 Rowan Strong, *Anglicanism and the British Empire c.1700–1850*, Oxford: Oxford University Press, 2007, p. 133.

40 Strong, *Anglicanism and the British Empire*, pp. 118–32, 175–6.

41 Claudius Buchanan, *Memoir of the Expediency of an Ecclesiastical Establishment for British India; Both as the means of Perpetuating the Christian Religion Among our own Countrymen; and as a Foundation for the Ultimate Civilization of the Natives*, American ed., Cambridge, MA: Hilliard and Metcalf, 1811, pp. 40–2.

42 Robert Eric Frykenberg, 'Episcopal Establishment in India to 1914', in Rowan Strong, ed., *The Oxford History of Anglicanism, Volume III: Partisan Anglicanism and its Global Expansion, 1829–c.1914*, Oxford: Oxford University Press, 2017, p. 301. Stewart J. Brown, 'Anglicanism in the British Empire, 1829–1910', in Rowan Strong, ed., *The Oxford History of Anglicanism, Volume III: Partisan Anglicanism and its Global Expansion, 1829–c.1914*, Oxford: Oxford University Press, 2017, pp. 56–61.

43 Claudius Buchanan, *Christian Researches in Asia: with Notices of the Translation of the Scriptures into the Oriental Languages*, London: T. Cadell and W. Davies, 1812, p. 35.

44 Frykenberg, 'Episcopal Establishment', p. 301. See Rammohun Roy, *An Appeal to the Christian Public, in Defence of the 'Precepts of Jesus' by A Friend to Truth*, London: n.p. 1823 [1820], pp. 122–30. See Strong, *Anglicanism*, pp. 186–7. J. N. Farquhar, *Modern Religious Movements in India*, New York: Macmillan, 1924, pp. 29–39. C. A. Bayly, *Indian Society and the Making of the British Empire*, Cambridge: Cambridge University Press, 1988, pp. 155–68. See Susan Bayly, 'The Evolution of Colonial Cultures: Nineteenth-Century Asia', in Andrew Porter, ed., *The Oxford History of the British Empire, Vol. 3: The Nineteenth Century*, Oxford: Oxford University Press, 1999, pp. 448–69.

45 Frykenberg, 'Episcopal Establishment', pp. 296–309. Farquhar, *Modern*, pp. 17–28.

46 Brown, 'Anglicanism', pp. 56–61. B. F. Westcott, 'The Universities in Relation to Missionary Work', in B. F. Westcott, *On Some Points in the Religious Office of the Universities*, London: Macmillan 1873, pp. 25–44. F. Max Müller, 'Westminster Lecture on Missions: Delivered in the Nave of Westminster Abbey, on the Evening of December 3, 1878', in F. Max Müller, *Selected Essays on Language, Mythology and Religion in Two Volumes*, London: Longmans, Green, and Co.,

1881, pp. 46–86. Nandini Chatterjee, 'Creating a Public Presence: The Missionary College of St Stephen's Delhi', in Chatterjee, *The Making of Indian Secularism: Empire, Law and Christianity, 1830–1960*, Basingstoke: Palgrave Macmillan, 2011, pp. 121–33. Daniel O'Connor, *A Clear Star: C.F. Andrews and India, 1904–1914*, New Delhi: Chronicle Books, 2005, pp. 37–8.

47 Westcott, 'Universities', p. 33.
48 Westcott, 'Universities', p. 39.
49 Stanley, *World Missionary Conference*, p. 219. J. N. Farquhar, *The Crown of Hinduism*, London: Oxford University Press, 1920.
50 Farquhar, *Crown*, p. 425.
51 Farquhar, *Crown*, p. 447.
52 Farquhar, *Crown*, pp. 447–52.
53 Farquhar, *Crown*, p. 447.
54 Farquhar, *Crown*, p. 446.
55 Farquhar, *Crown*, pp. 29–33.
56 Ananda K. Coomaraswamy, *Essays in National Idealism*, New Delhi: Munshiram Manoharlal, 1981 [1909], p. 139.
57 Coomaraswamy, *Essays*, pp. 138–52.
58 Lamin Sanneh, *Translating the Message: The Missionary Impact on Culture*, Maryknoll, NY: Orbis, 2004 [1989], p. 1.
59 See Robert S. Heaney, *Post-Colonial Theology: Finding God and Each Other Amidst the Hate*, Eugene, OR: Cascade, 2019, pp. 124–42.
60 See Robert S. Heaney, *From Historical to Critical Post-Colonial Theology: The Contribution of John S. Mbiti and Jesse N.K. Mugambi*, Eugene, OR: Pickwick, 2015, p. 212.
61 Sanneh, *Translating*, p. 207.
62 See Judith Becker, 'Introduction', in Judith Becker, ed., *European Missions in Contact Zones: Transformation through Interaction in a (Post-)Colonial World*, Göttingen: Vandenhoeck and Ruprecht, 2015, p. 12.
63 See also Ogbu Kalu, *African Pentecostalism: An Introduction*, Oxford: Oxford University Press, 2008.
64 John Karanja, 'Cultural Origins of the Anglican Church in Kenya', in William L. Sachs, ed., *The Oxford History of Anglicanism, Volume V: Global Anglicanism, c.1910–2000*, Oxford: Oxford University Press, 2018, pp. 171–95.
65 Sanneh, *Translating*, p. 31.
66 Frykenberg, 'Episcopal Establishment', p. 312.
67 Ivan M. Satyavrata, *God Has Not Left Himself without Witness*, Eugene, OR: Wipf and Stock, 2011, p. 123.
68 Satyavrata, *God*, p. 102.
69 Satyavrata, *God*, p. 110.
70 Satyavrata, *God*, pp. 91–125.

71 Cited by Satyavrata, *God*, p. 109.
72 Satyavrata, *God*, p. 112.
73 E. M. Wherry, *The Muslim Controversy: Being a Review of Christian Literature written in the Urdu Language for the Propagation of the Christian Religion and the Refutation of Islam*, London: Christian Literature Society, 1905, pp. 35, 43, 29.
74 Wherry, *Muslim*, pp. 15–66.
75 See Heaney, *Post-Colonial*, pp. 124–59.
76 Robert Edgar, 'New Religious Movements', in Norman Etherington, ed., *Missions and Empire*, Oxford: Oxford University Press, 2005, pp. 216–37.
77 Sanneh, *Translating*, p. 190.
78 O'Connor, *Clear Star*.
79 Cited in Frykenberg, 'Episcopal Establishment', p. 315.
80 Isichei, *History*, p. 10.
81 Hinga, *African, Christian, Feminist*, p. 68.
82 Ezigbo, 'Jesus', p. 57.
83 Ezigbo, 'Jesus', p. 57.
84 Cited in Heaney, *Historical*, p. 121.
85 See also Mercy Amba Oduyoye, 'Critique of John Mbiti's View on Love and Marriage in Africa', in Jacob K. Olopuna and Sulayman S. Nyang, eds, *Religious Plurality in Africa: Essays in Honour of John S. Mbiti*, Berlin and New York: Mouton de Gruyter, 1993, p. 355.
86 Ezigbo, 'Jesus', p. 57.
87 Heaney, *Historical*, p. 121.
88 Sanneh, *Translating*, p. 233.
89 Mbiti, *Bible and Theology in African Christianity*, Nairobi: Oxford University Press, 1986, p. 163.
90 Keith Kyle, *The Politics of the Independence of Kenya*, London: Macmillan, 1999, p. 27.
91 Bengt Sundkler and Christopher Steed, *A History of the Church in Africa*, Cambridge: Cambridge University Press, 2000, pp. 889–90.
92 See Carolin Elkins, *Britain's Gulag: The Brutal End of Empire in Kenya*, London: Pimlico, 2005; David Anderson, *Histories of the Hanged: Britain's Dirty War in Kenya and the End of Empire*, London: Phoenix, 2006 [2005]; Daniel Branch, 'The Enemy Within: Loyalists and the War Against Mau Mau in Kenya', *Journal of African History* 48 (2007), p. 292.
93 David Maxwell, 'Decolonization', in Norman Etherington, ed., *Missions and Empire*, Oxford: Oxford University Press, 2005, pp. 285–306 at 285–6, 290, 298–9.
94 Warren, *Caesar*, pp. 30–41.
95 Maxwell, 'Decolonization', p. 286.
96 Hanciles, *Beyond*, p. 375.

97 Bosch, *Transforming Mission*, pp. 329–34.
98 Frykenberg, 'Episcopal Establishment', pp. 21, 313.
99 Timothy C. Tennent, 'Building Christianity on Indian Foundations: The Theological Legacy of Brahmabāndhav Upādhyāy (1861–1907)', Thesis, University of Edinburgh, 1998, p. 369.
100 Tennent, 'Building', pp. 26–9, 371–88.
101 Cited by Tennent, 'Building', p. 380.
102 Tennent, 'Building', pp. 7–29, 380–8.

7

Distinctive and Faithful Practice

Contextualization has been defined and illustrated in terms of locally adaptive and faithful Christian practice. We have defined contextualization as hybridization, translation and resistance. The gospel was always received in conversation with cultural, religious and philosophical thought and practice. Hybridization was a particular, and often contentious, process of contextualization. It signalled the construction of a body of thought and witness distinct, yet in continuity, with pre-existent teaching and ritual and distinct, yet in continuity, with an imported faith. Hybridization, though unstable, often opened up fresh visions and articulations of the divine. Hybridization was witness. Translation brought the word of God in Jesus Christ to the hearts of believers and cultures in a myriad of places in history. Contextualization was hope. Resistance against acculturation honoured local theological practice and undercut paternalism. Contextualization was discernment.

What would it mean for Anglicans not only to see these practices as constitutive of mission history but as a resource for future promise? That is the purpose of this chapter as we define the promise of the Anglican Communion in terms of witness, hope and discernment. Each of these categories, already seen in the practice of Anglican mission, will be defined along with key implications for a Communion defined as the fellowship of communities of practice, liturgy and proclamation.

Witness in Communities of Practice

As we have already seen, a post-war critique of imperialism meant the modern witness of Anglicanism came under scrutiny especially by theologians from the so-called Global South. The broader modern missionary movement also came under scrutiny in an era of rising nationalisms and emerging nations. One broad response to this criticism, associated with the modern missionary movement and the ecumenical movement, was a shift to 'mission of God' (*missio Dei*) theology. Anglicans contributed to this shift and were influenced by this shift. Herein lay a theological turn that would influence generations of leaders and international consultations, resourcing an understanding of promise springing from the very being of God and God's own witness in history. In this section, we explain what *missio Dei* theology means and how it might further shape Anglican witness as a Communion made up of communities of practice.

The Shift to the Missio Dei

The international ecumenical understanding of mission emerged in post-war Germany. In 1952 the International Missionary Council, a continuation group of Edinburgh 1910, met in the town of Willengen and inspired a shift to *missio Dei* theology. Since that date, conciliar Protestants, and later other Christian traditions, increasingly embraced ways of thinking and speaking in terms of God's mission. It remained the summary term for post-colonial understandings of mission in the ecumenical movement into the twenty-first century. It was criticized as a term that was ambiguous and without a thoroughgoing theological explication.[1] There was merit in such criticism. However, in the absence of a dogmatic outworking, it has held together a broad range of Christians within and beyond the ecumenical movement. For Johannes Christiaan Hoekendijk, *missio Dei* theology was 'global and pluriform'. What was not needed, he argued, was a clamour for a 'precise, rather formal and one-track idea'.[2] The Willengen statement made a clear appeal to the Trinitarian nature of God as missionary thus displacing human agency from the centre of mission. For some, *missio Dei* language could be used to say something about the very nature of God. Christians understood the oneness of God in

Trinitarian terms where the eternal flow of love in God could be thought of as a 'sending' from Father to Son to Holy Spirit. God in God's nature is, therefore, a missionary God. There was a sense that, after Willengen, one could even say that God *is* mission.[3]

The major contribution of this renewed appeal to *missio Dei* language and thinking was an intentional and determined commitment to emphasize that God was the agent of God's own mission. The Church was not the agent of mission but was the fruit of God's work.[4] The Church did not exist to do mission but existed in God's mission. In the first instance, the Church did not take heed of or participate in mission to meet human needs or to ensure the Church's continuance or expansion. The Church owed its existence to God's mission and its ongoing existence to its participation in God's mission. The conference statement declared that mission had its source in the triune God in creation, in the mission of Christ to sinners and in the Spirit's mission of drawing believers to worship. Famously, Willengen declared, there 'is no participation in Christ without participation in His mission to the world. That by which the Church receives its existence is that by which it is also given its world-mission. "As the Father hath sent Me, even so I send you."'[5] When the Church failed to recognize this divine source, the Church entered into all kinds of alliances that led to the gospel being distorted. In such circumstances, often associated with imperial and colonial expansionism, the Church became not a witness to the grace of God but a counter-witness. This shift in theology had very real practical implications. A more critical approach to mission, along with this theological shift, fuelled a modern intercultural ecumenical movement and influenced Roman Catholic thinking about the nature of the Church during the second Vatican Council (1962–5).[6]

This shift to *missio Dei* theology resourced two distinct understandings of mission. Arising particularly in the 1960s, one perspective laid the emphasis on the larger mission of God at work in the world beyond followers of Christ and the Church. God was at work in all traditions, religions and cultures. For this reason, we can refer to this understanding of *missio Dei* theology as inculturationist. This view made the role of the Church problematic in relation to the missional agency of God. For the most radical thinkers, like Hoekendijk, the Church was but one means to point to God and humanize society. In such a view, proselytism could be seen as imperialist and the role of the Church could be seen as a hindrance to God's humanizing mission. Given a belief that God was at work in all places, and that the Church could hinder that work, great energy was put into schemes for education, political involvement and welfare. This line of thought led the World Council of Churches to set up the 'Special Fund to Combat Racism' in 1969. The fund soon became associated with anti-apartheid witness and work in South Africa. It was used, in part, to send financial support to 'secular' groups fighting against the violence of the apartheid state. The WCC's admission that white-dominated churches were implicated and thus impotent in the face of racism, along with its funding of 'illegal' organizations in South Africa, was too much for some and they left the organization.[7] But here was one clear practical outworking of a theology of the *missio Dei*.

In contrast, an approach that maintained a necessary place for the life and work of the institution of the church emerged. This view we can call an institutionalist approach to *missio Dei* theology. The Church is reconciled to God and becomes a reconciling presence in history. In its most conservative form, an institutionalist approach denied salvation outside of the Church. The movement of God's re-creation is to the Church and through the Church into the world. A normative understanding of mission meant, therefore, the establishment of the Church in a particular area. When that was done, the mission was complete and the work to safeguard and promote its integrity, presence and influence was a distinct type and phase of ministry.

In 1953 Bishop Lesslie Newbigin, a key author of the Willengen statement, warned against the extremes of either an inculturationist or institutionalist *missio Dei* theology. For him, both an 'unchurchly mission' and an 'unmissionary Church' were monstrosities.[8] The identity of the Church and the witness of the Church must be kept together. The Church is the new creation of God made visible in history and it is made present in history as it participates in God's witness to creation. Yet, while the Church is central, God remains sovereign always 'going ahead' of God's people. Thus, the work of ecumenism, intercultural theology and inter-religious cooperation speak to the importance of God's work of reconciliation in God's world among all people.

Five marks of mission have become important to Anglicans at least since the 1990s. The five marks set out the call of the Church to proclaim the gospel, form new believers, respond to human need, transform unjust structures and safeguard creation.[9] Arguably, despite the work of the broader ecumenical movement, this was an understanding of mission largely unaffected by *missio Dei* theology. Leading Anglicans and Anglican gatherings became conscious of this criticism. In 2004 the Church of England published its widely influential report, *Mission-Shaped Church (MSC)*, which reflected *missio Dei* language and drew from the priorities defined by the five marks of mission.[10] At the 2008 Lambeth Conference Bishop Michael Doe prepared a resource for the participants that defined an Anglican approach to mission as beginning with the nature and work of the Trinity. The theme of the conference was 'Equipping Bishops as Leaders in God's Mission', it had a 'decidedly missiological focus' and the official report concluded that it was successful in that the 700 bishops gathered drew closer together and 'therein is hope for the Anglican Communion and its faithfulness to the *missio Dei*'.[11] In 2012, Archbishop Rowan Williams spoke of mission as the work of God and a 'great current of divine transforming love'.[12]

A key impact of this broad acceptance of *missio Dei* theology had been a desire to do deeper contextual mission on the site of Anglicanism's initial emergence. The Church of England's *MSC* – lauded and lamented by scholars, leaders and church members – was one example of this. Inherent in the movement was, in our terms, the recognition that the 'Anglianism' that forestalled the promise of Anglicanism internationally had the very same impact nationally. The story had come full circle. 'Anglianism' had negative repercussions not just beyond England but within England. This 'Anglianism' rested on the institutional status of the Church within the state, exhibited an inwardly focused ministry of inherited structures and ministries, and was shaped by a predominately white leadership that implied or demanded assimilative practices of formation.[13] Against the rhetoric of a 'national' Church and the growth of the population in England, the attendance at Sunday services was well under one million. Prior to World War Two, nearly three-quarters of infants were baptized in the Church. By 2017, about 20 per cent of the population were baptized Anglicans. Statisticians assumed the Anglican share of the population would continue to decline and with falling numbers the questioning of the established nature of the Church would intensify.[14]

Within the Church of England there was no agreed upon analysis of the problem, no consensus in mission theology and no uncontested strategy for renewal. Alongside the tradition's inherited forms, new church-plants, 'fresh expressions', 'missional communities' and 'pioneer leadership training' attempted to bring to the fore a renewed commitment to contextualization. The institutional and inculturationist controversies in mission beyond Britain had come home. MSC did not have answers to the nature and call of church witness in modern Britain and may even have avoided key questions. However, the controversy and contestation it provoked around the issues of best practices of contextualization mirrored the history and the reality of the Communion. The modern situation for Anglicanism exhibited no international or intercultural settlement or consensus.

We argue that to search for consensus in, for example, a covenanting document or other confessional means in formal theological texts or in the strengthening of the existing Instruments of Communion is doomed to fail. Not only is it doomed to fail, it runs against the grain of a Communion that was created in intercultural mission practice and intercultural adaptations. We argue that the gift of Anglicanism centres on its adaptability or contextualization. Its promise is further seen in what we call inter-contextualization founded on a conviction that God is the agent of God's mission. What might the implications of this be for the Church of England and the Anglican Communion? We argue that a communion of witness is predicated upon a plurality and diversity of communities of witness. Rather than see institutional and inculturationist approaches as binary opposites, a focus on witness emerging from 'communities of practice' reconfigures the relationship.

Communities of Practice

Anglicanism pre-dates theorizing on communities of practice, but a central tenet of this field of study is the conviction that practice and belief positively relate one to the other.[15] Anglican practice, across distinct cultures and times, is about consistent and intentional action in ritual, testimony, learning and care that builds community in light of God's life-giving mission.[16] We take part in ritual or testimony because of faith commitments that Christ is present and transforms our lives. At the same time, in the actions of ritual and testimony our faith commitments are deepened and expanded. The concept of communities of practice is proffered in order to highlight and facilitate life-giving relationships through creative constellations of institutions, innovations and learning.

A community of practice is 'a group of people held together not primarily by structures or oversight but by common concern, common challenges, common commitment . . . who deepen their knowledge through continued interaction'.[17] What binds such a community together is not primarily formal or bureaucratic instruments but a collegiality of learning, formation and mission. The collegiality of the bishops is associated with the idea of a *collegium* of leaders sharing common goals or skills. *Collegium* becomes 'college' and with that an association of people brought together for education and formation.[18] At the very first Lambeth Conference, Archbishop Longley was clear that he was calling the bishops together for collegial fellowship and mutual learning. Arguably, the idea of communities of practice is in the Anglican DNA.

A community of practice is a group of people who have constructed a domain defined by a series of issues or concerns on the way to discerning a set of practices to transform their domain.[19] They do not need to meet face-to-face regularly but are held together by what they learn as they seek to transform shared concerns and issues.[20] Mission agencies, diocese-to-diocese partnerships, renewal movements, even networks within the Anglican Communion (centred on issues such as family, environment, gender justice, and youth) can be seen as communities of practice. Each community signifies and grounds fellowships of formation, learning or 'aliveness' around key issues and across cultural contexts. Recognizing the Communion in a communities-of-practice approach does not deny territorial configurations of Anglicanism in provinces. Such an approach to communion, however, is not determined by those territorial configurations. There would be a recognition of the already existing reality of trans-territorial Anglicanism and the inherent interculturality of shared domains. In truth, this trans-territorial and pluralist Anglicanism – existing amid porous boundaries between geographical, cultural, political and social locations – is not a theoretical construct. It describes an already existing reality. Anglicans exist in multiple domains and cross between multiple communities of practice. Even if an ongoing bureaucratic Communion sought to police such boundary crossings it would not be possible. A reconfigured and reconfiguring Communion exists de facto. The problem has been that centralized bodies and Instruments of Communion have largely been unable to conceive of a tradition that takes account of this. The same bodies have certainly been unable to articulate a future promise of Anglicanism amid competing and conflicted communities of practice. The powerful Global Anglican Future Conference (GAFCON) was a case in point.

The first GAFCON, meeting in Jerusalem in 2008, claimed to represent more than two-thirds of world Anglicanism.[21] At the time of the second conference in Kenya (2013), and in the wake of a recent terrorist attack in Nairobi, the new Archbishop of Canterbury, Justin Welby, preached at All Saints Cathedral.[22] According to some reports, this was not well received by all of the 1,300 participants and the 'Nairobi Communique' made plain that defence of their understanding of orthodoxy would trump any 'human authority'.[23] GAFCON returned to Jerusalem in 2018. With almost 2,000 participants, it declared itself the most representative and racially diverse gathering of Anglicans since the Toronto congress in 1963.

This was a significant movement with its own networks bringing people together not only around conservative sexual ethics but also around issues that included social development, church planning, women's ministry and theological education.[24] In a Communion defined by the convening of communities of practice the exclusion of groups like GAFCON would seem untenable. What 'inclusion' would mean for the Instruments of Communion and what process of inclusion would be needed is, of course, complex and controversial. Considering GAFCON an Anglican community of practice – we are assuming here legitimate ordinations – is a place to begin. This beginning recognizes GAFCON as a fellowship within the Anglican tradition brought together by a variety of common convictions and priorities. It recognizes that as a community of practice it is not of itself the Anglican Communion. For the Communion is not less than an aggregate of communities of practice.

We are not unrealistic. It is unlikely that all parts of the GAFCON movement would respond positively to an understanding of communion as a fellowship of communities of (mission) practice. Not all parts of GAFCON would react positively to a process of formal recognition by the Instruments. Equally, not all parts of the Anglican Communion would welcome such an open posture by the Instruments towards GAFCON. Nonetheless, communion as the fellowship of communities of practice does demand such a posture. This posture reconfigures understandings of relationships on the basis of a differentiated communion focused on mutuality of ministry priorities and ministries. We argue that given the extant partnerships that exist in the Communion across very different cultural and theological traditions such reconfiguration represents an already present reality. Communion as a fellowship of communities of practice better represents the grassroots and contextualized Anglicanism at work in the world. It represents the tradition in more comprehensive and practical ways than does the high-level disputations found both within GAFCON and the Communion.

The Anglican Communion would exist in this model as the gathering together of a plurality or differentiation of communities of practice. As a fellowship of such communities, gatherings would focus on the 'living process' of learning to create a repository for such knowledge. Such communion as the bringing together of communities of practice would, inevitably, be disputatious. Mature communities are not necessarily stable communities.[25] That there has always been contestation in Anglicanism and that there continues to be conflict is not necessarily a sign of dysfunction. This cannot be underlined enough especially against a wall of noise that would pronounce the Communion broken or breaking down. Further, a communion of practice (constituted by communities of practice) would lift the unnecessary and unrealistic expectation that the Instruments of Communion can construct and/or police identity.

A traditional mode of preventing institutional breakdown was to depend on bureaucratic means, which, in effect, was to lean on the institution more in a time when the institution was under threat. This cannot work. It will not work for the Anglican Communion. Centralized or top-down directives did not create the Communion and they will not necessarily prosper the Communion. Pronouncements or resolutions from the Archbishop of Canterbury, the Secretary General, the primates, the Lambeth Conference or the Anglican Consultative Council cannot, in practice, create cohesion or common vision. We argue that to lay this on any of these Instruments is to fail to learn the lessons of Anglican mission history and contextualizations of the gospel.

Rather than create cohesion, the primary role of the Instruments in this model is to convene communities of practice for the sake of renewed practices of witness. One lesson surely learned from the GAFCON movement was that more representative international and intercultural gatherings were needed. To what extent the Instruments are convening Instruments and are fit for the purpose of convening wider, more diverse and more representative gatherings, for the sake of formation in witness, we leave as an unanswered question. At the very least, a reconfigured Communion as the convention of communities of practice must aim even to outdo the version of diversity evident in a movement like GAFCON.[26]

An Anglican Communion that is the convening of communities of practice (defined, for example, according to common concerns, ministry focus, history, churchmanship or theology) is a distinct and fresh vision for the promise of Anglicanism. This is not a Communion centred on a confessional document nor structured according to top-down or centre-out authorities. As will be seen below, it is a Communion that nonetheless seeks to discern the will of God in the light of the risen Christ. It is a Communion where Instruments of Communion are not preoccupied by policing boundaries but bringing together sisters and brothers in ministry for hopeful discernment and mutual growth in the mission of God.

Communities of practice as constitutive of the Anglican Communion is one way to live into a theology that charts a middle way between institutionalist and inculturationist models. In our terms, Anglican communities of practice further define what we have called catholicity from below. This is not an image of communion that dichotomizes between institutionalist or inculturationist discernments of the *missio Dei*. We seek a different, imaginative and practicable sociality for Anglicans. Charles Taylor brings together this practicability and imagination in what he calls a 'social imaginary' that may well speak to the further promise of a reconfigured Communion:

> I speak of 'imaginary' (i) because I'm talking about the way ordinary people 'imagine' their social surroundings, and this is often not expressed in theoretical terms, it is carried in images, stories, legends, etc. But it is also the case that (ii) theory is often the possession of a small minority, whereas what is interesting in the social imaginary is that it is shared by large groups of people . . . (iii) the social imaginary is

that common understanding which makes possible common practices, and a widely shared sense of legitimacy.[27]

The Communion exists in the practice and imagination and hope of 'ordinary' believers all over the world. The Communion exists in this practice whether dispersed or convened.[28] For Anglicans, such social imaginary is fundamentally theological and centred on worship. That is to say, communities of practice are communities of liturgy from which springs hope even amid conflict.

Hope in Communities of Liturgy

Communion is not less than a convening of Anglican communities of practice. But it is more than this. Anglicans seek to be in communion. In the midst of cultural shifts, demographic changes, political instabilities, privilege and poverty people continue to submit to baptism. Believers continue to break bread together and to testify to the grace of God found in Christ. They continue to shape social practices and communities that make a difference in the neighbourhood and in the nations. In short, hope remains in the Anglican Communion.

Hope is not the work of human conniving or politicking. It is the work of God. It is the grace of God among us broken open in word and sacrament. It is fellowship based on the witness and work of Jesus Christ. It is, to use the biblical word for communion, *koinonia*. At a very basic level, communion is the Church assembled around the richness of the Word broken open and the generosity of the cup poured out in outward-turning anticipation of the return of her Lord. Communion is eucharistic, evangelical and eschatological.

Communion is Eucharistic

To emphasize contextualization, as we have been doing, is to say something about the particularities of the faith received in distinct social, linguistic, cultural and philosophical settings. At the same time, it is to recognize a general pattern inherent in the mission of the Church. The witness of the Church, throughout history, always involves translation, adaptation and demonstration of the gospel. At a further and 'higher' level, an emphasis on contextualization says something about God's own witness of God's self. The Christian faith is embodied. God comes to us in Christ. We are joined to Christ in material and tangible ways. We are submerged in waters of baptism. We take, bless, break, give, eat and drink.[29] In doing so, though we are many, reasons Paul, we become one because we all share in the one bread (1 Cor. 10.17). In this baptismal submission and eucharistic sharing we are constituted, in communion, as the Church of Christ.[30]

In baptism we are incorporated into Christ's body, which is the very promise of what is yet to come – communion in God's life in a perfected human community (Rom. 6.4; Rev. 21.3).[31] This is the work of the Holy Spirit. Baptism is that fundamental sign which says we neither choose nor construct the Church. Rowan Williams puts it more positively: 'what unites us with other human beings is not common culture or negotiated terms of co-operation ... but ... the regard of God upon us'.[32] We are 'caught up in solidarities we have not chosen'.[33] In such solidarity – wrought not by ourselves but by the work of God – social, cultural and racial barriers are unveiled by God as human constructs. The breaking in of God's reconciliation means the breaking down of these constructed barriers.

> As many of you as were baptized into Christ have clothed yourselves with Christ. There is no longer Jew or Greek, there is no longer slave or free, there is no longer male and female; for all are one in Christ Jesus. (Gal. 3. 27–28)

For Paul, communion at the table of the Lord is seen in the cup of blessing as *koinonia* in the blood of Christ and *koinonia* in the body of Christ (1 Cor. 10.16).[34] Communion is liturgical community and communion is embodied in eucharistic sharing. We are in communion when we come together to break the bread given to us by the Lord who, in the Spirit, is always and only the host. The Church is the Church at the table of the Lord.

At the heart of the Anglican Communion are people who have wagered their lives on the hope of resurrection and the return of the risen Christ. A hopeful heart remains. There is commitment that God has broken into history and God will bring all things to a just end. There is hope, in other words, that the end (*eschaton*) of the story defines the beginning and the middle of the story. Such hope Christians call *eschatological*. There is eschatological significance at work when followers of Jesus gather around the table of the Lord. The end breaks in and the future is poured out before our very eyes. The end is enacted in the present. The local assembly is joined with the heavenly assembly in a unity of heaven and earth and in a unity of the now and the not yet. This unity is the risen Jesus Christ ascendant and present to his Church. The assembly is transformed in public as God's grace comes to us in hands empty of any claim to self-satisfaction or self-justification. At the Lord's table we 'receive one another with Christ and Christ with one another; we at once receive Christ and the Church in which we receive him'.[35] That is to say, we do not birth communion by agreement, affinity or agenda. It is all gift. It is all God's grace. It is the mission of God.

This emphasis on the grace of God is central to the gospel and is often associated with a shift of theological language and priority associated both with liturgical renewal and missional renewal. The mission belongs to God coming to the world in the Son and, in the power of the Spirit, drawing people to a renewed and renewing community that, in turn, seeks to be water, and bread, and wine for a parched and hungry world.[36] We recognize, of course, that we often fail to enact the vision of unity and grace that has been opened to us in the paschal mystery. Williams reminds us that gathering at the altar puts us at the table of the risen Christ, but it also puts us in the place of the unfaithful disciples (Luke 22.14–34).[37] The liturgy anticipates such unfaithfulness and failure and within a rhythm of gathering and being sent and of receiving God's word and responding to it – there too is penitence for our failings. Communion as liturgical assembly evokes humility and it evokes witness in penitential mode.[38]

As the disciples in Emmaus were brought to the table by Jesus this same table fed them for the road (Luke 24.13–35). The table of the Lord always leads to the way of the Lord. There is taking, blessing, breaking, receiving and going. The Church, assembled around the Lord's table, centres itself on the promises of the Lord's presence. It centres itself on the rejected stranger and the disappeared foreigner (Luke 24.18). Thus, the rejected and the disappeared become present to the assembly in the reconciling life and presence of the risen Christ.

We take, bless, break, receive, go. We go determined that this feast will not fall into farce. We go in hope that Word and sacrament has changed us. We rise from the table and go onto the road as if our going was a sharing of bread and a pouring out of wine for the life of the community, the neighbourhood and the nations. The communion that is experienced as eucharistic is good news for the world. It is evangelical. Jesus said to them: 'You are witnesses of these things. Repentance for forgiveness of sins is to be proclaimed beginning from Jerusalem.' (Luke 24.47–48)

Communion is Evangelical

The gospel is summarized in that Easter proclamation: Alleluia! Christ is risen. He is risen indeed! We are saved by the grace of God found in Christ (Eph. 2.4–10). Our witness then is not to the healing we can bring to the world but to the healing we have found in the gospel. We are reconciled to God in Christ and, in the power of the Spirit, God creates a new and renewing communion. This is not idealism. While only seen and experienced in part, it is a deep spiritual reality (1 Cor. 13.9–10). God has spoken. God's word brings forth creation (Gen. 1.3–26). God's word calls forth a people as witness of God's grace (Gen. 12.1–2). In the face of sin, God's word comes through the lives and witness of the prophets. In these last days, God's word comes to the world incarnate in the life and testimony of Jesus Christ (Heb. 1.1–2; John 1.14).

Communion is good news. It is evangelical. It is the proclamation of the God revealed in Christ and it is the promise of God acting in Christ to reconcile the world to God's self. For some scholars, this evangelical understanding of communion is not simply good news of God's grace to an erring humanity. Communion is the very nature of God. We can say then that the very revelation of God, the word of God and the table of the Lord call us to communion. They call us to proclaim this communion to God's world. The Word and the table of the Lord lead to the way of the Lord. They lead to the road. They shape a people of witness and call a people to witness. It is the proclamation of the gospel which brings koinonia with the Father in the Son and, thus, *koinonia* with sisters and brothers (1 John 1.1–3). Because of God's grace, it is by faith that we enter into the *koinonia* of baptism (Phil. 3.10–11).[39]

The witness of communion and this call to communion exist amid the vicissitudes of world affairs and the pluralisms of competing ideologies. By 2015 the number of adherents to Christian faith had grown to more than 30 per cent of the world population and continued to grow in ever more diverse and fragmented ways.[40] The promise of Anglicanism has been that it can hold together a diverse expression of the faith. Anglo-Catholics, charismatics, liberals, evangelicals, progressives, conservatives and those who seek to transcend labels and labelling all rightly claim the pluralist and contextualist heritage of Anglicanism. Yet each strand is always called to testify how their contextualizations are explications of the gospel of Christ.

As the second decade of the twenty-first century came to a close, it was not clear if a movement like GAFCON would be any more successful at holding a disparate and diverse group together than the more long-standing Instruments of Communion. There were already examples of strain within the fellowship, particularly over the ordination of women and questions around authority and jurisdiction.[41] It was unclear where successive generations of adherents, especially in countries with liberal social attitudes and policies like the United States of America, would stand on divisive issues so important at its genesis like the nature of same-sex relationships. Would a founding declaration like GAFCON's 'Jerusalem Statement' (2008), elevating heterosexual marriage to doctrinal status, suffice for future generations?[42] We fear it will not suffice and that fracturing within the movement is inevitable.

An evangelical communion cannot eschew proclamation. Too often, however, proclamation is seen as the polar opposite of dialogue. This is not the case and it cannot be the case within the Anglican Communion. A renewed understanding of witness to one another and to the world is needed, and the idea and practice of prophetic dialogue is one means towards the renewal of Anglican promise. Prophetic dialogue arises from the field of mission studies (missiology) with a particular focus on witness amid religious pluralism. We take it here to have implications not only for inter-religious witness but also for intra-religious witness.

Prophetic dialogue is an idea and practice that can nourish Anglican fellowship and promise. Defining the term, Stephen Bevans and Roger Schroeder note that it came to prominence at a meeting of the missionary congregation of the Society of the Divine Word (SVD) in 2000. The term arose in intercultural contestation across deeply contextualized perspectives. On the one hand, Asian members of the SVD sought to define witness as 'dialogue'. On the other hand, Latin American members wanted the emphasis placed on the 'prophetic'. Consensus emerged when the congregation hit upon the term, 'prophetic dialogue'.[43] For Bevans and Schroeder this meant an emphasis on evangelical proclamation of God's saving power in Christ modelled according to God's own patient, respectful, dialogic mission.[44]

God's fullest revelation of God's self comes to us not in the shape of a treatise but in the flesh, words and ministry of Jesus of Nazareth. God enters into the context and contestation of human history. God calls us to conversion in conversation. There is dialogue at the heart of God's mission in Christ. God

DISTINCTIVE AND FAITHFUL PRACTICE

comes to us in the life of a young Jewish man, comes to us in the particularity of geography, culture and language. God's revelation in Jesus speaks with the accent of a northerner from Galilee. God crosses the expanse of glory in dialogue. God's testimony of God's self as love is embodied in ways that we can see, hear and touch.

Scripture paints for us a rich vision of divine dialogue. The Nazarene conversed and questioned in the Temple and synagogue (Luke 2.41–52; 4.16–31), healed a centurion's servant (Luke 7.1–10), taught amid the scene caused by a woman anointing his feet (Luke 7.36–50). He constantly told parables, confronted Legion (Luke 8.26–39), argued with the Pharisees and Sadducees (Luke 11.37–54; 20.27–47) and testified in words and silence during his trial (Luke 22.66–23.12). Even on the cross, Luke tells us, Jesus reached out in words of forgiveness to fellow convicts and to his persecutors (Luke 23. 26–47). Each one of these dialogic moments was about testimony across difference. The differences were about who was considered learned or unlearned, who was an insider and who an outsider, what was clean and unclean, who had power and who was powerless, what was orthodoxy and what was blasphemy. Such dialogue in no way dilutes the divine nature of Christ. It is the very form of God's prophetic word to humanity.

The testimony of God in the gospel of Christ is dialogue and it is prophetic. It is a testimony grounded and wrought in local idiom, careful listening and truth telling. As God comes to us in prophetic dialogue, the Church is called to go to the world in the same spirit. We are called to testify to one another in the same spirit. How such prophetic dialogue might be embodied and honoured and open up new visions for the working of the modern Anglican Communion will be submitted in the final section of this chapter as we consider the nature of collegiality within Anglicanism. Suffice it to say, the prophetic dialogue inscribed in Scripture and embodied in the witness of the Church testifies both to the revelation of God in Christ and the continuing call of the Church to explain and live that Word in distinct settings. It is testimony to the truth of Christ and the ongoing work of God's mission. But neither the dimness of our vision nor the incompleteness of our experience can diminish the truth and promise of God's reconciling mission. The very definition of communion as liturgical and evangelical assembly points to the promise of fulfilled communion with God at the last (Rev. 21. 1–4) and admits to the unfinished purposes of God in the Church.

Communion is Eschatological

We have already met the word 'eschatological' in the context of the Eucharist. It also relates to the ongoing and unfinished project of the Church. In the words of Scott MacDougall, the promise of communion is 'anticipatable but not totally realizable' in the present.[45] There is promise and provisionality in the witness and structures of Anglicanism. Kathryn Tanner recognizes that the Spirit of God is at work in the historical processes of the Church's contextualizations and contestations. This is the heart of Anglican promise and our understanding of the centrality of contextualization. God is at work in the Communion.

This appeal to the work of the Spirit, in light of the eschatological hope, does not mean that these contextualizations and the witness of Anglicans have some sort of 'indefeasible certainty or uncontestable veracity'. Rather, something 'about the human is changed through the working of the Spirit, but it is not the fully finite character of our acts'.[46] In short, there is the need for ongoing reformation in the life of the Church and Communion. The hope of such reformation cannot be realized if we cut ourselves off from one another on fantasy islands of supposed doctrinal purity. In the proclamation of a risen Saviour there is also the waiting for his return and a searching after his fuller will for the Church.

This eschatological dimension to an Anglican understanding of faithful witness and practice forms in us a 'bold humility'.[47] We are bold to testify to one another and to the world. The eschatological also means that we do not see the full picture. The Church seeks to align itself with the healing will of God, but it does so incompletely and partially. There is confidence, but there is also humility. There is innovation, but there is always the need for interdependence across time and place. The Church, as we have already seen, has aligned itself with particular wicked powers and programmes that now have been abandoned. The witness of the Church in the world and to the world is bold, and it is unfinished. But it is also and always penitential.[48] Anglicans need to recover a form of testimony that is marked by deep listening. But more than rich and intentional listening is needed – humility and penitence must also become its witness.

In foundational and formative documents of Christianity, the Church is considered 'holy'. Particularly strong or high views of the Church stress its superiority above human societies. It is perfect and sinless.[49] Historical catastrophes, including racist nationalisms, anti-Semitism, genocide and war have demanded that Christian theologians re-examine such an elevated view of the Church. A pilgrim Church is pictured in the Vatican II document *Lumen Gentium*. It journeys towards God's promised end of 'full perfection'.[50] In the meantime, it is open to God's spirit revealing its complicities in sin. Its holiness is not its own achievement. Its sacred nature is not won by its own work. It is the gift of God. What makes the Church holy is God's presence in her midst continually reconciling her to God's self. Its holiness is found in its continual turning towards the grace of God amid the histories of her life-giving testimony and death-dealing deeds. The renewing gift of holiness from God is part of the story of the Church and demands a process of discernment where, across differences, the Church is always open to correction and reformation. Such a call to discernment is inherent in a church birthed by God's inbreaking kingdom in the hope of God's kingdom fully breaking in.

Not everyone in the Communion will enter into discernment in the same way. The empowered will need to listen more. In Communion structures, the empowered certainly are those who have constructed and benefitted from white theology. In centres of formation, especially in the so-called Global North, there is continued need to take seriously the theological vision and voice beyond white theology. White Christians need to sit in the seat of discomfort, listening and listening again to the work and witness of theologians beyond the West. This also requires a recognition that power relations are not static. In the past, 'Anglicanism' served England's understanding of God's purpose in history. Centres of power understood, for example, in terms of setting agenda and/or in controlling financial resources remain important in determining those with power in the Communion. Such power differentials, however, are complex and range over a variety of human relationships and institutions. These differentials can change throughout history: the victors can become the vanquished. They can change according to context: the membership of a meeting or the rules of a meeting can be reconstituted to ensure that a minority becomes a majority. They can change within a given context: a variety of groups can be more intimate with centres of power or more remote from centres of power. This is the case even in countries that vaunt their ideologies of equality while perpetuating systems of representation that actually disadvantage some groups more than others.

We have already seen these complex power relations at work in the history of Anglicanism. Sometimes conservative bishops are marginal in the decisions made in the work of the Communion. Sometimes they are central. Sometimes progressives can visit their will on others. Sometimes they seem powerless to effect change. As will be seen below, better processes of consensus-building can be envisioned that will institutionalize in Communion gatherings a deeper practice of listening and discernment across power differentials. Tanner is correct. The Spirit that raised Christ from the dead and interrupted human history with God's future is the same Spirit at work in the Church. The eschatological nature of communion is not 'pie in the sky' escapism. It is an invitation to the all too human, and at times painful and disheartening, process of discernment wherein 'even in our ignorance of it, God's Spirit is making its way in and through' us.[51] What model of discernment, then, will serve the promise of Anglicanism in light of so great an eschatological hope?

Discernment in Communities of Proclamation

The Anglican Communion is the witness and convening of communities of practice. The Anglican Communion is the witness and convening of liturgical assemblies gathered around the ministry of the bishops. As the Church of Christ, between the ages, the Communion is part of the unfinished work of God in the world. Communities of practice nourished at the Lord's table and sent out into the world know well that their pilgrimage in the mission of God is incomplete. We await the coming of Christ all the while seeking to discern his will and proclaim his gospel. But, how is this discernment to be done faithfully? For the Anglican Communion, two forms of discernment can be identified. In this section, we will examine collegiality and conciliarity as forms of discernment and then, against current trends, call not for more robust forms of authority in the Communion but call for a deeper practice of consensus-building.

Conciliar Discernment

The Church as liturgical assembly gathers around the bishop. Of course, this is normally not the case *in fact*, but it is how the Church is understood *in principle*. A diocese is gathered around a presiding bishop who in himself or herself gathers together the identity of the Church as a baptized person, as a deacon and as a priest. This localized gathering, in liturgical setting, is also an embodied sign of apostolicity. That is to say, the Church gathers in order that it might be sustained for its sending mission. For sending is what apostolicity means. The Church, however, while not being less than local (contextual) is also universal (inter-contextual). One expression of that catholicity is seen when the bishops meet together.

In conference, the bishops embody the locality and locatedness of the Church to one another and in doing so represent to one another, and the world, the catholicity of the Church.[52] In Anglicanism, since 1867, the expression of this catholicity is made manifest in the Lambeth Conference. We have already outlined how this conference came about and how it continued to be a site where representatives of local expressions of Anglicanism could meet but also could be in conflict. In recent years there has been a move to interpret the Lambeth Conference retroactively as a 'council' and, thus, construct a form of 'conciliarism' that would give to such gatherings more authority in the workings of modern Anglicanism. We argue that such a move may have some theoretical coherency but that only a weak sense of conciliarity ever functioned in Anglican history and a more robust form cannot function in the contemporary world.

For Paul Avis, the central conviction of the tradition of conciliarism is the tenet that 'responsibility for the well-being (the doctrine, worship, and mission) of the Church rests with the whole Church' and it is his conviction that a robust form of conciliarity will usher in new Anglican promise. Conciliarity meant an emphasis on representation, consent, constitutional authority and the common good.[53] On the one hand, Henry VIII threatened conciliarism on the Pope but chose instead to directly curtail the power of the Holy Father. Article XXI of the Church of England's historical theological framework recognizes that councils depend on the blessing of princes, that they are fallible and that Scripture remains the authority.

On the one hand, Archbishop Thomas Cranmer remained emotionally attached to the ideal of a General Council. Hooker saw General Councils to be a counterweight to papal sovereignty. On the other hand, Archbishop Nicholas Ridley opposed the idea of a universal council because it was not commanded by Christ nor found in Scripture.[54] The Church of Henry and Elizabeth did not run on conciliar lines but by 'autocratic methods of monarchical Erastianism'.[55] The English Reformers further compromised appeals to a thoroughgoing conciliarism in that they rejected the Council of Constance (1414–18), which was widely adjudged to be the most impressive council of the late Middle Ages. Given its anti-Catholic tone, the Reformers much preferred the Council of Basel (1431–49), which was marred by controversy and descended into farce.[56]

Paul Valliere defines conciliarism in plain terms as 'decision-making by means of councils'.[57] Councils were one of the 'signature institutions' of the Christian tradition. However, the early modern period between the seventeenth and nineteenth centuries saw a loss of conciliarism.[58] It was not until the twentieth century in post-imperial Russian Orthodoxy, in post-World War One WCC Protestant ecumenism and in Vatican II Roman Catholicism that conciliarism was revived. What was at work in the WCC was a soft conciliarism. It did not represent an instrument of church government, though it did emphasize the collaborative and dialogic nature of councils.[59]

As we have already seen, when Archbishop Longley called the first Lambeth Conference, he was adamant that the conference was neither a synod nor a council. Valliere depicts the first Lambeth Conference as a 'monument to Anglican ambivalence about conciliarism'.[60] Since Longley's injunction, the collegial nature of the Lambeth Conference has remained. It has been a convening of bishops under the presidency of Canterbury to confer, to pray, to worship, to study Scripture and to be formed in deeper ways for the call of Christian witness. Despite this, some high churchmen wanted to argue for a conciliar Anglicanism, and that is precisely what Richard Watson Dixon (1833–1900), Mandell Creighton (1844–1901) and Neville Figgis CR (1866–1919) did.[61]

Over against Colenso, depicted as an 'anti-conciliar bishop', some sort of process to save the Communion from the 'chaotic pluralization of the Anglican tradition' was sought.[62] On this view, the 1867 conference is seen as defending the 'historical doctrines' and practices of the Church and thus it 'can be seen as a conciliar event in a non-juridical mode'.[63] For Valliere, Anglican conciliarism is needed because of doctrinal and disciplinary controversies within the Communion.[64] He is clear that 'the laws of ecclesiastical polity that Anglicanism needs today are laws of conciliar polity'.[65] Twentieth-century Anglicans, argued Avis, moved in this direction.

Anglicans were not only key to the modern missionary movement, they were also leaders in an emerging ecumenical movement. Leaders including Bishop, later Archbishop, William Temple

(1881–1944), Bishop George Bell (1883–1958) and Bishop Oliver Tomkins (1908–92) contributed to the emergence of the WCC and its form of conciliarity in the twentieth century.[66] Lambeth 1948 repudiated all ideas of 'central authority for the whole Church', affirming rather the 'General Councils of Bishops'. Lambeth 1968 affirmed the centrality of episcopal collegiality but set this within the apparent conciliar character of the Church and particularly the discernment of the faithful (*sensus fidelium*). The 1978 conference underscored the importance of prayerful discernment. In 1988 the 'gradual and dynamic process' of reception over time was recognized as the Church responded to decisions made by synods and councils. For Avis, Anglicans had an 'affinity' with the conciliar tradition.[67]

Building on this apparent nineteenth- and twentieth-century legacy towards conciliarism, the Inter-Anglican Standing Commission on Unity, Faith and Order (IASCUFO) produced *Towards a Symphony of Instruments* (2018) as an attempt to make more explicit what Anglicans believed about the nature of an international and intercultural Church. More specifically, the document sought to provide a clearer rationale for the existence and purpose of the Instruments of Communion (the Archbishop of Canterbury, the Lambeth Conference, the Primates' Meeting and the Anglican Consultative Council) with the intention of giving them more authority than had been previously the case. This move is clear in key sections of the text.

Admitting to Longley's original vision for the conference, *Towards a Symphony* assures readers that this did not mean it was simply a 'talking shop'.[68] Of course, in making such a denial the rhetorical effect was to imply precisely this possibility. To make such an intimation in light of the oft-reported collegiality found in intercultural fellowship at Lambeth Conferences is, at the very least, a dramatically reductionist insinuation. That the implication could be made that bishops from around the Communion meeting together – in liturgical and eucharistic assembly seeking to be further equipped for witness – was insignificant demeans the fellowship the document seeks to strengthen.

DISTINCTIVE AND FAITHFUL PRACTICE

The rhetorical force of the implication is to move opinion towards a practice of conciliarism for the Communion. *Towards a Symphony*, however, remained quite cautious on the possibility of a deepening conciliarity. Not so Avis.

Avis depicts the Lambeth Conference along with the more recent innovations of the Anglican Consultative Council (1971) and the Primates' Meeting (1979) as 'conciliar institutions' because they have universal structures of consultation. The Lambeth Conference exhibits a 'conciliar principle' in that it is honoured as having moral authority for all Anglicans and that its resolutions are offered to the provinces for adoption. In practice, however, Anglicans have become increasingly aware of an 'authority deficit'. Moral authority, it appears, is no longer effective and some path between provincial autonomy and universal jurisdiction needs to be found.[69]

Avis, citing the work of Norman Doe, discerns an imbalance in Anglican polity. Juridical order resides in the provinces with only moral order residing at Communion level. Given that Anglicanism emerged from missionary engagement it is no surprise that a 'voluntaristic, persuasive ecclesiology . . . pertains to the Communion'. In contrast, a 'binding, canonical ecclesiology' pertains in the provinces. Avis adjudges that what is needed is a closer integration of the moral and juridical orders.[70] A step towards such integration was taken in 2002. At a meeting in Canterbury, the primates identified an 'unwritten law' or a set of 'principles' that arose out of studied commonalities across provincial canon law. Such principles are suggestive of an Anglican common law (*ius commune*). The primates went as far as to wonder if this was not a fifth instrument of unity.[71] Stretching the term beyond its normal sense, Doe considers this expert study of international canonical law, and the principles it suggests, a 'grassroots' movement that will resource closer 'global ecclesial communion'.[72]

Avis, while reading Doe, goes beyond him when claiming that a 'fundamental Anglican canon law already exists, albeit in a latent form'. Avis wants a move beyond latency to a codified 'core canon law' for the Communion that would have to be incorporated into the legal system of each province.[73] This is an unexpected application of conciliarism. We argue that such moves will not usher in a deeper sense of Anglican promise. This legalistic approach will not win the day. It is impracticable not least because each province would have to consent to the process and any body of law that might emerge.

Collegial Consensus as Discernment

In this section, we argue that deeper practices of discerning consensus and consensus-building are vital to the renewal of Anglican promise. Rather than imagine or reimagine gatherings such as the Lambeth Conference, the Anglican Consultative Council (ACC)[74] or the Primates' Meeting as 'quasi-conciliarity', we see them as what they have always been – collegial gatherings. Unlike others who might want to make explicit the conciliar nature of Anglicanism, or simply assert the conciliar nature of the Lambeth Conferences, Valliere adopts a forward-looking posture.

Valliere simply concludes that conciliarism 'belongs to the future of Anglicanism, not to its past. It is an aspiration, a call to leave the cozy nest of provincialism and grow up as a communion.'[75] Consequently, Valliere does not read conciliarism into the past of Anglicanism but exhorts Anglicans to create councils. It is not clear to us that seeking to create, for the first time, a series of international Anglican councils, is any more practicable than the legalistic approach to Anglican promise of the previous section. We argue first for a deeper sense of the *collegium*. For there only exists an 'authority deficit' if a more centralized or legalistic understanding of Anglicanism is presumed. Seeing, as we do, the past promise of Anglicanism in its adaptability and contextualization, we are not now going to identify these very same processes as stumbling blocks to further promise. In short, Anglicanism does not suffer from an authority deficit. It suffers from a consensual deficit. In the major gatherings of world Anglicanism, the answer is not for

Instruments to accrue more power but to enter deeper into discernment amid difference.

We do not necessarily envisage new structures and we certainly do not envisage increased powers for present structures. Leaving aside whether or not Anglicans want to call a future and more broadly representative convention, what is needed for the *collegia* – gathered especially in the representative gatherings of the Lambeth Conference and the ACC – is a process that represents their discernment and deliberations better than has been achieved so far in Anglican history. For if the Communion is to be more demonstrably a fellowship of proclamation amid conflict, then a renewed process of discernment is needed. This we argue is the latency already at work in Anglicanism between complete freewheeling provincial autonomy and images of enhanced authority for the Instruments.

The very WCC that key Anglican leaders helped to found currently operates a system of consensual decision-making that the Communion would do well to heed. Janice Love notes that for many the council's parliamentary style was but one contextualization of decision-making and not the dominant way of decision-making in the cultures that make up the WCC. This may well be the situation at Lambeth Conferences. Many, she observed, 'have lamented the way this style forces participants into adversarial yes or no stances' when such stances do not represent the mind or spirit of the convention accurately and thus, hamstring the witness of the gathering.[76] Because of the reality of impaired communion and because of deeply held differences along with a commitment to communion, the WCC has adopted a consensus decision-making process for its gatherings.

There are different models of consensus-building, but there are common traits.[77] In broad terms, consensus decision-making displaces so-called 'parliamentary style' decision-making. Instead of casting 'yes' or 'no' votes, participants indicate, by use of an orange card, if they 'warmed' to a particular idea or, by raising a blue card, signalling that they were feeling doubtful, uncertain or resistant to an idea or argument.[78] At least five outcomes are possible in a consensus-building model:

- A consensus is reached if all participants are in agreement (unanimity).
- A consensus is reached if most agree and those who are in disagreement recognize that all positions have been fully heard and that the proposal represents 'the mind of the meeting'. If this is the case, the minority give their consent and consensus is reached.
- The meeting recognizes there are a range of opinions on the subject at hand. These various views are incorporated into the proposal (and not just recorded in the minutes).
- It is agreed that the matter is postponed.
- The meeting agrees that no decision can be reached.[79]

Such consensual decision-making allows for constituent bodies to hold conflicting views within a commitment to communion. It allows for diversity and disagreement to be held in communion without endangering that Communion. Unlike more legalistic approaches, no presumptions about the loyalty of one province are made in this embodiment of communion. Will this likely result in fewer Lambeth resolutions and a more deliberate and slower pace for Communion conventions? Yes. But the pronouncements or resolutions that are made come from a renewed practice of deeper listening and are genuinely more representative of the mind and will of the Communion.

Proposals for more robust (legalistic) processes of conciliarity have gained momentum in recent years because of conflict in the Communion. The threat to the Communion is particularly related to debates on human sexuality and the emergence of what increasingly look like parallel structures designed to deepen fellowship among socially conservative Anglicans. What promise might discernment as consensus bring to these current difficulties? Consensus decision-making is the practical and practicable middle way that the Communion has been searching for at the level of legalistic or philosophical abstraction.

Consensus as discernment will inevitably mean fewer pronouncements and resolutions. However, the decisions and statements would represent the mind of the Communion.

Subsequent to the gathering these resolutions would be sent to the provinces to be received or ratified. 'Received' would mean that a province recognizes this is the voice of the tradition at this time. 'Received for ratification' would mean a particular resolution or priority would be adopted, through proper canonical processes, and be integrated into the priorities and governance of that province. Given that Lambeth Conferences meet every ten years, provinces would likely be in a position to report back to the conference on the processes of reception (or dissent) in their setting, thus providing a means of relating the 'moral order' of the Communion with the 'juridical order' of the provinces. Moral authority and juridical authority, thus, relate in consensual ways without the latter creeping into the former in ways that were not envisaged for the gatherings of world Anglicanism.

If this consensual deficit is identified broadly within the Communion and discernment as consensus-building is adopted, what further practical implications might this have for the promise of Anglicanism? To begin to answer that, we return to the polarizations within twenty-first-century Anglicanism. Suffice it to say that, along with consensual deficits in this period, there were relational deficits also. No appeal to law can heal such ailment. A process of consensus is a commitment to discern the will of God in conference. When consensus is reached in unanimity, witness means testifying to a common mind. When consensus is reached without unanimity then there is also space for lament and even dissent. Where there is failure of consensus then the testimony of the Communion is its brokenness, its failure to reach consensus, or its witness is its silence as it waits on God. A province, in the wake of a Communion convention, such as the Lambeth Conference, may receive but not ratify the mind of the conference. That province would then, according to its juridical rights and responsibilities, be a dissenting province unrepresentative of Anglican thought in that regard. In a consensus model, this would not mean that this province was in impaired communion or under threat of banishment. This dissent would not be seen as political dysfunction. It would, in a very practical manner, point to the eschatological reality that we live in an age between the ascension of our Lord and the return of our Lord. The Church remains God's unfinished work.

In the controversies of the twenty-first century, then, the Episcopal Church in America could (in conference) at one and the same time recognize the present mind of the Communion on matters of sexual ethics while dissenting from that view (option ii above). No great legal powers would need to accrue to Canterbury, Lambeth, the primates, or the ACC to juridically pronounce that the Episcopal Church did not represent the mind of the Communion on matters of human sexuality. The Episcopal Church, as a full and functioning member of the Communion, would dutifully confirm the common mind in conference and, with gladness, itself dissent from the common mind in this matter in her own context and mission. By virtue of consensus in conference, and by virtue of her discernment, the Episcopal Church would not represent the Anglican Communion position on this matter. To what extent this vision of a consensus-building Communion is 'conciliar', or could represent conciliarity 'as far and wide' as is possible, is not our concern, nor is it a concern we feel should be prioritized.[80] A collegial Communion has been the model and a consensus-building model of Communion seems to both stand in continuity with that ethos and provide a practicable process to deepen that ethos. But how far and how wide might Anglicans be prepared to take this collegiality?

As we have already suggested, GAFCON cannot be ignored. Indeed, through proper consensual decision-making processes, GAFCON could be officially invited to (re)join the Communion. If they wished to join, then a number of options could be considered. They could be received as a renewal movement and a religious order within the Communion. They could be received and 'mapped on' to the Communion in ways not dissimilar to the multidimensional oversight at work in the Church of Aotearoa/New Zealand or by an arrangement not dissimilar to the Convocation of Episcopal Churches in Europe that exists alongside the Church of England's Diocese in Europe. It may well be that such an invitation – followed inevitably by negotiations with Anglican primates, the ACC and the Archbishop of Canterbury – could be rebuffed. Be that as it may, a collegial and consensus-building Communion would have the ongoing capacity to welcome these dissenting voices to the *collegia*. If the invitation were continually rebuffed, then GAFCON would be confirming its identity and ethos not as a renewal movement within a consensus-building Anglicanism but as a dissenting tradition beyond it.

Amid the crises of the twentieth and twenty-first centuries, many believers held on to the conviction that the Anglican Communion was a gift. It remained a fellowship of Christian practice, Christian liturgy and discernment oriented to the *missio Dei*. Yet, ministries of contextualization, resourced across cultural and theological contexts, are ever in need of renewal in the light of the God who will make all things new. In that hope and expectation, Anglicans, in solidarity with all Christians, await the consummation of God's ongoing but as yet unfinished work. In this time between the ages, Christians are called to enter into deep discernment for the sake of faithful witness and practice. Anglicans, in particular, have wrestled with how faithful discernment for the sake of faithful practice might be undertaken. We argue that Anglicans have at least three options when it comes to visions of practice that firmly ground Anglican promise.

First, Anglican histories can be read in search of greater authority, though latent and implied, for the long-standing and latter-day Instruments of Communion. Second, the Communion can succumb to centralizing impulses and create new bodies with more juridical authority. For example, a pan-Anglican synod, a universal canon law or a centralized worldwide tribunal could be imagined. We reject such moves because they stand in tension with the mission history of the Anglican Communion in its contextual diversity, because they intermingle moral and juridical order in corrosive ways, and because they are impracticable. A third option becomes necessary. Practicable processes of consensus decision-making at the Communion level are urgent. Communion expressed in consensus-building will more sharply define processes of reception and dissent without unchurching any part of the Anglican family. It is this third option that this chapter has sought to elucidate. For it is a practical form of promise more consistent with the history and nature of an intercultural and international Anglicanism.

Notes

1 See John Flett, *The Witness of God: The Trinity, Missio Dei, Karl Barth, and the Nature of Christian Community*, Grand Rapids, MI: Eerdmans, 2010.

2 Johannes Christiaan Hoekendijk, 'Mission – A Celebration of Freedom', *Union Seminary Quarterly* 21:1 (1966), p. 139.

3 For a critical appraisal, see Flett, *The Witness of God*, pp. 35–77.

4 David J. Bosch, *Transforming Mission: Paradigm Shifts in Theology of Mission*, Maryknoll, NY: Orbis, 1998 [1991], p. 390.

5 Norman Goodall, ed., *Missions Under the Cross: Addresses Delivered at the Enlarged Meeting of the Committee of the International Missionary Council at Willingen, in Germany, 1952; with Statements Issued by the Meeting*, London: Edinburgh House, 1953, p. 190.

6 Stephen B. Bevans and Roger P. Schroeder, *Constants in Context: A Theology of Mission for Today*, Maryknoll, NY: Orbis Books, 2004, pp. 289–90. This influence is seen particularly in the document *Ad Gentes*, available online at www.vatican.va/archive/hist_councils/ii_vatican_council/documents/vat-ii_decree_19651207_ad-gentes_en.html [accessed 5 April 2019].

7 Baldwin Sjollema, 'Combating Racism: A Chapter in Ecumenical History', *The Ecumenical Review* 56:4 (2004), pp. 470–9.

8 Lesslie Newbigin, *The Household of God: Lectures in the Nature of the Church*, London: SCM Press, 1953, pp. 147–8.

9 Cathy Ross, 'Mission', in Mark D. Chapman, Sathianathan Clarke and Martyn Percy, eds, *The Oxford Handbook of Anglican Studies*, Oxford: Oxford University Press, 2016, pp. 504–16.

10 Graham Cray and Mission and Public Affairs Council, *Mission-Shaped Church: Church Planting and Fresh Expressions of Church in a Changing Context*, London: Church House Publishing, 2004. See Justin Lewis-Anthony, 'Contested Church: Mission-Shaped, Emerging and Disputed', in Martyn Percy with Ian S. Markham, and Francesca Po, eds, *The Study of Ministry: A Comprehensive Survey of Theory and Best Practice*, London: SPCK, 2019, pp. 403–19.

11 Ian T. Douglas, 'Equipping for God's Mission: The Missiological Vision of the 2008 Lambeth Conference of Anglican Bishops', in David Craig, ed., *Equipping Bishops as Leaders in God's Mission: Reports from and Reflections on the Fourteenth Lambeth Conference of the Bishops of the Anglican Communion, 16 July–4 August 2008 at the University of Kent at Canterbury*, London: Anglican Consultative Council, 2015, pp. 5, 16.

12 Ross, 'Mission', pp. 507–8.

13 In 2015, 3.4 per cent of Church of England clergy were 'non-white'. Harriet Sherwood, 'Church of England to create bishop for minority ethnic community', *The Guardian*, 27 March 2017, available online at www.theguardian.com/world/2017/mar/27/church-of-england-to-create-bishop-for-minority-ethnic-community [accessed 3 April 2019].

14 David Voas, 'The Church of England', in David Goodhew, ed., *Growth and Decline in the Anglican Communion: 1980 to the Present*, London: Routledge, 2017, pp. 269–91.

15 Alasdair MacIntyre, *After Virtue*, second edition, Notre Dame, IN: University of Notre Dame Press, 1984, pp. 187–91. See Pierre Bourdieu, *Outline of a Theory of Practice*, trans. Richard Nice, Cambridge: Cambridge University Press, 2017 [1977]; Terry Rey, *Bourdieu of Religion: Imposing Faith and Legitimacy*, London: Routledge, 2014 [2007], pp. 44–56; Catherine Bell, *Ritual Theory, Ritual Practice*, Oxford: Oxford University Press, 1992, pp. 19–46.

16 Craig Dykstra and Dorothy C. Bass, 'A Theological Understanding of Christian Practices', *Lifelong Faith* (Summer 2008), pp. 3–18. Kathryn Tanner, *Theories of Culture: A New Agenda for Theology*, Minneapolis: Fortress Press, 1997.

17 Etienne Wenger, Richard McDermot and William M. Snyder, *Cultivating Communities of Practice: A Guide to Managing Knowledge*, Boston, MA: Harvard Business School Press, 2002, p. 4.

18 A more juridical version of 'collegiality' is also possible, but this is not what we are intending here. See Norman Doe, *Canon Law in the Anglican Communion: A Worldwide Perspective*, New York: Oxford University Press, 1998, pp. 124–6.

19 Wenger, McDermott and Snyder, *Cultivating*, p. 27.

20 Wenger, McDermott and Snyder, *Cultivating*, p. 4.

21 Mark D. Thompson, 'The Global Anglican Future Conference', in Ian S. Markham, J. Barney Hawkins IV, Justyn Terry and Leslie Nuñez Steffensen, eds, *The Wiley-Blackwell Companion to the Anglican Communion*, Chichester: Wiley-Blackwell, 2013, pp. 739–49.

22 The Archbishop of Canterbury's sermon is available online at www.youtube.com/watch?v=oQPQyOigbpc [accessed 4 April 2019].

23 Christopher Craig Brittain and Andrew McKinnon, *The Anglican Communion at a Crossroads: The Crises of a Global Church*, University Park: The Pennsylvania State University Press, 2018, pp. 66–7. GAFCON, 'The Nairobi Communique', 26 October 2013, available online at www.gafcon.org/news/nairobi-communique-and-commitment [accessed 4 April 2019].

24 Available online at www.gafcon.org/networks [accessed 4 April 2019]. See Esau McCaulley, 'Why GAFCON Matters: Thoughts on the Opening of GAFCON 2018', *Covenant*, available online at www.livingchurch.org/covenant/2018/06/19/why-gafcon-matters-thoughts-on-the-opening-of-gafcon-2018/ [accessed 4 April 2019].

25 Wenger, McDermot and Snyder, *Cultivating*, p. 96.

26 See Stephen Noll, *The Global Anglican Communion: Contending for Anglicanism 1993–2018*, Huntington Beach, CA: Anglican House, 2018, pp. 239–49.

27 Charles Taylor, *A Secular Age*, Cambridge, MA: Belknap Press of Harvard University Press, 2007, pp. 171–2.

28 See Robert S. Heaney, *Post-Colonial Theology: Finding God and Each other Amidst the Hate*, Eugene, OR: Cascade, 2019, pp. 160–6.

29 Paul McPartlan, 'The Body of Christ and the Ecumenical Potential of Eucharistic Ecclesiology', *Ecclesiology* 6 (2010), p. 158.

30 Paul Avis, *The Identity of Anglicanism: Essentials of Anglican Ecclesiology*, London: Bloomsbury T&T Clark, 2008, pp. 102–17. Robert W. Jenson, *Systematic Theology: Volume 2: The Works of God*, Oxford: Oxford University Press, 1999, pp. 187–227.

31 Jenson, *Systematic Theology: Volume 2*, p. 311.

32 Rowan Williams, *On Christian Theology*, Oxford: Blackwell, 2000, p. 212.

33 Williams, *On Christian Theology*, p. 213.

34 The Inter-Anglican Standing Commission on Unity, Faith & Order (IASCUFO), *Towards a Symphony of Instruments: A Historical and Theological Consideration of the Instruments of Communion of the Anglican Communion: Unity, Faith & Order Paper No. 1*, London: Anglican Consultative Council, 2018, pp. 6–10.

35 Jenson, *Systematic Theology: Volume 2*, p. 222.

36 Robert F. Taft, 'What Does Liturgy Do? Toward a Soteriology of Liturgical Celebration: Some Theses', in Dwight Vogel, ed., *Primary Sources of Liturgical Theology: A Reader*, Collegeville, MN: Liturgical Press, 2000, pp. 142–4.

37 Williams, *On Christian Theology*, p. 204.

38 See James W. Farwell, *The Liturgy Explained*, new edition, New York: Morehouse, 2013, pp. 32–3.

39 IASCUFO, *Towards*, pp. 6–10.

40 Conrad Hackett and David McClendon, 'Christians remain world's largest religious group, but they are declining in Europe', *Pew Research Center*, available online at www.pewresearch.org/fact-tank /2017/04/05/christians-remain-worlds-largest-religious-group-but-they-are-declining-in-europe/ [accessed 25 April 2019].

41 See Mike Woods, 'GAFCON conservative Anglicans face tensions over women bishops ahead of June meeting', *Christian Today*, 5 March 2018, available online at www.christiantoday.com/article/ gafcon-conservative-anglicans-face-tensions-over-women-bishops-ahead-of-june-meeting/126866.htm [accessed 25 April 2019]. Tim Wyatt, 'Jesmond robust in defence of its new curate-bishop', *Church Times*, 12 May 2017, available online at www.churchtimes.co.uk/ articles/2017/12-may/news/uk/jesmond-robust-in-defence-of-its-new-curate-bishop [accessed 25 April 2019]. Anglican Church in North America, 'A Statement on the Election of Church of Nigeria Bishops for the Diocese of Trinity', 18 January 2019, available online at www.anglicanchurch.net/?/main/page/1776 [accessed 25 April 2019].

42 GAFCON, 'The Complete Jerusalem Statement', 22 June 2008, available online at www.gafcon.org/resources/the-complete-jerusalem-statement [accessed 25 April 2019]. The statement itemizes 14 'tenets of orthodoxy which underpin our Anglican identity'. Between recognition of the three orders of ordained ministry and an acceptance of the 'great commission', the eighth tenet acknowledges God's creation as 'male and female and the unchangeable standard of Christian marriage between one man and one woman as the proper place for sexual intimacy and the basis of the family. We repent of our failures to maintain this standard and call for a renewed commitment to lifelong fidelity in marriage and abstinence for those who are not married.'

43 Stephen B. Bevans and Roger P. Schroeder, *Prophetic Dialogue: Reflections on Christian Mission Today*, Maryknoll, NY: Orbis Books, 2011, p. 59. Michael Amaladoss used the phrase in 1992. See Michael Amaladoss, 'Mission as Prophecy', in James A. Scherer and Stephen B. Bevans, eds, *New Directions in Mission and Evangelization 2: Theological Foundations*, Maryknoll, NY: Orbis, 1994, p. 72.

44 Bevans and Schroeder, *Prophetic Dialogue*, p. 61.

45 Scott MacDougall, *More than Communion: Imagining an Eschatological Ecclesiology*, London: Bloomsbury T&T Clark, 2015, pp. 256–7.

46 Kathryn Tanner, *Christ the Key*, Cambridge: Cambridge University Press, 2010, pp. 280–1.

47 Bosch, *Transforming Mission*, p. 489.

48 For a fuller account of penitential witness, see Heaney, *Post-Colonial Theology*, pp. 124–59.

49 See Pope Pius XII, *Mystici Corporis Christi* (1943), pp. 14, 63; available online at http://w2.vatican.va/content/pius-xii/en/encyclicals/documents/hf_p-xii_enc_29061943_mystici-corporis-christi.html [last accessed 21 June 2019]. *Catechism of the Catholic Church* (1992), p. 867.

50 Vatican II, *Lumen Gentium* (1964), VII:48. Available online at www.vatican.va/archive/hist_councils/ii_vatican_council/documents/vat-ii_const_19641121_lumen-gentium_en.html [last accessed 21 June 2019].

51 Tanner, *Christ the Key*, p. 299.

52 IASCUFO, *Towards*, p. 32.

53 Paul Avis, *Beyond the Reformation? Authority, Primacy and Unity in the Conciliar Tradition*, London: T&T Clark, 2008, pp. 184, 143.

54 Avis, *Beyond*, pp. 134–48. Hooker, *Ecclesiastical Polity*, VIII, vi, 3, 8, 11.

55 Avis, *Beyond*, p. 141.

56 Avis, *Beyond*, p. 141.

57 Paul Valliere, *Conciliarism: A History of Decision-Making in the Church*, New York: Cambridge University Press, 2012, p. 7.

58 Valliere, *Conciliarism*, p. 10.

59 Valliere, *Conciliarism*, pp. 10–15. Avis, *Beyond*, pp. 156–205.

60 Valliere, *Conciliarism*, p. 186.

61 Avis, *Beyond*, pp. 154–5.

62 Valliere, *Conciliarism*, pp. 192–3.

63 IASCUFO, *Towards*, p. 25.

64 Valliere, *Conciliarism*, p. 214.

65 Valliere, *Conciliarism*, p. 16.

66 Avis, *Beyond*, pp. 165–6.

67 Avis, *Beyond*, pp. 167–8.

68 IASCUFO, *Towards*, p. 29.

69 Avis, *Beyond*, p. 169. Valliere, *Conciliarism*, pp. 196–7.

70 Avis, *Beyond*, p. 172.

71 Norman Doe, 'The Contribution of Common Principles of Canon Law to Ecclesial Communion in Anglicanism', in John Rees, ed., *The Principles of Canon Law Common to the Churches of the Anglican Communion*, London: Anglican Communion Office, 2008, pp. 98, 105.

72 Doe, 'Contribution', pp. 105, 110, 97.

73 Avis, *Beyond*, p. 173.

74 The ACC is the most representative of Communion-wide gatherings, meeting about every three years.

75 Valliere, *Conciliarism*, p. 219.
76 Janice Love, 'Can We All Agree? Governing the WCC by Consensus', *Christian Century* (November 1, 2002), p. 8.
77 WCC, 'Interim Report on Consensus Procedure', 2 September 2003, available online at www.oikoumene.org/en/resources/documents/central-committee/2003/interim-report-on-consensus-procedures [accessed 11 April 2019]. Pauline Barnes and Elizabeth Nash, *Consensus Decision-Making in the United Reformed Church: A Review to Date with Some Recommendations for the Future*, United Reformed Church, UK, February 2011, available online at www.urc.org.uk/images/MissionCouncil/May%202011/consensus_procedure_-_review.pdf [accessed 11 April 2019]. Kerry Strayer, 'Considering Consensus: Is Agreement Possible?' *Vision* (January 1, 2007), pp. 62–70.
78 Barnes and Nash, *Consensus*, pp. 11–16.
79 WCC, 'Interim Report on Consensus Procedure'.
80 Avis, *Beyond*, p. 167.

Conclusion

Our pursuit of a clear statement of Anglicanism's promise has led us from confusions and diffuse meanings of the term 'Anglican' through unrealized ideals of church life and partial forms of consensus to divergences and divisions. We have framed the promise of Anglicanism in broad historical and theological terms, at first tracing the early and medieval Christian development of the idea. We located the origins of Anglican promise in the contextual rise of the Church of England during the Protestant Reformation. We also noted that the English Church, and the Anglican world which its ideals have encouraged, had their roots in distinctive aspects of English religious experience before the Reformation.

We have seen how Anglicanism became rooted in English experience, reliant upon the Church's status as religious establishment. We have shown that the Church of England and its progeny have never been complete. Even as its life unfolded, the Church's belief and practice were contested. Even when its role as English establishment seemed secure, its adherents never agreed on its shape and its relation to society. No conclusive form could be achieved. The ideal of comprehension, for example, endured without being secured in explicit form. Nevertheless, we believe the promise of Anglicanism was at work amid the contestation. Promise has been as much a journey as a destination.

As the Church expanded beyond England, it faced forms of adaptation to new social conditions, illustrated by the necessity of the office of commissary in the American colonies. Even as a chaplaincy to English expatriates in emerging colonial settings, the Church's forms and functions varied. As mission to indigenous peoples arose, the need for adaptation increased, widening the variations in church life and deepening the potential for divisions over them. It was in this arena of mission that it became possible to speak of Anglicanism as a distinctive expression of Christian faith. In cross-cultural witness and in intercultural exchange, a tradition beyond England arose. Mission became a principal aspect of the promise of Anglicanism. Mission and intercultural relations embodied the journey on which Anglicans had embarked.

Two realities accompanied the Church's participation in mission. First, the task of rooting the Church in unfamiliar cultural contexts became apparent. Contextualization became the principal mark of Anglican life, the reality that arose repeatedly as Anglicanism grew and as the world changed in light of colonization, modernization and then decolonization. Second, as Anglican intercultural relations deepened, the ideal of the Church's catholicity became a principal basis for defining what it meant to be Anglican. Because of mission, the Church developed in a myriad of contexts. In turn, contextualization entailed processes that gave birth to a tradition beyond what we have called 'Anglian'. The Church was becoming Anglican, that is intending to be rooted in various contexts but also intending to be catholic in its intercultural relationships and theologies. A new basis for being Anglican emerged; a sense of catholicity from below became integral to its promise. English historical precedent offered marks of church life, which were reapplied, refashioned and resisted elsewhere. However, Anglicanism aspired to be catholic because of such intercultural exchange, not despite adaptation and contestation.

The ideal of achieving Anglican catholicity fuelled efforts at becoming a communion of churches. As one step towards the realization of this ideal, Anglican mission developed a notable focus on bishops. We have given examples of the roles bishops have taken in mission, including being its principal initiators in a variety of contexts. Philander Chase in Ohio was an early instance of a missionary bishop. His ability to secure financial support in England could be cited as an example of Anglicans being in communion with one another. The Church he envisioned was not simply defined by life in Ohio, or in the United States. It intended to be rooted contextually yet not solely defined by such roots. Over time, Anglican bishops worked at creating indigenous ministries and, with further church development, a few indigenous bishops were consecrated. Anglican episcopacy began to step beyond cultural and racial limits.

The reality of decolonization forced the issue of the Church's enculturation. Fresh emphasis upon mission, upon being in communion and upon the Church's practice as the centre of its identity arose. The Church continued to spread, becoming more reliant upon internal, contextual impetus than upon direction from without. This was a welcome and necessary development. But it complicated the Anglican pursuit of being in communion by elevating the priority church leaders gave to its local, contextual character. Such emphasis was necessary as the Church in newly independent circumstances sought resources to build its life. All too often, there was continued dependency upon aid from the resource-laden Global North, which thus controlled in implicit ways even after the formal end of colonialism. The pursuit of promise became obscured by disparities of church life from one part of the globe to another.

The Anglican story has habitually been told from a certain perspective. That is, it has been recounted from the view of those in the Global North, its promise seemingly embedded in the Church as religious institution, defined by the outlook of the upper echelons of its institutional hierarchies. The story can be made to seem consistent, the institutional Church summoning uniform standards and expressions, calling its fledgling branches towards greater efficiency in their organization and consistency in their practices; a summons that is never fully realized. Such paternalism is a recurring reality in mission history. But the pursuit of catholicity has required more than dependence upon Global North provinces for the resources other provinces require. Those who sent aid could not presume to speak for those who received it. Those who received aid questioned its efficacy as they identified rich resources in their own settings. Anglican fault lines have arisen where indigenous voices and their worldviews have been disregarded. The Global North does not know what is best for the rest.

History is not simply the record of ideals fully realized and consensus triumphantly declared in institutional guise. The Anglican story is replete with instances of fragmentation and conflict. Ironically, we see Anglican conflict, or 'contestation' as we have termed it, as the proper approach to grasping Anglicanism's promise. Contestation has arisen as Anglicans have been compelled to respond to social realities that test the adaptability and veracity of church life. Even within particular contexts, diverse responses to social realities have signalled the onset of contestation as consensus over faithful response has been elusive. The propensity to contestation has increased as Anglicans in one or another context have questioned the appropriateness of church life elsewhere. We do not equate contestation with division. Contestation is inherent in contextualization. Contestation refers to a readiness to contend for certain aspects of Christian belief and practice, which are seen as integral to Anglican life in particular form. Division has been the conclusion that one must separate from those with whom one disagrees because of differences. We view contestation as inevitable and even life-giving to Anglicanism. As a religious tradition and an ecclesiastical institution, its variegations make contestation a fact of common life. On the other hand, we view division as Anglicanism's gravest threat. The distinction is stark.

The story of Anglican division has become a history of its own. The sources of conflict have varied, the precipitating factors often arising in the Church's social environments and compelling responses over which Anglicans have differed. The onset of political upheaval, for example, has been a prominent dividing point. The 'Glorious Revolution' of 1688 was not deemed glorious by all in the Church of England. The resulting Non-Juror schism enlisted even the Archbishop of Canterbury. Over time, the impulse to divide from one another intensified, especially as social and political change took unprecedented forms. We read this history less as a series of external threats to Anglican life than as a series of challenges to Anglican consensus about the Church's proper expressions of its faith and relation to society. Thus, in North America in the late nineteenth century, the Reformed Episcopal Church arose as the Episcopal Church seemingly compromised its Protestant heritage in a rush to adopt Catholic ceremonial. Similarly, in South Africa, the breakaway Church of England in South Africa resisted the formation of the Church of the Province of South Africa as a separate jurisdiction. Later renaming itself the Reformed Anglican Church of South Africa, this body aligns itself with the conservative end of Reformed Christianity and with traditionalist groups in the Anglican world.[1] The phenomenon of Anglican division has not been limited to North America and the British Isles. Such points of friction have increasingly become intra-Anglican, the stakes for church life becoming higher. Late twentieth-century conflicts have increased the number of competing forms of Anglican life. Consensus seems elusive, especially if presumed to entail uniformity more than unity.

The turn from contestation to division seemingly disrupts any notion of promise. The challenges facing Anglicanism, as both institution and faith tradition, are manifold without the spectre of continued division, to the extent of some embracing competing forms of assembly. The fact of division is embodied by the rise of GAFCON as an alternative form of international assembly. GAFCON was fostered by dissenting expressions of Anglicanism. The challenges faced by Anglicans, and the resulting divides, are similar to the challenges other Christians face. But the expanse, contextual focus and extent of differences over crucial issues give Anglican life complexities few Christian confessions face. What accounts for this disruptive turn? Why have historic patterns of Anglican contestation escalated to the point of alienation and division?

Anglicans have disagreed repeatedly over the proper embodiment of their ideals. Woven through the differences recent issues have embodied, there has been the reality of Anglicanism becoming enculturated in a myriad of contextual settings after the end of the colonial era. There has also been the shaking of the Church's presumptions about its institutional forms and social role in the Global North. Repeatedly the issue has presented itself as the Church's relation to culture. A widespread search for faithful social grounding, for authentic forms of enculturation, has shaped the priorities and styles of church life in its varied contexts. In turn, such steps towards adjusting the relation between Church and context have intensified Anglican frictions. For instance, the acceptance of homosexual persons into the Church in one Anglican province can appear to be abandonment of the faith in another. Intensified searches for fresh ministry and witness in one context can seem to be compromise for others. The contextual nature of Anglican mission and ministry has become a conundrum for intra-Anglican relations. It seems more apt to speak of crisis than of promise in Anglican life.

The underlying dynamic transcends the particular issues of liturgical change, ordination of women or the recognition of homosexual persons. Avid proponents as well as those who differ with equal fervour succumb to a similar *'mentalité'*. That is, they are prone to an outlook upon the faith and the Church which becomes the seedbed of division. In a word, Anglicans have become susceptible to a 'sectarian' outlook. We trace the rise of fissiparous tendencies to the advance of this outlook at all levels of Anglican life.

The term 'sect' typically denotes a religious group within or apart from a larger and more diverse religious entity.[2] A sect represents people who consciously set themselves apart in order to foster or to protect a qualitatively different pattern of belief and practice animated by distinct values. Often people choose to affiliate, or to create, such groups for the sake of specific ideals which they perceive to be under threat. Sectarian identity can feature a precisely stated purpose, stringent criteria of affiliation and high symbolic boundaries to demarcate the group. Precise qualities of belief and practice gain import and may become the basis of excluding those who differ or whose allegiance is deemed insufficient.

Often, in order to enhance sectarian identity and to distinguish the group from the wider world, themes of purity may be invoked. Purity embodies the ideal of holding genuine belief, following prescribed rules and roles, and preserving oneself intact from beliefs or actions, individuals or circumstances that are taken to represent compromise.[3] By one account, 'purity' occurs 40 times in the Hebrew Bible, referring to an emptying out or being clean. It is tinged with moral as well as ritual import. Purity can also mean innocence, the antithesis of guilt. It entails faithfulness to God's covenant and obedience to God's law. The New Testament contrast is only slight. There, moral purity has entirely replaced ritual purity.[4] It has become a matter of uprightness, patience, reverence, endurance. Such ideals apply to personal as well as group life.

The theme of purity is an inevitable component of sectarian identity. It represents the intention of securing a particular vision of religious life, one which requires that specific ideals become literal facts. Not simply the pursuit of an ideal, the sectarian intention works to distinguish religious identity from the corrupting influence of the world. Indeed, the 'world' can serve as a vague reference for all that would stain the purity a sectarian outlook intends to protect. Alarm at possible compromise and deep commitment to foster certain ideals do not mean that a sect, or sectarian outlook, is reserved for a group with few members located in one place. The sectarian outlook can encompass large numbers of adherents spread over a wide expanse. In this age of rapid connection and social media, the limiting factor of geography has receded. But even before such rapid links became possible, ideals of a sectarian sort could be carried from one locale to another. Religious groups of various kinds, including orders, movements and communities, show aspects of sectarian outlook, whether they are at war with the world and the rest of the Church or not. It can suffice to elevate aspects of Christian tradition, social intention and practice without challenging the Church's broader bounds.

It could be argued that a sectarian impulse has been a by-product of Anglicanism's contextual focus. In the midst of social and political upheaval, such a tendency has been evident. Amid the rise of new nations from colonies, the Church has been compelled to define itself in novel circumstances. There has been an added threat when extremist political movements

CONCLUSION

have arisen or dominant religious groups have turned assertive, further relegating Anglicans and other groups to minority status. In response, the Anglican response has often been to accommodate church life to the culture, in the process striving to enhance its social ministries and to clarify what are deemed to be defining aspects of Anglican identity. In some circumstances, where Anglicans are a barely noticed minority, congregations can assume the dynamics of extended families. Such has often been the case in mission circumstances. The sectarian instinct can be presumed to safeguard identity and solidarity.

But the sectarian impulse has grown as intra-Anglican conflict over pivotal matters of faith and practice has deepened. In the current situation of Anglican division, parties to the conflict display aspects of sectarian *'mentalité'*. Some contenders fear the world is oppressing groups of people whose lives should be affirmed. The Church must shed its worldly prejudices, move beyond exclusion and embrace those whom the world has denigrated. Other contenders for the Church's purity are driven by a sense that there has been surrender of faithful identity to the world's priorities. All parties conclude that there has been religious and moral compromise, both perceive worldly corruption, but of different sorts. Both intend literal realization of specific religious ideals. They equate their ideals with the authenticity of the Church's life.

Prompted by such sectarian instincts, movements of protest against the tenor of church life have divided the Anglican world by claiming that theirs is the true Christianity and the genuine form of Anglicanism. In effect, all such groups claim to be the rightful heirs of Anglican promise. Alternative institutional expressions of Anglican life are apparent, some trying to retain links to the Church against which they protest, some simply leaving its jurisdiction. In recent decades, as the tenor of Anglican discernment and disagreement has increased, there has been a great readiness to disagree by leaving to form dissenting fellowships and even competing forms of church structure. Division is apparent from local, contextual levels outward to new church bodies to international assemblies such as GAFCON. Anglicans compete vigorously against one another, perhaps more than against their religious and social rivals.

The search for ways to define Anglican life, to set boundaries on the limits of proper faith and practice, has been embodied in the rise of synods. The setting of limits and the pursuit of Anglican promise have hardly been the same thing. However, the rise of synods has been understandable. English reliance upon Parliament, and fitfully upon Convocation and then a General Synod, helped to set such a precedent. The age of democratic revolution and the expansion of Anglicanism beyond England made synodical governance necessary. As the idea of being in a communion shaped by the gospel dawned, international forms of Anglican assembly also arose. As we have depicted, the organization of the Lambeth Conference and later of the Anglican Consultative Council have been further expressions of a desire to discern God's will in representative and worshipful assembly.

Yet, it has been in synodical gatherings that sectarian intentions and the hope of unity have collided. Some Anglicans, intent on realization of their specific ideals of faith and church life, have confronted others intent on endorsement of contending ideals. The path towards Anglican promise has appeared to lead towards legislative vindication, a conclusive triumph over one's opponents and dismissal of them and their errant convictions. Anglicans have shown a troubling impulse to exclude, to dismiss those who differ, in the name of Christ.

What should such gatherings seek? In what ways could they be aligned with Anglican promise more than Anglican division, with the best in Christian faith and church life rather than with contradictions of them? Anglicans have sought a kind of balance, a consensus that would allow for variation yet link the local and the universal, the ideal and the real, the disparities between contexts, in an overarching unity. We contend that unity does not require uniformity. But unity has become elusive as the setting of boundaries and a readiness to exclude has become the intention and the strategy. Instead, what would it look like if the pursuit of promise was the priority of Anglican life, and specifically the goal of Anglican assemblies?

CONCLUSION

The legislative turn of Anglican synods misses much of the purpose of synodical assembly in the Christian world as well as in secular, democratic counterparts. There has been useful recent work on the role of democratic assemblies as the world has become pluralistic. In his review of works on 'Discourse and Democracy', David Franz observes that 'part of democracy's promise is the claim that it will provide a context for discussion between those committed to radically different visions and ways of talking about the common good'. Franz believes that democracy in the modern world is based on the assumptions that public reasoning produces greater social good and that the authority of reason facilitates toleration rather than coercion 'as a way of making peace between people with deep differences in a polity'.[5] The emphasis, especially for the Church, should be to discern steps towards a common mind with mission together as a particular priority. Contestation must be conducted in prayerful discernment as a search for renewed communion.

However, the idea of an authoritative and tolerant public reasoning proves elusive. The processes of democratic assembly can be clogged by those who intend final triumph over their ideological foes. In this regard, church assemblies prove no different from secular ones, when vindication rather than promise becomes the intention. Franz notes that 'discourse for the purposes of persuasion and rational agreement . . . requires social discipline and the channelling of emotions and conflicts into constructive argument'. In other words, what people stand for matters more than what people viscerally oppose. The late Robert Bellah, an Episcopalian, spoke of 'habits of the heart', that is, qualities which transcend argumentation in favour of discourse. Bellah and other authors have posed democracy's fulfilment as an emphasis upon civility, and cultivation of 'the social and cultural contexts necessary to sustain civility'. Anglican promise requires no less.

We have held that Anglican promise is more journey than destination. At this juncture, the pursuit of promise requires transforming this faith tradition's centrifugal forces into centripetal ones. But movement towards a refreshed view of the

Anglican centre cannot rely upon uniformity. Instead, unity requires a different approach, one that may frustrate some because of its porous boundaries and inconclusive processes. We are informed by the work of Adam B. Seligman and Robert P. Weller on finding unity amid pluralism. Speaking of broader religious and social worlds than the Anglican one, they see ambiguity as a facet of contemporary pluralism. Because ambiguity 'is built into our experiences and relationships . . . we have to impose an order of some sort in order to live'.[6] This is not simply the problem these authors address, it is the Anglican conundrum: how can we have boundaries porous enough to learn and witness to the world and defined enough to make our witness to promise distinct from the world?

The terms that Seligman and Weller choose to depict the tension between ambiguity and order resonate with Anglican experience. People live in particular contexts, they note. Rules and boundaries acquire added importance because of life's dissonance. It becomes tempting to equate ambiguity with defilement, a loss of pure belief and community, and to blame others for the perceived decline. But ambiguity can be embraced. It represents potential more than threat. Ambiguity reflects the realization that there are alternate points of view, that experience varies, that order can be pliable to be humane. Boundaries must look outward as well as inward. That is, they must encourage shared values. Rigid conceptions of order are defied by the plasticity of social worlds and by the heightened awareness of pluralism that characterizes twenty-first-century life. A common culture can arise out of the contestation that marks such encounters. It is an inevitable contestation, we add. The choice in such occasions lies between the intention to divide and the pursuit of common life. The choice is unavoidable.

What then could common life mean? How would it unfold? Seligman and Weller cite two ways forward. On the one hand, they speak in general terms of ritual. In a generic sense, they define ritual as formal, iterated acts. While dramatizing ambiguity, they argue, ritual also opens up the possibility of empathy. This becomes possible, we add, because ritual creates times and places for experience of the sacred. Amid the world's messiness, in explicitly Christian terms, the sacredness of ritual is the call to God's grace that relativizes difference and demands fellowship amid embodied difference. The central category is empathy because it represents readiness to see the world as others do and so to benefit together.[7]

In turn, ritual proposes the possibility of shared experience. Even though people live in specific contexts, it is possible to live together with new, shared meaning. Bracketing out the divisive potential of difference, shared experience can be built, with ritual creating frameworks for mutual discovery. In the process, ideals are confronted by the complexities of reality. Simple explanations and solutions prove insufficient; boundaries can be used to restrict rather than to build. However, we urge that boundaries must be used to make communities clearly focused in their identity and their mission. Anglican contestation often concerns the nature and location of boundaries. What and how do they embrace? Who and what do they exclude? Contestation, we add, is inherent because of the reality of difference. There is no shortcut to the unity we identify with Anglican promise. Difference cannot be diluted, nor should it be. The intention is to stand together in the midst of difference. In this sense, contestation of an empathic and dialogic sort is desirable; it is the way towards promise. Boundaries must help to focus our collective intentions, not to restrict the possibility of inclusion.

Seligman and Weller's work underscores our key points. We argue that Anglicanism is bounded by Christian faith and tradition, but that our boundaries retain openness to those who are different. We have maintained that in intercultural encounters and processes of discernment common faith and mission arise. Indeed, we emphasize that Anglicanism has arisen on the basis of contestation about its incomplete realization and efforts to elicit a greater sense of promise in the midst of processes of contextualization. Intercultural discernment towards God's just end can be our response to the world's ambiguities and challenges. Our common commitment to discern God's guidance together makes us Anglican. Common prayer is our basis and our hope.

We conclude by asking if such a heightened empathy is possible. Can Anglicans embrace contestation as a virtue that unites? Can difference enrich rather than impede? We suggest that movement towards promise now must entail a readiness to heed the experience of others and to build common life on this basis. We see signs of such possibility in deeper practices of consensus-building. Formally and informally, there are signs of Anglicans linking parishes and dioceses across differences that might otherwise be insurmountable. There have been extensive explorations of context to context, grassroots to grassroots relations in mission. Often, such relations bypass church structures for the purpose of shared, personal ties. We observe that Anglican mission arose in such a fashion, the SPG and the CMS eventually gaining recognition by the Church as institutions.

The purpose of such connections has not been to legislate nor to draw boundaries that divide. The purpose has been to build common ritual and shared experience. In the process, people find space for common discernment, explore what they can do together and build respect that overcomes cultural and theological divides. The state of the Church at its institutional levels cannot be disregarded. But while debate flows, countless people who call themselves Anglican live their lives, offer their prayers to God, seek to enhance faith community and find ways to work together without fully agreeing with one another. They sense promise that does not require the elimination of difference. Indeed, promise is enriched by difference and even the contestation which it can fuel. Through the struggles of our common life, the grace of God becomes present.

Notes

1 Allen Guelzo, *For the Union of Evangelical Christendom*, State College, PA: Penn State University Press, 1994. Herbert Hammond, 'The Church of England in South Africa and the Anglican Communion', *Churchman* 102:3 (7 August 1988), pp. 251–8.

2 William H. Swatos, Jr, ed., 'Church-Sect theory', available online at www.hirr.hartsem.edu/ency/cstheory.htm [last accessed 16 June 2019].

CONCLUSION

3 Cf. Mary Douglas, *Purity and Danger*, London: Routledge, 1966.

4 'Purity', in *Baker's Evangelical Dictionary of Evangelical Theology*, available online at www.biblestudytools.com/dictionary/purity [last accessed 16 June 2019].

5 David Franz, 'Bibliographic Review: Discourse and Democracy', *The Hedgehog Review* 6:3 (2004), pp. 85–92.

6 Adam B. Seligman and Robert P. Weller, *Rethinking Pluralism: Ritual, Experience, and Ambiguity*, Oxford and New York: Oxford University Press, 2012, p. 4.

7 Seligman and Weller, *Rethinking Pluralism*, p. 145.

Index

acculturation 155
  resistance to 167–71
Africa
  as cultural construct 141
  independence 170–71
  religion 65–9, 77, 121–5, 157–8
African American missions 156–7
Akinyele, A. B. 66
ambiguity 230
Anglianism 57–60, 78, 186–7
Anglican Communion 203
Anglican Congresses 110
Anglican Consultative Council 110
Anglicanism
  coherence 117–47
  emergence 57
  identity ix–xii, xv, 59, 101, 143
  international expansion xxii, 60–62, 84–91
  non-English language 76
  see also catholicity; communion; contextualization; GAFCON

apartheid 185
apostolic life 23, 26
apostolicity 203
atonement 70
Augustine of Canterbury 16–17
Augustine of Hippo 14–16
Australia 90
Avis, Paul 204, 207–8
Ayandele, E. A. 124–5
Azariah, V. S. 125–6

Banerjea, Krishna Mohan 164–5
baptism 194
barrenness 168–9
Barry, Alfred 153
Basil of Caesarea 12–13
Baxter, Richard 37–8
Bayne, Stephen 111, 112
Belize 99
Bell, George 206
Bentinck, William 159
Bevans, Stephen 198
Bible translation 77
  King James Version 35
  Mandarin 121, 156

INDEX

bishops
  in Africa 65, 72, 74
  collegiality 188
  conciliarity 203–8
  and contextual change 113–14
  in the early church 14
  elected 85
  in India 46, 90
  missionary 84–92, 95–6
  in North America 63, 84–9
  and power 202
  in Reformation England 34, 37–8
  see also Lambeth Conference
Blomfield, Charles James 94–5
Blyden, Edward 132
Book of Common Prayer xv–xvi, xxv–xxvi, 30
  baptism for overseas converts 58
  prescribed by 1662 Act 38
  translations 121
Boone, William James 155–6
Bourdieu, Pierre 53
Bray, Thomas xxi–xxii, 43–4, 84
Brazil 156
Brent, Charles Henry 155
Britain, national identity 50–52
Broughton, William 90
Brown, Peter 24 n8
Buchanan, Claudius 159
Buganda 122

Calvin, John 27
Cambridge Mission to Delhi 100
Canada 85, 87–8, 113
canon law 207–8
Carey, William 58, 139, 152
Cartwright, Thomas 34
caste system 140, 159–60
Catholic Emancipation 64, 94
catholicity xxii, 103–5, 221
  and mission xxiii–xxiv, 101–2, 222–3
Celsus 11
Celtic Christianity 16
Chambers, George 134–5
Chase, Philander 86–7
Chicago-Lambeth Quadrilateral 103
China 121, 155–6
Church of England
  at the Restoration 37
  becomes more than English 36, 46
  Convocations 102
  decline 187
  establishment 1, 29, 34, 39, 44–5, 50
  origins 30–32
Church Mission(ary) Society 46, 64, 85, 152–4
Church and politics 15–16
  in Reformation England 29–30, 35
Church of the Province of South Africa 77–8

circumcision 170
Claggett, Thomas John 63
Clapham Sect 46, 52, 90
Clarendon Code 38
Cluny 21–2
Colenso, John William 57, 66–74, 77–8, 97, 104–5
collegial consensus 208–212
Colley, Linda 50–52
Colonial Bishoprics Fund 95
colonialism 45–7, 60–62, 71–2, 101, 137–43, 151–2
  and mission 153–5, 158–60, 171–2
commerce, and mission 152
commissaries 43, 84
communion xxii–xxiii, 103–6, 110–114
  and eschatology 200–202
  and eucharist 194–7
  and mission 150–76
communities of liturgy 193–6
communities of practice 182–93
comprehension xi, 37
conflict 3
Connecticut 45, 62–3, 86
consensual decision-making 208–213
contestation xii–xv, xviii–xx, 49–50, 75, 150, 223
  and tradition 2–4
contextualization xix–xxvi, xxiv, 60, 128–32, 143–4, 150–51, 221
  communities of witness 187–8

criticism of mission 160–62
  as resistance to acculturation 167–71
  as translation 138–40, 163–7
conversion
  and culture 138–9, 144–5, 155
  in early middle ages 16–19
  in east Africa 133, 164
  mutual 69, 78, 172
  in South Asia 125–6
Convocations 102
Coomaraswamy, Ananda K. 162
Corfe, John 156
Corporation Act 38, 64, 94
Cotton, George Edward Lynch 160
Councils of the Church 203–8
Cranmer, Thomas 30, 204
Creighton, Mandell 205
Crowther, Samuel Ajayi 57–8, 65–7, 75–6, 123–5
Crummell, Alexander 132

Danaher, William 113
dialogue 198–9
discourse 28, 41, 141–2
dissent 38–9, 94
division, theological and moral 3–5
Dixon, Richard Watson 205
Doane, George Washington 88–9, 92

INDEX

Doe, Michael 186
Doe, Norman 207
Drake, Francis 60
Duff, Alexander 139
Duffy, Eamon 30

East Africa Revival 132–6
East India Company 158–60
ecclesia 10
Egypt 144–6
Elizabethan Settlement 33–4
Emancipation Act 64, 94
enculturation 128, 136, 224–5
Episcopal Church (USA) 63–4, 85–6, 88–9, 117, 211–12
eschatology 195, 200–202
establishment 34–5, 39, 44–5, 50, 94–5, 120
eternal punishment 67, 69–70
eucharist 70–71, 194–7
 in the early church 10–11
evangelicalism 42, 48
Ezigbo, Victor I. 157–8, 168–9

Farquhar, J. N. 161
Fay, Lydia Mary 155–6
Figgis, Neville 205
Fisher, Geoffrey 110
Foucault, Michel 28
Francis of Assisi 22–3
Franz, David 229
Frykenberg, Robert Eric 160, 165
fulfilment theology 161
Fulford, Francis 102

GAFCON (Global Anglican Future Conference) 189–92, 197–8, 212–13, 224
 1st (Jerusalem, 2008) 189, 198
 2nd (Kenya, 2013) 189–90
 3rd (Jerusalem, 2018) 190
Gahini 133–5
Gairdner, William Temple 144–5
Garden, Alexander 45–6
Gener, Timoteo D. 155
Gladstone, William Ewart 94
Gordon, Patrick 44
Gray, Robert 67, 68, 73, 90, 97–8
Great Ejection 38

Haidt, Jonthan 5–6
Haiti 156–7
Hall, Ronald xvi, 146
Hammond, Henry 36, 37
Harper, Susan Billington 125
Harrab, Thomas 57
Heber, Reginald 140, 159
Henry VIII (King of England) 29–30
Herbert, George 61
Hinduism 161
 scriptures 165–6, 173
Hinga, Teresia Mbari 157, 168
Hobart, John Henry 87
Hoekendijk, Johannes Christiaan 183, 185
holiness, of the Church 201
Holly, James Theodore 156–7

homosexuality xviii, 225
Hong Kong 146
Hooker, Richard 32–3, 204
Hooper, John 33
hope 193, 195
Hopkins, John Henry 101
hybridization 173–4, 182

IASCUFO (Inter-Anglican Standing Commission on Unity, Faith and Order) 205
imperialism
  and God's work 152
  theology of 153–4
  see also colonialism
India 46, 90, 100, 125–6, 158–62
  Christian theology 172
  language use 140
  see also caste system; Hinduism; *sati*
indigenous church leadership 45, 117–19
Inglis, Charles 85, 153
initiation rites 128–30
Instruments of Communion 206, 208–9
International Missionary Council 183
Isichei, Elizabeth 155, 167
Islam 145–6, 166–7
Ives, Levi Silliman 92

James VI (King of England) 61
Japan 117–18, 156
Jewel, John 31

Johnson, James 124–5
Jones, Richard 122

Karanja, John 136, 164
Keith, George 44, 45
Kemper, Jackson 88
Kennaway, John H. 152–3
Kenya 136, 164
Kenyatta, Jomo 169–70
Kenyon College 87
Kikuyu 136, 164, 170
Kimathi, Dedan 170
koinonia 194–5, 197
Korea 156

Lahiz, Maulvie 'Imad ud-din 166–7
Laing, Catriona 144
Lambeth Conferences 102–110, 204–5, 210–211
  1st (1867) 58, 102–4, 188, 205
  2nd (1878) 75
  7th (1930) 105–6
  10th (1968) 205
  11th (1978) 205
  12th (1988) 71, 103, 205
  14th (2008) 186
languages, and colonialism 138–40
Latin America 156
latitudinarianism 39–40
Laud, William 35
Lewis, John Travers 102
Li, Florence Tim Oi xvi
liberation 170
libraries 43

INDEX

liturgical revision xv–xvi, xxv–xxvi
Long, William 97–8
Longley, Charles Thomas 73, 102
Louisiana 86
Love, Janice 209
Lucas, Vincent 129–30
Lumen Gentium 201
Luther, Martin 26–8

MacCulloch, Diarmaid 32–3
MacDougall, Scott 200
McIlvaine, Charles 92
Mackenzie, Charles Frederick 99
Macrorie, W. K. 97
Malawi 99
Maryland 43
Massachusetts 45
Mau Mau 170
Maurice, F. D. 67, 97
Mbiti, John S. 77, 157, 168, 169
Meade, William 92
Methodism 52
Middleton, Thomas 46, 90
missio Dei 40, 183–8
mission xii, xx, xxiii–xxiv
 Anglican overseas 40–48
 and colonialism 153–5, 158–60, 171–2
 and communion 110–111, 150–76
 criticisms of 151–62
 fields 114 n3
 five marks 186
 and trade 152, 158

Mission-Shaped Church 186–7
missionaries, criticized 68–9
missionary bishops 84–92
missionary societies 46, 59, 100
Montanism 24 n6
morality 5–6
 see also sexuality
Mountstephen, Philip 78
Mudimbe, V. Y. 141
Müller, F. Max 160
Museveni, Yoweri 135
Mutual Responsibility and Interdependence 110–114
mutuality 106–7, 113–14

Natal 67, 72
national identity 50–52
New Zealand 90, 91
Newbigin, Lesslie 185–6
Ngidi, William 68
Niger Mission 65–6
Non-Jurors 39

O'Connell, Daniel 94
Oduyoye, Mercy Amba 169
Ohio 86, 87
Origen 11
Otey, James Hervey 87
Oxford Movement 90, 91

Padwick, Constance 144–6
Pan-Anglican Congress (1908, London) 110
Parker, Matthew 34
Paul (St) 9–11
Peel, J. D. Y. 136

Pels, Peter 138
penance 19
Pennsylvania 85
peripheries 20–23, 49, 52–4
Peterson, Derek 133–5
pluralism 230–31
Podmore, Colin 110
Polk, Leonidas 89
polygamy 71, 97, 103
power 202–3
Prayer Book *see* Book of Common Prayer
preaching 45–6
Prevost, Elizabeth 144
Prevost, Samuel 63, 153
promise
  in the Bible 7–11
  in the early church 11–12
  meanings x–xi, 1–23
prophetic dialogue 198–200
Puritans 34–5, 37, 44
purity 225–6

Radner, Ephraim 105–6, 112–13
reading rooms 45
Reformation 26–34
reformation of manners 42
reformation (ongoing) 200
resistance to acculturation 167–71
Ridley, Nicholas 204
ritual 230–31
Robinson, Armitage 59

Rock, David 156
Roman Catholic Church
  emergence 16–18
  medieval reforms 21–2
Rwanda 133–4

Śankara 173
Sanneh, Lamin 122, 123, 136, 163, 167
Sarum Rite 21
sati 159
Schereschewsky, Samuel Isaac Joseph 121, 155–6
Schroeder, Roger 198
Scott, Thomas 58, 152
Seabury, Samuel 63, 85
Secker, Thomas 45
sectarianism 226–7
Seligman, Adam B. 230–31
Selwyn, George Augustus 90, 103
sexuality xvii–xviii, 2, 3, 198, 211–12, 225
Sheldon, Gilbert 36, 37, 38
Skipper, Dora 133
slaves 62, 65, 94
Smith, Benjamin Bosworth 87
social transformation 9, 17
Society of the Divine Word (SVD) 198
Society for Promoting Christian Knowledge 43, 84
Society for the Propagation of the Gospel 43–4, 45, 52, 61–2, 84–5, 100

INDEX

South Africa 90, 96–9
Spencer, Aubrey 88
Steere, Edward 99–100
Stephenson, Alan 59
Stock, Eugene 152–3
Stoner-Eby, Anne Marie 129–30
Strachan, John 87–8
Strong, Rowan 61–2
Sundar Singh, Sadhu 167
synodical government 74, 85, 91, 97–8, 228–9
synthesis 33

Tait, Archibald Campbell 73, 74
Tanner, Kathryn 200, 202
Tanzania 129–30
Taylor, Charles 192–3
Taylor, John V. 122
Temple, William 205–6
Tertullian 12
Test Act 64
Thornton, Douglas 144, 145
Tiffin, Helen 142
toleration 37, 38–9
Tomkins, Oliver 206
Tozer, William George 99
trade, and mission 152, 158
tradition, and contestation 2–4
translation
  and contextualization 163–7
  and mission 138–40
  see also Bible translation
Trinitarian theology 184

Tucker, Henry St George 117–18, 147
Twells, Edward 96–7

United States of America 84–7
  imperialism 155
  treatment of Native Americans 154
unity 107–8
Universities' Mission to Central Africa 99–101
Upadhyay, Brahmabandav 172–4

Valliere, Paul 205, 208–9
Vedas 165–6
Venn, Henry 57, 64–5, 95, 122, 123
vestments 33–4
Virginia 43, 84, 117
Virginia Company 60–61

Warren, Max 113, 153–4
Welby, Justin 78, 189–90
Weller, Robert P. 230–31
Wesley, John 42
Westcott, Brooke Foss 160
Weston, Frank 121–2, 129
Wherry, Elwood M. 166
White, William 63, 85, 106, 153
Whitefield, George 42, 45–6, 52
Whitehead, Henry 126
Whittingham, William 101–2
Wilberforce, William 46

Wilken, Robert Louis 11, 15
Willengen statment 183–4
Williams, Channing Moore 156
Williams, Rowan 186, 194
Wilson, Daniel 140, 159
women's ordination xvi–xvii
Woodward, Josiah 42
World Council of Churches 206
consensual decision-making 209–210

Special Fund to Combat Racism 185
World Missionary Conference (Edinburgh, 1910) 144

Yelle, Robert 139, 140
Yieh, John 146
Yoruba 136

Zanzibar 99, 121–2
Zink, Jesse 110–111
zones of influence 171

www.ingramcontent.com/pod-product-compliance
Lightning Source LLC
Chambersburg PA
CBHW021939290426
44108CB00012B/896